OXFORD STUDIES IN SOCIAL AND
CULTURAL ANTHROPOLOGY

CULTURAL FORMS

The Anthropology of Landscape

This book is published by Oxford University Press thanks to the general editorship of Howard Morphy, University Lecturer in Ethnology at Oxford and Curator at the Pitt Rivers Museum, and Fred Myers, Associate Professor of Anthropology at New York University.

The Anthropology of Landscape

Perspectives on Place and Space

EDITED BY

Eric Hirsch and Michael O'Hanlon

CLARENDON PRESS · OXFORD

OXFORD
UNIVERSITY PRESS

Great Clarendon Street, Oxford OX2 6DP

Oxford University Press is a department of the University of Oxford.
It furthers the University's objective of excellence in research, scholarship,
and education by publishing worldwide in

Oxford New York

Athens Auckland Bangkok Bogotá Buenos Aires Calcutta
Cape Town Chennai Dar es Salaam Delhi Florence Hong Kong Istanbul
Karachi Kuala Lumpur Madrid Melbourne Mexico City Mumbai
Nairobi Paris São Paulo Shanghai Singapore Taipei Tokyo Toronto Warsaw

with associated companies in Berlin Ibadan

Published in the United States
by Oxford University Press Inc., New York

© the several contributors 1995

First published in hardback and paperback 1995

British Library Cataloguing in Publication Data
Data available

Library of Congress Cataloging in Publication Data
Data available

ISBN 0–19–828010–6 (Pbk)

5 7 9 10 8 6 4

Printed in Great Britain
on acid-free paper by
Biddles Ltd., Guildford and King's Lynn

PREFACE AND ACKNOWLEDGEMENTS

This volume had its origins in a conference convened by Eric Hirsch and Alfred Gell on 'The Anthropology of Landscape', held at the London School of Economics and Political Science on 22–3 June 1989. The fact that contributors from a range of disciplines found as much to talk about as they did suggested that this was a topic whose time had come and that the proceedings merited publication. Alfred Gell's commitments prevented him from acting with Eric Hirsch as co-editor; subsequently Michael O'Hanlon, who had been a discussant at the original conference, joined Hirsch in this capacity.

With the exception of the introduction, all the chapters were initially presented at the conference and all were substantially revised for publication. The introduction arose out of a 'position statement' produced prior to the conference and has developed in conjunction with the revisions of the individual essays. Sadly, Nicholas Green, the author of the first of the essays, did not live to see the publication of the volume; however, he revised his essay before his tragic death from an AIDS-related illness.

The original conference also benefited from the contributions of the other discussants. Here we would particularly like to thank Brian Morris, Jonathan Parry, Dick Werbner, and James Woodburn. Stephen Daniels also presented a paper at the conference, but due to prior commitments he was unable to include his contribution here. The Press's anonymous reader provided especially helpful comments on two separate drafts of the volume. After the volume's acceptance by the Press, we learned the identity of the reader so are able to offer our particular thanks to Jimmy Weiner. Linda Frankland also provided invaluable assistance over the period of revision. Finally, we would like to thank Peter Momtchiloff and Jenni Scott no less than the contributors themselves, for their support and patience during the volume's long gestation for which, while there may be no excuses, there are plenty of reasons.

The original conference was made possible by a grant from the Economic and Social Research Council to whom we are most grateful.

E.H.
M.O'H.

CONTENTS

LIST OF FIGURES

NOTES ON CONTRIBUTORS

MAURICE BLOCH is Professor of Anthropology at the London School of Economics, University of London. His research interests are the ethnography of Madagascar and the anthropology of cognition. His most recent books are *From Blessing to Violence* (Cambridge University Press, 1986), *Ritual, History and Power* (Athlone Press, 1989), and *Prey into Hunter* (Cambridge University Press, 1992).

ALFRED GELL is Reader in Anthropology at the London School of Economics. He has conducted fieldwork in Papua New Guinea and central India. He has written three monographs: *Metamorphosis of the Cassowaries* (Athlone Press, 1975), *The Anthropology of Time* (Berg, 1992) and *Wrapping in Images: Tattooing in Polynesia* (Clarendon Press, 1993). His current interest is in the anthropology of art.

PETER GOW is Lecturer in Social Anthropology at the University of Manchester. He has conducted fieldwork in Peru and Brazil and is the author of *Of Mixed Blood* (Clarendon Press, 1991).

NICHOLAS GREEN, who died while this volume was in preparation, was Lecturer in Art and Cultural History in the School of Art History and Music, University of East Anglia. His book *The Spectacle of Nature: Landscape and Bourgeois Culture in Nineteenth-Century France* was published by Manchester University Press in 1990.

ERIC HIRSCH is Lecturer in Social Anthropology in the Department of Human Sciences, Brunel University. He has conducted fieldwork in Papua New Guinea and more recently in south-east England. He is the co-editor of *Consuming Technologies* (Routledge, 1992), a co-author of *Technologies of Procreation* (Manchester University Press, 1993) and is currently completing a monograph based on his fieldwork in Papua New Guinea.

CAROLINE HUMPHREY is Lecturer at the Department of Social Anthropology, University of Cambridge, and a Fellow of King's College, Cambridge. She has research interests in the current social transformations in Russia, Mongolia, and Northern China, and is the author of *Karl Marx Collective: Economy, Society and Religion in a Siberian Collective Farm* (Cambridge University Press, 1983).

ROBERT LAYTON is Professor of Anthropology at the University of Durham. His research interests include the anthropology of art, indigenous rights, social change, and social evolution. His publications include *Uluru: an Aboriginal History of Ayers Rock* (Institute of Aboriginal Studies, 1986) and *Australian Rock Art: A New Synthesis* (Cambridge University Press, 1992).

HOWARD MORPHY is Lecturer in Anthropology at the Institute of Social and Cultural Anthropology, University of Oxford, and Curator at the Pitt Rivers Museum there. His research interests are in art and material culture and the ethnography of Australia. His most recent book is *Ancestral Connections* (University of Chicago Press, 1991).

MICHAEL O'HANLON is an Assistant Keeper in the Ethnography Department of the British Museum. His research interests are in visual anthropology, objectification and the ethnography of New Guinea. He is the author of *Reading the Skin* (1989) and of *Paradise: Portraying the New Guinea Highlands* (1993), both from British Museum Press.

CHRISTOPHER PINNEY is Lecturer in South Asian Anthropology at the School of Oriental and African Studies, University of London. He has conducted fieldwork among village resident industrial workers in central India and published on early anthropological photography and contemporary Indian photography. He is currently completing a historical and ethnographic study of mass-produced popular Hindu art.

TOM SELWYN is Senior Lecturer in Social Anthropology at the Roehampton Institute, London, where he co-ordinates postgraduate studies in the anthropology of tourism, and directs a programme of work on the social and cultural implications of tourism for the EC. His interests also include South Asia and the Middle East, political anthropology and symbolism. His *The Tourist Image: Myths and Myth-Making in Tourism* is published by Wiley in 1995.

CHRISTINA TOREN is Senior Lecturer in Anthropology and Psychology at Brunel University. Her main research interest is in cognition as a microhistorical process, particularly with regard to Fiji, where she has carried out extensive fieldwork. She is the author of *Making Sense of Hierarchy: Cognition as Social Process in Fiji* (Athlone Press, 1990).

Introduction

Landscape: Between Place and Space

===

ERIC HIRSCH

This Introduction and the essays that follow explore the concept of landscape from an anthropological perspective. Unlike 'exchange', 'ritual', 'history' and other concepts which have figured centrally in anthropological debates in recent years, landscape has received little overt anthropological treatment.[1] In this respect landscape shares a similar status to the body in anthropology, that despite its ubiquity it has remained largely unproblematized: 'the majority of researchers have in effect simply "bracketed" it as a black box and set it aside' (Lock 1993: 133). Yet landscape has a submerged presence and significance in anthropological accounts in two related ways. 'Landscape' has been deployed, first, as a framing convention which informs the way the anthropologist brings his or her study into 'view' (i.e. from an 'objective' standpoint—the landscape of a particular people). Secondly, it has been used to refer to the meaning imputed by local people to their cultural and physical surroundings (i.e. how a particular landscape 'looks' to its inhabitants). The black box of landscape requires 'opening' and its contents themselves brought into view.

Dresch has recently commented on how the first of these uses of landscape functioned as a standard framing device in the classic monographs of the 'British school' of social anthropology. As he notes (Dresch 1988: 50) '[t]errain is woven into book after book', a convention Malinowski used to create a participatory effect in his monographs on the Trobriand Islanders ('Imagine yourself suddenly set down . . . alone on a tropical beach . . .' (Malinowski 1922: 4).[2] The convention was reproduced by the subsequent generation of Malinowski's students, such as Firth and Fortes (Dresch 1988: 51–2). In each case, the people are portrayed initially as if seen in a recognizable landscape or picturesque view. But this 'objective', outsider's perspective is soon left behind in order to capture the native's point of view.

This second way in which 'landscape' has been used can also be illustrated by numerous examples drawn from recent ethnographies. Keesing (1982: 76) provides a relevant exposition midway through his monograph on the Kwaio when discussing the topic of ancestors:

The landscape of the Kwaio interior appears, to the alien eye, as a sea of green, a dense forest broken periodically by gardens and recent secondary growth, and an occasional tiny settlement . . . To the Kwaio eye, this landscape is not only divided by invisible lines into named land tracts and settlement sites; it is seen as structured by history.

There is thus the landscape we initially see and a second landscape which is produced through local practice and which we come to recognize and understand through fieldwork and through ethnographic description and interpretation.

A principal aim of this volume follows from these two related ways of considering landscape: the conventional (Western) notion of 'landscape' may be used as a productive point of departure from which to explore analogous local ideas which can in turn be reflexively used to interrogate the Western concept. As Parkin (1991: 7) has suggested, it is through this process of 're-casting cultural ideas and analytical concepts in terms of the light they may throw on each other' that anthropology can succeed in its widest goal as a comparative discipline.

The word landscape was introduced into the English language in the late sixteenth century as a technical term used by painters. It came from the Dutch *landschap* and was known in English for some time as 'landskip'. The painterly origin of the landscape concept is significant. What came to be seen as landscape was recognized as such because it reminded the viewer of a painted landscape, often of European origin. Keith Thomas has documented this development in England between the sixteenth and early nineteenth centuries. It was particularly during the eighteenth century that this appreciation took a self-conscious hold in the English context: 'The initial appeal of rural scenery was that it reminded the spectator of landscape pictures. Indeed the scene was only called a "landscape" because it was reminiscent of a painted "landskip"; it was "picturesque" because it looked like a picture' (Thomas 1984: 265).

This ideal or imagined world as depicted in various genres of landscape painting (Poussin, Claude, Salvator Rosa) was linked to the perception of countryside scenery and its subsequent improvement (through landscape gardening, estate management, etc.): the goal was to achieve a correspondence between the pictorial ideal and the countryside itself. This tendency is reflected in the way the landscape concept is applied to an ever wider range of domains of social and cultural life.[3] The late nineteenth-century development of the garden city is perhaps exemplary here. As Thomas (p. 253) noted: 'Ebenezer Howard drew on a long tradition when he proclaimed in the 1890s that "town and country must be married".'

The interest of Howard's call lies in its goal of uniting in a single place what are otherwise seen as mutually exclusive alternatives: an aspiration achieved by the suburban middle class during the nineteenth century and the working class during the twentieth century (Cosgrove 1984: 267–8). On the one hand there are the social and economic opportunities of the town (hard labour and material rewards) and on the other hand there is the country, offering the possibilities of an Arcadian, idyllic existence (cf. Cronon 1991: 368 for an analogous contrast but from the 'rural' perspective). As Thomas (1984) has documented in the English context, life in the first has long been seen as a way of realizing the potential embodied in the second; today this takes the form of the house with a garden, the allotment, the country cottage, the home in the suburbs, the retirement cottage. There is a relationship here between an ordinary, workaday life and an ideal, imagined existence, vaguely connected to, but still separate from, that of the everyday. We can consider the first as 'foregrounded' in order to suggest the concrete actuality of everyday social life ('the way we now are'). The second we can consider as a 'background', in order to suggest the perceived potentiality thrown into relief by our foregrounded existence ('the way we might be').

Defined in this way, then, 'landscape' entails a relationship between the 'foreground' and 'background' of social life. This, after all, is what is achieved in the idealized world of the painted representation; the painted picture allows us to discern this within the painting itself and/or in the relationship between the viewer of the painting and the painted representation. The argument presented here suggests that the Western convention of landscape representation is a particular expression of a more general foreground/background relationship that is found cross-culturally. As we shall see, however, social life can never achieve the timelessness of a painting, although as the essays that follow show this is often what is striven for in particular cultural contexts (albeit in most cases, without the use of canvases as such).

This definition shares similarities, I think, with the argument recently advanced by Carter (1987). In *The Road to Botany Bay*, Carter takes issue with what he calls 'imperial history': the form of history which 'reduces space to a stage' upon which actors enact significant historical events such as those leading to Australia's 'discovery' and 'settlement'. In its place, Carter (p. xxii) advocates a 'spatial history'—a history of 'the spatial forms and fantasies through which a culture declares its presence'.

Carter's argument is that only mistaken teleology allows us to see early travellers to Australia as arriving in a land waiting to be 'discovered' and later settled. What a traveller (such as Cook) did was to 'bring into view' a land redolent with the European experience from which he had originated. One of the themes explored by Carter is the trouble such travellers continually had in bringing the country into focus: in constituting in new territory a recognizable conjunction between their 'here and now-ness' and a background or horizon to which this could be related. The way in which Australia was named and settled corresponded to this positing of a relationship:

It depended on positing a 'here' (the traveller's viewpoint and orientation) and a 'there' (. . . the horizon). And where such viewpoints did not exist, they had to be hypothesized, rhetorically asserted by way of names . . . Mountains and rivers were culturally desirable, they conjured up pleasing associations. But, more fundamentally, they signified differences that made a difference. They implied the possibility of viewpoints, directions . . . (Carter p. 48)

In Carter's account the relationship between a 'foreground' (here and now, place) and a 'background' (horizon, space) is not incidental to the history and narratives of Australia's colonization: it is central to the way it was conceived, enacted, and, as Carter stresses, is continually re-enacted in the present day. His argument applies not merely to the Europeans who named and settled Australia but also to the Aborigines who are so often peripheral or silent in the traveller's accounts. Although the 'journeys' of the traveller ('discovery' and 'settlement') and of the Aborigines ('the Dreaming') were predicated on different cultural logics, both involve positing a relation between a foreground actuality and a background potentiality. As Carter suggests, 'what he, the nomad, black or white, symbolised, when he wrote or danced or simply made tracks, was not the physical country, but the enactment of a historical space' (p. 349). What was continually re-enacted in these historically and geographically adjacent, but culturally different contexts, were the forms of relations thought to have brought the country into view in the first place (see Munn 1973a).

Although landscape has been singled out here as a distinct cultural idea and analytical concept it is in fact difficult to isolate it from a number of related concepts, including place and space; inside and outside; image and representation.[4] Each of these related concepts, which themselves take on a local aspect, corresponds to one of the two poles of the notion of landscape outlined above. The two poles can be arranged in tabular form:

foreground actuality	↔	background potentiality
place	↔	space
inside	↔	outside
image	↔	representation

The concepts on the left side of the table roughly correspond to what we would understand as the context and form of everyday, unreflexive forms of experience (Bourdieu 1977), while the concepts on the right roughly equate to the context and form of experience beyond the everyday. These latter are often imagined as standing apart, as relatively separate and detached though never completely disconnected. I have referred to this as perceived 'potentiality' ('the way we could be'). The purest form of potentiality is emptiness itself, and it is interesting that sacred sites and places are sometimes physically empty[5] or largely uninhabited, and situated at some distance from the populations for which they hold significance.

Although the items in the table above have been arrayed in two columns, it is important that they are not regarded as unconnected. They are, rather, moments or transitions possible within a single relationship, analogous to the experience of a person momentarily losing his/her way on a familiar journey before relocating him/herself by reference to an external perspective; or to the 'empty place' which periodically fills the 'foreground' experience before receding to its customary 'background' location. The Kaya, the empty ritual capital of the East African Giriama, described by Parkin (1991) is of this form: it is a source of restorative power, but has long been vacated and is divorced from the everyday experience of most Giriama. Though physically distant it shares similarities with the local homestead: like the homestead it can become contaminated and in need of purification. Parkin describes how an analogous method of animal sacrifice is performed both in the homestead and in the Kaya. When performed in the homestead, the background potentiality of the Kaya is foregrounded into everyday experience. And when performed at the Kaya, the diverse experiences of foregrounded place are channelled towards this sacred centre as if to achieve, momentarily, the experience of potentiality, of life as independent and powerful like the Kaya, only to recede into the background and return the Giriama to their fragmented quotidian existence. What is being defined as landscape here is the relationship seen to exist between these two poles of experience in any cultural context. Landscape thus emerges as a cultural *process* (see Ingold 1994: 738).[6]

The conception of landscape proposed here is one rather different from that developed in related disciplines, such as geography, where debates about landscape have, of course, a greater prominence. Ingold (1993: 154) has recently drawn attention to this difference as exemplified in the work of Daniels and Cosgrove (1988: 1), two geographers at the forefront of research in this area, who define landscape as 'a cultural image, a pictorial way of representing or symbolising surroundings'. As Ingold points out this definition is one which emphasizes landscape as essentially static, as the denial of process (see Cosgrove 1984). The problem with this definition is that it takes one pole of experience intrinsic to landscape (the representational) and generalizes this experience into landscape *tout court*. While it is certainly the case, depending on the cultural and historical moment, that men and women attempt to realize in the foreground what can only be a potentiality and for the most part in the background, Daniels and Cosgrove's definition neglects what, by contrast, exists as a part of everyday social life. Their definition only captures one half of the experience intrinsic to landscape, ignoring the other half and the cultural processes of which both poles of experience are a part and through which both are brought into relation. A key question, it would seem, is which socio-cultural factors make for the denial of process, a question to which I will return in the concluding section of the Introduction.

The intention of the remainder of this Introduction is to draw out from the essays that follow a set of common themes which illustrate in greater detail the definition of landscape as cultural process sketched above. Through discussion of the cross-disciplinary literature outlined in each section, my aim is to develop an anthropological perspective on the debates about landscape which have been more central in disciplines such as geography and art history; a second goal is to provide a framework for the cross-cultural comparative study of landscape: a framework which has been lacking both in anthropology and in these related disciplines.

Nature into Landscape

The idea of 'nature', Raymond Williams argues, is probably one of the most complex in the English language (1972: 146). Much of his work has been concerned to clarify the social, political, and textual dimensions of the notion as it has changed over time in the English/British context. Together with the more recent writings of Keith Thomas (1984), Williams has done much to clarify the emergence of the appreciation of 'landscape' which, as noted, took hold throughout Europe between the sixteenth and nineteenth centuries (see Lovejoy 1964: 15–16). It is, of course, during this same period that what we now refer to as anthropology had its origins, and anthropology draws on the same common intellectual background which led to the emergence of an explicit idea of landscape in the Western context. An anthropology of landscape needs to be clear about this relationship.

Collingwood identified three relatively distinct periods in European conceptions of nature (1960: 3–13; see also Olwig 1984: 1–10). He argued that the idea of nature prevalent during these periods derived from analogies drawn from the realm of human society. Where the concept of nature that was prominent in medieval representations encompassed humanity—Nature was God's creation and humanity part of it—the place of humans was less certain in the conception of nature which came to prevail in the post-Renaissance period.[7] That more secular and rational idea of nature depended on a new and singular abstraction—the abstraction of humans themselves (cf. Foucault 1970). And further, this abstraction was related to another set of processes—the increasing intervention of humans into what was imagined as 'natural': in the form of science, agricultural improvement, and the industrial revolution.

One concomitant of the process of ever-increasing intervention in nature was the simultaneous generation of new ideas of separation, such as that between subject and object. It was around these new ideas of separation that the Western idea of landscape emerged. This has been observed by art historians on the one hand, and by geographers focusing upon spatial and material change on the other. In Chapter 1, Nicholas Green examines a particular historical example of this process in early- and mid-nineteenth-century France (cf. Green 1990). Green argues that the growing appreciation of the countryside which he describes for nineteenth-century Paris cannot be accounted for either by the opening up of the countryside or by changes to it—although these factors were undoubtedly significant. What Green argues to have been more important, rather, was the contemporary proliferation in Paris of landscape pictures, tour guides, advertisements for houses in the country, and a more general desire for immersion in the countryside. As he suggests: 'it was the material conditions and the cultural developments germane to the capital that generated those vocabularies of looking which were capable of bringing nature into visibility as a significant form of social experience'.

Green's analysis foregrounds two intersecting ideologies which impinged on the everyday experience of Parisians during this period: a concern over the unhealthy state of Paris after the cholera epidemic of the 1830s, and the proliferation of 'sights' such as arcades and dioramas in strategic parts of the city. The 'potentiality' thus brought into focus was the health-giving benefits of immersion in the countryside and the 'landscape' itself as a key form of spectacle, particularly as portrayed in the dioramas (see Crary 1990), which themselves fostered a particular kind of looking. What was stressed, particularly in the guides and advertisements for the countryside, was less the 'picture as text' and more a way of seeing that was structured by various domains of metropolitan life in Paris. Green's chapter is an elegant plea to art historians, geographers, and anthropologists alike to abandon their traditional attitude towards the pictorial: 'It is time to have done with a commonsense that claims the visual as the primary property of pictures.'

The rise of landscape painting as a distinctive genre predates the period dealt with by Green by several centuries. A theme highlighted by accounts of the genre's emergence, which Green also brings out, is the manner in which a positive relationship is constructed between the experience of a viewing 'subject' and the countryside as a desirable 'object' to behold. As the place of humans in nature became more open to question than it had previously been, the relationship between 'foreground' and 'background' in visual representations of this period was gradually transformed.

Gombrich (1966: 108–9) has proposed an institutional explanation—as opposed to this stylistic one—to account for the rise of the landscape genre. He suggests that landscape painting arose out of the merging of two cultures of visualization and the forms of representation valorized by each. As we shall see below these traditions of visualization are deployed differently in the artworks produced during European exploration and colonization in the Pacific: historical developments that importantly shaped the subsequent use of the landscape idea in anthropology and related disciplines (see Smith 1985: ix–x).

Gombrich's argument is useful to summarize here as it has been influential in debates about landscape in the neighbouring discipline of geography (cf. Cosgrove 1984: 22–5). Art historians have long noted the proliferation of landscape paintings in early modern market cities such as Antwerp. To account for this development they suggested that in such market-dominated contexts artworks were no longer produced primarily for individual commissions but through anonymous demand.[8] Instead, Gombrich traced the conceptualization

of 'landscape' to the aesthetic theories of Alberti and his foundational text of
Renaissance visual representation, the *Ten Books on Architecture*.[9]

Alberti had canonized the idea of art as an autonomous sphere of human
activity, which should be treasured for its psychological effects. One of the
ways in which such effects could be generated was through the depiction of
pleasing 'sights' such as the countryside. This formulation can be linked, in
turn, to the Albertian definition of the picture as a framed surface or pane
situated at a certain distance from the viewer who looks through it at a second
substitute world or 'stage'.[10] In contrast to this 'southern' tradition, there
existed a 'northern' tradition of visualization, an 'art of describing' (see Alpers
1989).[11] This latter tradition is not predicated on an Albertian 'pane'; instead,
the emphasis is placed more on the craft of empirical representation. The
prevalence of maps, map-like representations, and pictures with a 'realist'
quality are expressive of this visual culture.[12]

Gombrich suggested, then, that landscape as a genre with widespread popularity arose as a consequence of a dominant 'southern' aesthetic theory appro-
priating the products of 'northern' realism (Gombrich 1966: 114). However,
this trend, and the emergence of the notion of landscape only became possible
when the individual subject came to be envisaged, following Alberti, as drawing
delight from pleasing sights in a self-conscious manner (cf. Williams 1973:
121). The emergence of the idea of landscape is further connected to the central
importance that would henceforth be attached to picturing, mapping, mir-
roring, representing the world as the only reliable way of knowing it (see Alpers
1989).[13]

Place and Space

It would be mistaken, however, to see these developments associated with the
Renaissance (particularly the rediscovery of linear perspective (Cosgrove 1985)
and the profusion of map-making) as heralding a radical and inseparable break
with previous forms of experience. The value placed on viewing the world in
Cartesian terms (i.e. 'non-subjective' geometric space) is part of a project of
making explicit what had previously, and in other cultural contexts, been more
implicit and not necessarily separated out as a distinct way of imagining oneself
as placed in the world.[14]

An analogous contrast between an emphasis on the particularities of place as
seen from a specific (subjective) vantage point and an emphasis on the study of
space, divorced as much as possible from a subject-position, has been of central
concern to the way the concept of landscape has been taken up in geography
and anthropology (Livingstone 1992: 290–300). The work of the American
geographer Sauer, especially his monograph *The Morphology of Landscape*
(1963), is a particularly clear example.

Sauer's notion of landscape derived from European trends in geography which took shape during the late nineteenth century (especially in relation to the emerging field of sociology). The debates between geography (as represented by the German Ratzel) and sociology (as represented by the Frenchman Durkheim) focused on what has come to be known as the 'society-milieu' relationship.[15] Sauer's monograph, a combination of insights and criticisms of the German and French schools, argued that culture shaped the natural landscape to produce a 'cultural landscape': 'The cultural landscape is fashioned from a natural landscape by a culture group. Culture is the agent, the natural area is the medium, the cultural landscape is the result' (Sauer 1963: 343).

The force of his argument was against environmental determinism (associated with Ratzel), but he considered that his attempt to formulate an objective procedure for the study and comparison of landscape could never succeed in eliminating the intrinsically subjective element: 'there remains an aspect of meaning in landscape which lies "beyond science", the understanding of which cannot be reduced to formal processes' (Cosgrove 1984: 17). There is thus a tension evident in the relationship between the subject-position of place and the non-subject-position of space in the way landscape has been taken up as an analytical concept. This is especially explicit in geography.

Gow's Chapter 2, on the Piro of Amazonian Peru, exemplifies the tension between these perspectives. The cultural shaping of Amazonia by indigenous peoples is hard to discern for people from temperate climates, since a distant horizon does not recede away from a point of observation. It is only when the forest has been extensively cut down and roads constructed that a relationship between place and distant space can be discerned by those unaccustomed to such surroundings.

By contrast, what the Piro 'see' when they look at the land is kinship. Gow describes how the Piro produce themselves as people through the production, circulation, and reciprocal sharing of food. He notes that just as kinship is produced in this manner, so the vegetation pattern that surrounds villages is seen as 'loci of kinship'. An important theme highlighted in this chapter and echoed in several others is that kinship and the land are mutually implicated (see Munn 1986; Cronon 1983). It is through the processes of implication that Piro notions of place and space emerge. This is made apparent to the Piro themselves through the endless stories that recount these implicating processes, a point also developed in Toren's chapter. Through situated narration, the 'here and now-ness' of place expands to a more distant horizon, constituted by past and ongoing relationships such as garden-making and home-building. At the same moment this enables the place of narration to have features of a distinctive vantage point or perspective on the horizon which encompasses these relations: features, in short, of 'space'.

But there is also an ambiguity in the relation between living humans and the land. The Piro must constantly make use of regenerated forest and new portions of the river. These spaces, however, are the source of sickness and death, embodied in the Piro concept of the 'bone demon'. From the 'foreground' of specific places, then, humans depend on these uninhabited spaces for potential gardens, villages, etc. The Piro shaman, by contrast, is able to enter these river and forest spaces through the use of the drug *ayahuasca* and to perceive them as filled with people. The shaman is thus able to see what other men and women cannot in their everyday experience, and to return from his shamanic voyaging with the knowledge required to cure the sick. The shaman bridges the relationship between proximate place and distant (largely invisible) space.

At first sight the situation described by Bloch in Chapter 3 on the Zafimaniry of Madagascar could not be more different. Among the Zafimaniry it would seem that it is the very presence of the trees which is the problem. Chopping the forest down is part of the process through which the Zafimaniry attempt to transcend the precariousness of their everyday life and to inscribe themselves more permanently on the land. In so doing, they attempt to take on some of the qualities of their ancestors. But despite the Zafimaniry's deforestative preferences there is a significant similarity between them and the Piro. In both instances there is an attempt to achieve a relationship with a background potentiality—to overcome the perceived precariousness of their everyday, situated existence. In the Piro context, this is through an enduring invisible space (regenerated forest), approached via the agency of the shaman who perceives it as a place filled with people; among the Zafimaniry, it is through a space which is temporarily occluded by forest until the latter is cleared to make way for visible villages filled with people. In both contexts the relationship between place (here in the sense of livelihood) and space (now in the sense of regenerative life) is accomplished through particular conceptions of mortality and immortality (see Bloch and Parry (eds.) 1982).

At marriage the Zafimaniry construct a house, and if the couple are fecund, the house itself becomes the focus of an increasingly large and clearly visible village. Bloch goes on to describe how Zafimaniry notions of altitude, clarity, permanence, legitimate political power, and genealogical seniority are all interrelated. Over time, the initially impermanent materials that are used to construct the house of such a founding couple are replaced by harder woods, immortalizing marital reproduction. After a period following their death, though, another material form takes shape, expressive of the rivalry between marriage and siblingship: stone megaliths are erected outside the boundaries of the village, immortalizing unchanging, static siblingship. And the dead themselves, in becoming an increasingly anonymous part of the surroundings, take on for their descendants that uncaring permanence which, in life, they had sought to transcend. More recently, the land has come to take on an even more fixed aspect as it becomes usable only for irrigated rice cultivation, and not the transient form of slash and burn agriculture which depends on regenerated forest.

The Picturesque

The Zafimaniry's delight in the 'good views' which deforestation opens up brings to mind an ambivalent set of Western attitudes. On the one hand, radical alterations of the land such as deforestation are seen as a form of environmental degradation. Places appear to lose their individual character, with no prospect of future regeneration.[16] On the other hand, such alterations can, from an alternative Western perspective, be seen as transforming 'nature' so it conforms to a pre-existing but positive image: making it appear picturesque (or alternatively, 'productive' (Thomas 1984: 267)). Both perspectives coexist in an uneasy tension, each creating the conditions for the other. Certainly, the idea of the picturesque proved to be a powerful framing device for the way in which non-Western cultures came to be perceived, represented, and colonized. Since the pioneering work of Bernard Smith and his analysis of the artistic works produced by Europeans during voyages in the South Pacific, we have come to appreciate in much clearer terms the close relationship between landscape (picturesque) representation and early forms of ethnographical description (Smith 1985: ch. 7).

An important finding in Smith's work is that European conventions of representation (both visual and textual) were transformed as a result of the encounters with peoples and places in this region. His work also exemplifies the tension in representational techniques mentioned in the previous section: between a picturesque mode premised on neo-classical ideas of Italian origin and a 'descriptive' mode associated with observation, empirical record-making and experimentation. It is the latter mode which predominated, for example, in the drawings of individual plants and animals (Smith 1985: 112). However, when it came to rendering the local inhabitants and their surroundings, the picturesque, Albertian mode was more to the fore. This reflected the attempt to represent 'native' peoples in terms of several predefined conventions associated with notions of Arcadia, Eden, primitivism, and 'savagery'.[17]

Smith argues that the tension between the convention of romantic depiction and more 'scientific' ethnological information resulted in the emergence of what he calls 'typical landscapes': representations that would evoke the sense of people and place characteristic of the area. What became explicit during this period was the notion that each country had its own peculiar type of landscape: a certain natural physiognomy, as Humboldt came to refer to it. In anthropology this was a view with which Boas subsequently aligned himself (Livingstone 1992: 291).

This transformation in representational emphasis, and the colonization of peoples of the region, play off one another in significant ways.[18] It is possible to see the initial debate among the 'theorists of the picturesque' (Gilpin, Payne Knight, Price) as anticipating in microcosm the colonizing tendencies that were to be such a feature of the nineteenth century. On the one hand, the picturesque was theorized as 'passive' and bound by rules for viewing (as experienced by the powerless traveller). On the other, and subsequently, the picturesque was theorized as 'active' (as enacted by the powerful colonialist). The first position is associated with the ideas and writings of Gilpin. The second arose in debates between Payne Knight and Price on the one hand and Repton on the other around the nature of landscape 'improvement' (Michasiw 1992).

The debate surrounding notions of the picturesque in Britain was a reaction both to the idealized landscapes painted by Claude, Poussin, and Salvator Rosa and to the then prevailing convention of the Grand Tour to which these paintings gave visible expression. In this sense, the debate concerned English/ British 'national identity'.[19] At the same time the debate about the picturesque in Britain anticipated a number of subsequent developments in the evaluation of the countryside (see Thomas 1984: 262).

As Smith (1985: 200–2) shows, Cook's voyages to the South Pacific were also having a profound effect on the English and European imagination at this time. As earlier suggested, people were coming to think not only that each region had its own peculiar type of landscape, but that the convention of the Grand Tour itself was geographically far too limited: '[the] possibility of adventures in distant colonies and the prospect of painting scenes never painted before, held more attractions than the visit to Italy'. In this regard, voyages to the Pacific often formed the prelude to world travel; India became a key destination for many.[20]

Pinney's Chapter 4 considers how the colonial tradition of the picturesque and picturesque painting in India became transformed into the visual form of the oleograph ('calendar art'). He explores the relationship between what is represented in oleographs and the industrial town of Nagda where his fieldwork was conducted and where many such oleographs are sold and 'consumed'.

In certain oleographs, the relationship between foregrounded place as representing traditional dimensions of existence exists in an uneasy, often disjoined relationship with the background space wherein modernity is represented. Pinney shows that this tension is not just a feature of the representational realm but is part of the lived experience of inhabitants of Nagda. In other oleographs, particularly those incorporating Hindu deities, a unified relationship between foreground and background is achieved. However, this internal unity is radically disjoined from the contemporary lived experiences of those who actually purchase the oleographs. Indian nationalism sparked off an attempt to resolve the disjunction between tradition and modernity and in a range of oleographs adopted the convention used for deities to represent a unified, fecund, and self-possessed nation: 'It is in this political fiction that horizon and foreground, space and place, coalesce momentarily'.

The political fiction that Pinney draws to our attention is a recurrent theme in the history of nation-states, but it is also, as Bloch shows in his chapter, one that does not depend on the nation-state for its existence. Pinney's chapter makes apparent the significant but ambiguous relationship between what is perceived to exist inside the representation and what outside. What is also highlighted in this context is the uneasy relationship between what the local people of Nagda perceive as inside their local 'landscape' and what the large industrial estate views as the boundaries of its domain.

Inside and Outside

Raymond Williams has been much cited as pointing out that it is 'outsiders'—estate owners, improvers, industrialists, artists—who have recourse to the notion of landscape, not those who actually live *in* the area in question. In *The Country and the City* (1973), Williams suggested that the conventional use of the landscape idea made apparent this ambiguity between inside(r) and outside(r). It is this ambiguity, for example, that prompted geographers to banish landscape from the vocabulary of geography in the post-World War 2 period (Livingstone 1992: 308).[21] More recently, Cosgrove (1984) has discerned in this ambiguity the ideological nature of the concept of landscape.

However, Williams' sharp distinction between 'insiders' who 'live' their landscape and 'outsiders' who entertain an objectified concept of it, is difficult to sustain. With its implications that the first are rooted in nature while the second have an understanding based exclusively on commercial/possession values (see Berger 1972), it savours of romanticism. Like 'place' and 'space', notions of 'inside' and 'outside' are not mutually exclusive and depend upon cultural and historical context.

Selwyn's Chapter 5, on the Israeli landscape, shows how ideas of inside and outside can shift radically in the context of national and wider geopolitical events. There is an interesting parallel between the interests of the nineteenth-century Zionists and Williams' vision of the 'insider' on the land, portrayed as closer to 'nature' and engaged in more 'authentic' forms of work. As Selwyn points out, Zionism was less a religious movement and more 'a socialist redemptive process grounded in physical life and work on the land'. The Zionists hoped to transform Jewish life from being based on a form of hollow commercialism in Europe (as outsider) to being a new and 'normal' set of relations between men, women, nature, and work on the land, based in Palestine (as insider).

Crucial to this transformation were the country's existing denizens, the Arab 'fellah' and the Bedouin. They were generally seen as 'authentic residents of the Bible' and some scholars claimed they were descendants of the biblical patriarchs. The image of insideness evoked by the Arabs, as a legacy of the Hebrew past, was one that earlier settlers hoped to re-enact through their entry to Palestine. The possibility of religious and national coexistence was sketched out by men such as Buber with these images in mind. But as Selwyn subtly shows, the centrality of landscape to Israeli ideas of the nation has, particularly since

Independence (1948), radically transformed the relationship between those perceived as inside and those perceived as outside. He explores this through three case studies and a historical sketch involving related conceptions of inside ('good'/'us'/Israeli) and outside ('bad'/'them'/Arab). What is understood as the contemporary Israeli landscape is the relationship sustained between these notions of insideness and outsideness and their historical transformation.

Underlying these transformations, Selwyn discerns a close relationship between notions of 'defending nature' and 'defending' the Israeli state. The landscape is now seen as a 'stage' which needs to be secured from two threats: the demographic expansion of the Arab population and the values of American consumerism. Ironically, as Selwyn notes, 'the landscape has now become a strategic metaphor in the reconstitution of the very values from which the early settlers attempted to liberate themselves'. The liberating potential previously imagined to reside in the Arab and Bedouin populations has been recast as an external threat.

The contemporary Israeli case involves a transformation of the relationship of inside and outside between two relatively separate peoples and religious traditions that were brought into relationship in one context. The tensions that emerged can be compared with the Mongolian case described by Humphrey in Chapter 6. But in this latter context the tensions emerge less around specific peoples than around competing notions of agency that are made visible by placing people in the world in radically different ways. Humphrey refers to these as 'chiefly' and 'shamanist' landscapes. These are not to be confused with separate 'societies', or with the landscape as a preconstituted entity of which there are chiefly and shamanist views. Rather, these are now latent, now manifest potentialities present throughout this cultural region. They emerge through the conjunction of certain ecological, political, and religious factors; moreover, they are anticipations of one another.

Humphrey points out that chieftainship and large centralized polities have tended to arise in the vast region of the central treeless steppes; shamanism has tended to occur in more 'peripheral' areas where grassland is interspersed with forests, mountains, and large rivers and lakes. But the ecology is only one factor. Her chapter argues that chiefly and shamanic landscapes are only contingently related to one another. The transformations from one mode to another entail differently conceived notions of inside and outside. In the chiefly mode this is focused around the 'vertical' domain—mountains being one example—and upon the repetition of moving ritual centres based on patrilineal descent. This in turn is linked to a repetitive toponymy and to the situational characterization of shamans (and women) as outsiders. The exclusion of shamans relates to the access they are believed to have to a spiritual realm that threatens to subvert the achievement of verticality and to replace toponymic uniformity with unrestricted variation. It is only when these repetitive centres can no longer be politically sustained that the background shamanic landscape becomes the ascendant mode.

What the shamanic mode celebrates is difference. Spiritual powers seen as inherent in the cosmos are channelled towards the person instead of the patriline. There is an emphasis on laterality and on movement in contrast to the repetitive toponymy of the chiefly mode. This is given visible expression at the death of shamans when they become spirits and are memorialized as specific place, instead of forgotten and erased from the land as happens in the chiefly mode. However, the structural tendency towards verticality and repetitive centredness is never far in the background: it is present as a potentiality ready to emerge again as the more dominant social and political form throughout this vast region.

The tensions and transformations documented in Humphrey's chapter at first sight seem very different from what we are accustomed to in the Western context. But at the same time, the tendencies inherent in the chiefly landscape—with its emphasis on the obliteration of spatial specificity, emphasizing repetitive temporal movement—brings to mind one of Marx's central tenets of the logic of capitalism: 'the annihilation of space by time' (cited in Cronon 1991: 92). In the Mongolian context an emphasis on social and cosmological verticality means that 'space [is] collapsed along the time axis'. According to the logic of capital, based on the dictates of technological and market efficiency and ever-increasing connections, geography (space) tends to become annihilated as a way of increasing the temporal flow of commodities. This process has been documented, for example, by Cronon (1991) in his exemplary study of the historical relationship between Chicago ('Nature's Metropolis') and the 'Great West'. He describes how an economic process which increasingly interrelates and integrates a 'landscape' ironically generates increasingly sharp disjunctions between 'inside' and 'outside', city and countryside.

In a similar manner there are countervailing tendencies in capitalism which, reminiscent of the shamanic mode described above, celebrate diversity in particular ecosystems. Here, the attempt is to transcend the homogenizing and depersonalized relationship between the experience of inside and outside which the logic of capital brings about (D. Harvey 1989: 254–9). Sets of such countervailing tendencies have a long history in, for example, England. Thomas has discussed the problem as it became more apparent during the eighteenth century. How, he asks, can one 'preserve wild nature and yet keep it out of the kitchen garden?' (Thomas 1984: 285).

As we saw in the previous section a similar problem was encountered by European travellers in the South Pacific who drew upon contemporary conventions of the picturesque in their attempt to represent native peoples. South Pacific Islanders were represented in such a way as to render their 'otherness'—their outsideness—so that it conformed to European visions. But this has never been a one-way process. Toren's Chapter 7 describes how the Fijians have come to render various Western institutions so that they conform to local ideas about the relationship between inside and outside: how precolonial ancestral powers (*mana*) inherent in the land and the cash-cropping and Christianity which accompanied colonialism, cohere in a single 'landscape'. It would be incorrect to view the former as more 'inside' and the latter as more 'outside'. Rather, Christianity and capitalist market relations are now encompassed by the spatiality of Fijian village life. Toren shows how this is revealed both through the Fijian practice of routinely remarking on the most ordinary events of village life and through more specific narratives.

   Her chapter includes an account of the foundation of an ancestral chiefly house (*yavu*). The *yavu* lies outside the movements of ordinary village life, but its outsideness is perceived as a potential of *mana*, one that finds living embodiment in the person of the paramount chief. It is in a similar manner that mission Christianity and capitalist cash-cropping are seen as potentialities to be brought within the Fijian relationships of inside and outside as construed through narrative. To view one as more 'traditional' and the other as more 'modern' and imposed from outside would be to ignore local processes of transformation. Thus the horizon and spatiality of village life has expanded to encompass both State and Christian ideology. But at the same time these changes continue to be expressed through local narratives and imagery which emphasize that such changes are 'in the way of kinship', 'in the way of the chiefs' and 'in the way of the land'.

Image and Representation

The Fijian example draws our attention to how narratives continually bring into focus the relationship between the foreground of place and 'insideness' and space and 'outsideness'. It is this recurrent, emergent process—expressed through imagery and metaphor—which a number of recent writers have seen as the central feature of local constructions of landscape (Basso 1988; Weiner 1991). The narrative dimensions of the Fijian example can also be counterposed to another tradition for analysing how people are seen to be related to their surroundings. It is one that took hold in the West after Descartes and has often been described as leading to forms of 'objectivism' in social inquiry (Bourdieu 1977). In fact, it was just such an emphasis on imagery and metaphor which came to be condemned by the Cartesian tradition, whose 'rationalistic programme involved eliminating from our . . . language . . . all figurative and metaphorical conceptions, all expressions that could be understood only by reference to images' (Hampshire 1969: 477). The goal of this programme was to find a secure basis of knowledge, untainted by all outside influences. The language that was aimed for may be referred to as a language for 'finding one's feet in the world'—knowledge as secure as an artefactual map. As has been suggested above, it is not accidental that the views of Descartes coincided historically with profound developments in cartography and the profusion of map-making for popular consumption in Western Europe.

There is, however, another line of thought in the Western tradition, against which Cartesianism was directed, which gives a central place to imagery, metaphor and 'common sense'. This is what has come to be known as the 'art of memory' (Yates 1992). For Vico, perhaps the most ambitious theorist in this tradition, knowledge was not, as it was for Descartes, to be found in anything pre-established either in people (*res cogitans*) or in the surroundings (*res extensa*). Rather it is found 'in socially shared identities of feeling they [people and surroundings] themselves create in the flow of activity between them' (Shotter 1986: 199, emphasis removed). The identities are what Vico calls 'sensory topics' (Greek *topos* = place). This term is chosen 'because [these identities] give rise to "commonplaces", i.e. to shared moments in a flow of social activity which afford common reference, and "sensory" because they are moments in which shared *feelings* for already shared circumstances are created' (ibid.). In contrast to the Cartesian tradition of knowledge and language, that of Vico might be referred to as the 'language of involvement'.[22]

The Cartesian view aims for a form of absolute positionality. The specifics of place are not of central concern, as the goal is to achieve clear and distinct map-like representations.[23] The Vichian view is more relativistic, giving a priority to images and placedness. At one level these two viewpoints appear to be irreconcilable. However, underlying the apparent difference is a link which can be highlighted by reference to the almost taken-for-granted practice of everyday movement, way-finding, and navigation. In fact, Gell (1985) has discerned a relationship between absolute and relative positions (between attachment to place and more detached space, between a sense of inside and an external vantage point, between images and representations). Gell develops this idea with respect to an important critique which Bourdieu makes of 'objectivism'. Bourdieu states:

It is significant that 'culture' is sometimes described as a *map*; it is the analogy which occurs to an outsider who has to find his way around in a foreign landscape and who compensates for his lack of practical mastery, the prerogative of the native, by the use of a model of all possible routes. The gulf between this potential, abstract space, devoid of landmarks or any privileged centre . . . and the practical space of journeys actually made, or rather of journeys actually being made, can be seen from the difficulty we have in recognising familiar routes on a map or town-plan until we are able to bring together the axes of the field of potentialities and the 'system of axes linked unalterably to our bodies, and carried about with us wherever we go', as Poincaré puts it, which structures practical space into right and left, up and down, in front and behind (Bourdieu 1977: 2).

Gell's point is that there is an underlying assumption in this quotation that the 'native' does not have recourse to 'maps' (cf. Harley and Woodward 1987: 505–8; P. Harvey 1980). Much of course depends on how a map is defined.

Gell suggests that in defining a map it is first important to distinguish between relative, subject-centred forms of knowledge (which he calls indexical) and absolute, non-subject-centred spatial knowledge (non-indexical). According to this distinction a map may be defined as 'any system of spatial know-ledge . . . which takes the form of non-[. . .] indexical statements about the spatial locations of places and objects' (1985: 278). Images, by contrast, are indexical forms of knowledge, in that they always have a sensory form. Thus, images 'are perceptually based beliefs about what is where in relation to a percipient subject' (p. 280). In contrast to Bourdieu, then, Gell argues that it is only on the basis of non-indexical knowledge (maps) that indexical knowledge (images) about current locations and objects are established.

For analytical purposes, while it is important to be able to distinguish between images and maps, in practice, as Gell (pp. 278–80) suggests, images and maps flow one into the other in mutually related ways. This is brought out with particular subtlety in a number of recent studies of Australian Aboriginal peoples which have drawn inspiration from Munn's study of the Walbiri (Munn 1973a). Her analysis of Walbiri graphic representations reveals how they are 'ways of depicting different spatial distributions of locales' and are thus sometimes referred to as 'maps' (Munn 1973a: 136). Morphy's Chapter 8 highlights this intrinsic relationship of image and map in the Yolngu context as it comes to be focused around the primacy of place. His chapter also presents an interesting variation of the Mongolian case discussed by Humphrey. In the Mongolian context diversity and change are related to the shamanic landscape while 'unchanging' structure results from the ascendancy of the chiefly form. In the Yolngu case, by contrast, contingent change is recurrently incorporated into ancestral, unchanging structure. The focal point of this process is local notions of place.

Much of Morphy's account is devoted to describing the manner in which conception of place has precedence over time in Yolngu ontogeny. This is evident in the structure of language where notions of 'emplacement' are par-ticularly prominent—analogous to the more familiar process of ancestral beings continually turning into place. However, this ordered and frozen world of the ancestral past is only re-created in personal experience through the movements made by persons and collectivities between places. Morphy speaks of the tracks created by ancestral beings, before they became transformed into place, as a 'mythological map'. The notion of 'map' should be noted here. It is a form of representation at once distant from the everyday field of experience of Yolngu men and women, but which is continually brought into this presentational field through narratives, songs, marriage practices, and ritual. Like a more conven-tional, artefactual map it is drawn upon for the purposes of orientation and action: whom to marry or not to marry, what to hunt and what not to hunt.

Morphy describes how this sense of orientation and action is also a product of kinship. As we have seen in a number of the essays discussed above, kinship and the land are involved in a process of mutual implication. In this Australian instance everyday images and the ancestral, mythological map 'flow' one into the other in what is conceptualized as a lifelong 'journey'. This is established at birth, reinforced at marriage, and completed during mortuary ritual. At birth the 'soul', a manifestation of ancestral power, is inside the person and at the death the soul returns to the ground, taking a unique route across Arnhem Land. Morphy quotes Munn (1973b: 199), who notes: 'In this sense, the Dreaming [ancestral past] is continually coming out of the ground and being re-embodied as a living entity, as well as continually returning to the ground in death.' Image (as lived experience) and map (as the marks on the land indicating potentialities for the life-course as well as its objectification at death) continually re-create each other.

In Arnhem Land then, birth, marriage, and death are particular moments in which what we refer to as the landscape of the Yolngu is made temporarily visible (as 'images') only to become part again of the invisible background of everyday practice (as ancestral map). These same processes are evident in the Western Desert, but as Layton makes clear in his Chapter 9, we find them differently articulated in this cultural context. This is a consequence of a different ecological situation (seasonal water in Northern Australia vs. irregular water supplies in the Western Desert). It is this ecological context which impinges on the distinctive style of Western Desert 'discourse' on which Layton focuses. His engagement with this discourse occurred while working on a land claim for Anangu people of Uluru (Layton 1986). The stance he adopts in his chapter arises from the problem of translating Western Desert discourse into legal or anthropological discourse.

As in the Yolngu context, the land of the Western Desert is thought of as having been created by ancestral beings during the *tjukurpa*, which Layton translates as the 'time of law'. When these local conceptions are brought under the scrutiny of the white Australian legal system intent as it is on specifying rights and boundaries, unanswerable questions arise: '"How wide is a dreaming track?" is, for instance, a nonsensical question which was posed at an earlier land claim hearing.'

Such a question reflects the Australian State's attempt to render local knowledge in a particular form: to imagine that a 'track' is a cartographic category and that it is possible to specify its 'width'. It is not that the inhabitants of the Western Desert do not have recourse to non-indexical maps of the kind Gell describes, it is just that they would not ordinarily separate out such image-based knowledge into legalistic 'objects' of discourse.

Layton's chapter can thus be read at two levels. At one level it is an attempt to demonstrate a problem of referential meaning: the manner in which the meaning of a word or phrase is shaped by the contexts of its production. This is a debate which goes to the core of current concerns about the limitations of post-modernism. He advocates a view of language where it is seen to have practical import; language is used to get things done (see Shotter 1986; Merleau-Ponty 1962).

Secondly, the chapter shows how image and map are interrelated differently in the Western Desert and in Arnhem Land. Again, Layton argues that this difference arises from the more precarious ecology of the former. In the Western Desert one is neither born into, nor does one return to, a place as part of an 'ancestral grid' or 'map'. Rather, one looks after or 'holds' a country. The map here, as a form of non-indexical spatial knowledge, engenders a different sense of orientation. It is less a grid of ancestral tracks for the prescription of marriage, hunting, etc., and more a facilitator for the extension of such practices in as many directions as possible (*along* ancestral tracks). The idiom of siblingship (of 'holding' a person and a place simultaneously) is the social mechanism through which this is achieved. The day-to-day experience ('images') of access to food and water exists in conjunction with the background potential of all the possible tracks that might be held. The Western Desert map is one based on the accumulation of relationships in contrast to the replication of a pre-existing pattern.

Although the differences between Western and Northern Australia have been stressed here, what is common to both regions is the high degree of visibility. A cultural value is placed on visuality, which is given iconic expression in the graphical symbolism analysed by Munn (1973a) in the Western Desert and in Arnhem Land by Morphy (1991). It is pertinent that anthropologists working in the forest environments of Papua New Guinea have drawn comparisons and contrasts with, for example, the Walbiri ethnography. Weiner, who worked with the Foi people of Papua, has recently commented on such parallels, focusing in particular on the inscriptive activities of men and women in their everyday movements, and in relation to the tracks of their ancestors as recalled through Foi place-names, dreams, and songs (Weiner 1991: 196–7). Central to both cultural contexts is the prevalence of iconicity: in the Walbiri context this is articulated graphically, in the Foi context, linguistically. The underlying basis of this difference is the point of departure for the final chapter by Gell, which draws upon his fieldwork among the Umeda people of New Guinea.

Among the Umeda, the relationship between everyday 'images' and the sense of a more encompassing representation ('map') is not engendered primarily through the use of sight. Gell argues that a dense forest environment of the sort that the Umeda inhabit imposes a 'reorganization of sensibility', different in kind from that which develops in more 'open' environments. Language here takes on a salience additional to that which it possesses in more visual cultures. Specifically, Gell suggests that in cultural/environmental contexts where a single sense modality is dominant (hearing, in the case of the Umeda, where sight is so often obscured by forest and 'views' so rare), then iconicity is a pervasive feature of language.[24]

In this highly audible world nothing that we would understand as a (visible) landscape is present—only partial glimpses (compare Gow's chapter). There is no central vantage point from which a synoptic view can be obtained. In the Umeda context that which is visible is by definition that which is physically close. Hiddenness takes the form not of invisibility but of inaudibility. The landscape that the Umeda inhabit is thus one of 'articulation', as Gell calls it:

This landscape is constructed out of the interface between two kinds of experience; distally it comprises a codification of ambient sound, that is, a soundscape, proximally it comprises the basic unifying armature of the body as a sounding cavity, sensitive to sound and, through the autokinetically sensed experience of verbal and mimetic vocalisation, productive of sound.

Gell describes the schemas in Umeda language which encode these two forms of experience. Through his description we are able to understand how the soundscape of the Umeda is bounded conceptually. At one physical extreme there is the 'vertical fence', made up by a tall local ridge, which suggests a background horizon. Phonologically this is encoded through rounded but constrained sounds suggestive of encircling limits. At the other physical extreme there is the proximate village knoll; phonologically this is encoded so as to express this opposite physical extreme. The encoding of these linguistic features is analogous to the physical movements through which the Umeda traverse their surroundings. In other words, the linguistic features have to be understood as arising from transient sounds and articulations: they have to be understood dynamically, as movements.

What Gell's chapter highlights is that the relationship between indexical 'images' and non-indexical 'maps' is one which is not restricted to *visual* forms. The auditory map of Umeda finds its physical manifestation in spoken language; the map is in a sense re-created through these auditory means. Through their speech, Umeda men and women express in language what they constitute through movement and through practical and ritual action: the most distant (least visible) and most proximate (most visible) dimensions of the Umeda landscape.

Gell's contribution thus brings us back to Green's discussion of nineteenth-century France presented above: the argument against the common-sense claim that the visual is the primary property of (landscape) pictures. Rather, the visual articulates differentially with the other sense modalities, depending on the precise social and historical context. In the French context it was developments associated with the metropolitan centre of Paris that created the conditions for bringing the countryside into view in a distinctive way. In a sense, as with the Umeda, it was the *lack* of spatial views (in urban Paris), together with other factors that stressed the experience of commercially produced spectacle, which facilitated the emphasis on visualizing nature as 'landscape'. In each context, landscape emerges as a form of cultural process.

Conclusion: Landscape as Cultural Process

The model of landscape developed in this Introduction is one predicated on the idea of landscape as process. The individual essays draw out this process ethnographically. More generally, it has been suggested that this process is one which relates a 'foreground' everyday social life ('us the way we are') to a 'background' potential social existence ('us the way we might be'). It is a process that attains a form of timelessness and fixity in certain idealized and transcendent situations, such as a painted landscape representation, but which can be achieved only momentarily, if ever, in the human world of social relationships. This last point requires further comment and also raises an issue which has been influential in the study of landscape outside anthropology.

Cosgrove (1984: 32) has argued forcefully that landscape implies the denial of process: 'it is process [that] landscape as an ideological concept formally denies'. Landscape, as discussed by Cosgrove, is based on a reading of the concept's historical emergence that emphasizes its visual, painterly dimensions. Landscape in this interpretation is a restrictive way of seeing which privileges the 'outsiders'' point of view, while sustaining a radical split between insiders and outsiders on the land: between those who relate 'directly' to the land and those who relate to it as a form of exchange value (Cosgrove 1984: 269–70).

It is certainly the case that the historical emergence of the Western notion of landscape implied ways of viewing and relating to the land and surroundings that were not previously explicit. It also gave expression to notions of inside and outside that were previously less evident. But to suggest that the landscape concept implies a denial of process is to confuse what appears to be striven for in artistic representations, gardens, and estates, and what, by contrast, exists as a part of everyday social practice (cf. Cosgrove 1993: 250–1).

We have seen above (and this is described in some of the essays that follow) that in certain contexts men and women endeavour to attain a timeless permanence reminiscent of that achieved in landscape painting: the 'picturesque' Zafimaniry villages and their apogee, the stone megaliths outside their boundaries, come to mind here. But as Bloch reminds us, these Zafimaniry attempts to overcome what they see as the uncaring permanence of the land result only in a pyrrhic victory: the permanent stones themselves become part of that uncaring environment. Or again, in a different setting, outside agencies such as the State attempt to impose on native categories and practice a fixity and permanence associated with an artefactual map as Layton describes for Western Desert Aborigines.[25] By contrast, the Mongolian case detailed by Humphrey shows how the tendency to deny laterality and movement (her 'chiefly' mode) coexists with a landscape mode that celebrates movement and toponymic difference.

The point, then, is that landscape is a process in so far as men and women attempt to realize in the foreground what can only be a potentiality and for the most part in the background. Foreground actuality and background potentiality exist in a process of mutual implication, and as such everyday life can never attain the idealized features of a representation. The attempt to transcend this limit, to deny process, brings us to questions of power and history as Cosgrove suggests. And it is in this context that the framework proposed here for the cross-cultural study of landscape becomes a part of wider theoretical concerns in anthropology and social theory more generally (cf. Dirks, Eley, Ortner (eds.) 1994).[26]

Although the framework proposed here has been generated through the opening up and 'unpacking' of the landscape concept, there has also been a refusal to specify a precise closure for the sets of related concepts that have emerged as a result. Place and space, inside and outside, and image and representation cannot be arranged further into a set of equivalences or exact homologues of one another, with landscape as their sum. This is because there is no 'absolute' landscape: the salience and relationship between place and space, inside and outside and image and representation are dependent on the cultural and historical context.

This last point returns us to an issue touched on at the beginning of the Introduction. There it was suggested that landscape holds a similar status in anthropology to that of the body: although ubiquitous, it has remained largely unproblematized (a situation, it is hoped, that has been partially remedied by the presentation here). However, Gell reminds us in his essay that, as with landscape, there is no 'absolute' body; the body is a locality, a form of ambience and a perceptual surround. Analogous to the body, then, the contextual and transformative nature of landscape emerges in all the essays; it is, perhaps, especially evident in Pinney's exploration of Indian oleographic representations. Here we find transposed on to a visual medium the tensions and contradictions enacted on a daily basis in the industrialized setting of contemporary India. At one moment there is an uneasy relationship between notions of foregrounded 'tradition' and a background of the 'modern' appearing in a single representation. At another moment, a stable representation of tradition seems to predominate, or again, one of modernity. Finally, the tension between tradition and the modern—foreground and background, place and space— appears to be momentarily resolved in a representation that encapsulates the political fiction of a unified nation. There is not one absolute landscape here, but a series of related, if contradictory, moments—perspectives—which cohere in what can be recognized as a singular form: landscape as a cultural process.

Notes

This Introduction has benefited from the comments and helpful suggestions of a number of people to whom I am most grateful. Allen Abramson read an early draft and his insightful comments proved very important in clarifying several key theoretical issues. He also very kindly agreed to comment on a much later draft. Several of my colleagues in the Department of Human Sciences, Brunel University, gave me their advice and encouragement; here I would like to thank Adam Kuper, Mark Nuttall, Ralph Schroeder, and Charles Stafford. In addition, the comments of Jonathan Benthall, Gustaff Houtman, and Tim Ingold were most welcomed, as were the comments from several contributors to the volume. Nicola Abel Hirsch listened and read as the argument of the Introduction took shape. Her patience and insights have proved invaluable. I am particularly grateful to my co-editor Michael O'Hanlon whose careful and thorough reading of several drafts of the Introduction has immeasurably improved not only its style but the argument as a whole. Many of the ideas contained in the Introduction were initially explored in a course of lectures titled 'Nature and Representation'. My appreciation goes out to the students who attended these lectures for their constructive criticisms and encouragement: Bryan Cleal, in particular, very kindly provided insightful comments on a draft of this text. For the errors in either fact or form that remain I have only myself to blame.

1. Since completing this introduction, the volume edited by Bender (1993) has appeared: independent evidence that the time has indeed come for landscape as an anthropological topic.
2. The entire sentence reads: 'Imagine yourself suddenly set down surrounded by all your gear, alone on a tropical beach close to a native village, while the launch or dinghy which has brought you sails away out of sight.'
3. See the entry under 'Landscape', *Oxford English Dictionary*, 2nd edn. viii. 628–9.
4. See also Alpers 1989; Barnes and Duncan (eds.) 1992; Barrell 1972; Buttimer and Seamon (eds.) 1980; Cosgrove 1984; Cosgrove and Daniels (eds.) 1988; Gell 1985; Tuan 1977.
5. For example, the British Cenotaph unveiled on Armistice Day, 1920 in Whitehall: 'Thus was created perhaps the first national holy site . . . neither Lloyd George nor Lutyens [the designer] . . . anticipated the spontaneous response of the people to the infinite meanings of emptiness . . . Thousands of the bereaved left wreaths at the makeshift altar, projecting their grief onto the void within . . .' (Laqueur 1994: 156–7).
6. At this point it is perhaps appropriate to distinguish my own definition from the Durkheimian distinction between the sacred and profane. Although the present formulation is linked to this tradition in its privileging of socio–cultural relations, the focus here is less on space as a reflection of social classifications (Durkheim and Mauss 1963), or as a form of mutual classification between the social and physical (Lévi-Strauss 1966). It also differs from those studies which focus on space as a feature of bodily and domestic relations that are 'worked at', analogous to the way a cultural text is shaped (Moore 1986; cf. Duncan 1990). Rather, it shares an interest with Parkin (1991: 9) in space (through its relationship with foreground place) as a background potentiality, often amorphous and, as noted, even empty. In other words, the emphasis here is upon processes of mutual implication rather than upon Durkheim's rigid dichotomy between sacred and profane space.
7. Thus during the period when Christian theology was a common point of reference, God was perceived as the first absolute and Nature his minister and deputy. Then

between the 17th and 19th c., the dominant idiom of nature shifted to that of a 'constitutional lawyer'; there was a preoccupation with the details of the 'laws of nature' and with their classification, prediction, and discovery (Thomas 1984). This emphasis on the 'law-like', constitutional quality of nature is further transformed through the advent of the theory of evolution: natural forms not only have a 'constitution' but a 'history'. The idea of nature is thus gradually transformed from the image associated with a 'constitutional lawyer' to that of a 'selective breeder'.

8. Friedlander, one of Gombrich's teachers, had suggested that the emergence of landscape painting itself could be seen in terms of the protrusion into the 'foreground' of what had previously been in the 'background' of pictures. Friedlander argued that this noticeable shift was precipitated by the Renaissance emphasis on 'humanism' and the dwindling of religious and mythological themes in paintings. Where in the medieval workshop there was a division of labour between figure painters, background painters, and still-life specialists, background painters now emerged as a specific (landscape) genre.

9. Published posthumously in around 1498.

10. The Arcadian landscapes of Poussin (1593–1665), for example, later exemplified this cultural value (Bann 1989: 100).

11. Alpers's argument about visual representation also points towards its relationship with material or socio-economic factors. She indicates how the mapping practice (what she calls a 'mapping impulse') prevalent in the Dutch context was conditioned by Dutch relationships with the land: conditions which were unlike those in England/Britain during the same period (this is brought out by Turner (1979) whose discussion of English poetry of the time focuses on its concern with issues of (landed) authority and possession).

12. The realist pictures produced by Vermeer, for example, such as the 'View of Delft' can be compared with the topographical prints which proliferated throughout Holland and Europe more generally during the 17th c. Where Vermeer represents an image as taken from a particular place (chorography), maps represent the world as arrayed in space, providing a measure and relationship between places (geography).

13. Alpers (1989: 133–8) has argued that the centrality of this map-making impulse can be traced to the reappropriation during the Renaissance of Ptolemy's conception of geography, first formulated during the 2nd c. AD. His conception involved the contrast (see n. 12) between 'chorography' (the subject-centred sense of place) and 'geography' (the non-subject-centred sense of a range of places).

14. Although some, like Cassirer, have suggested a radical separation between so-called 'mythical' and 'geometrical' space, 'closer examination show[s] that mythical space is dependent upon "geometric" strategies of reference and consistency, just as geometric space relies upon "mythic" strategies of subjective position and observation' (Noyes 1992: 29).

15. As Buttimer (1971: 28) has noted:

> Both Ratzel and Durkheim treated society from an organismic viewpoint. For the geographer, social groups were like biological cells in symbiotic relationships with their natural habitat and expressed a natural impulse to expand territorially.

> For the sociologist, they were the product of collective consciousness crystallised in an institutional framework. Relations to environment or natural habitat did not figure directly in Durkheim's analytical framework.

Burke (1990: 109) has discussed how the opposition to Ratzel was carried on in the French tradition of geography by Vidal and later Febvre. However, this continued to define itself differently from the Durkheimian legacy:

> The Durkheimian tradition encouraged generalization and comparison, while the Vidalian approach concentrated on what was unique to a particular region.

16. For a recent instance see e.g. the *Guardian*, 5 Sept. 1992.
17. Similar representational tensions were also becoming visible much closer to home (see Barrell 1980).
18. For work on the picturesque in colonial India see Tillotson 1990: 141–51.
19. Gilpin, for example, questioned whether it was necessary to venture beyond Britain in order to find picturesque beauty. He argued that the English/British wilderness (e.g. Cumberland) offered such experiences much closer to home. But there were limits to the scenic grandeur of Britain which invited the 'improver'. The notion of the improver emerged from the critique of Gilpin's work by Payne Knight and Price. These later theorists endeavoured to make the picturesque more philosophically sophisticated (by allying it with the then current theory of Associationism). They were also engaged in a running debate with the landscape improver Repton. As Michisaw (1992: 84) observes:

> The conscious project of Gilpin's picturesque is the re-enchantment, not the re-design, of the domestic landscape. It is only in the second phase that this project is itself domesticated, transforming a transformed England (and by extension, Western Europe) into a norm.

20. An omission from this Introduction (as well as essays of this volume) is a consideration of landscape processes and landscape representation in China and Japan. In the Chinese context there is a vast literature on various schools and traditions of landscape painting (cf. Bryson 1983: 87–92). This literature has largely been the province of Sinologists. By contrast, geomancy, or divination processes by means of lines, figures and points on the land, has a large anthropological literature (see Feuchtwang 1974). In the Japanese context mention should be made of the important text by Higuchi (1983) which documents the existence of seven 'landscape-types' that dominate the visual and spatial structure of Japanese city and countryside contexts.
21. This led in subsequent decades to a reaction against such 'objectivist' conceptions and an emphasis on the 'insiders'' viewpoint (Cosgrove 1984: 33–8). The notion of landscape was central to this re-conception, and became part of a phenomenologically inspired terminology used to describe geographical experience (e.g. Lowenthal 1961; Relph 1976; Tuan 1977). Here, the focus was on the study of the everyday, immediate and original relationships persons have with their surroundings. Drawing on the 20th-c. Continental tradition of existential philosophy (Heidegger, Merleau-Ponty, Sartre) Relph, for example, developed a geographical terminology for the description of 'being-in-the-world' (Relph 1985; see Weiner 1991 for a similar trend in anthropology).

22. This is what Shotter (1986: 208) has referred to as 'knowing-from'; that is, knowing from within a situation. Our use of everyday language implies a placedness and locatedness—a speaking from 'organized settings' of the ongoing situation (cf. Berlin 1969; Edie 1969).
23. 'In Cartesian space, objects hold positions which are defined absolutely, not in relation to the presence, in the same space, of the epistemic subject' (Gell 1985: 273).
24. Gell similarly draws attention to the pervasiveness of iconicity in American Sign Language, an instance in which sight is dominant.
25. Gow highlights a similar dilemma focused around a map/land claim between the Piro and the State.
26. One important area of focus is the existential gap between foreground actuality and background potentiality, place and space and so on, and the manner in which this is spanned and co-ordinated in specific contexts. The nature of this gap has been theorized from one cultural and historical vantage point by Jameson in his account of post-modernism—see in particular his discussion of 'cognitive mapping' and the 'spanning' and 'co-ordinating' capacities of power/ideology (Jameson 1991: 51–2, 415–17). It has been theorized from a different cultural and historical vantage point by Strathern in her synthetic account of Melanesian sociality—see in particular her discussion of the 'anticipated outcome' (Strathern 1988: 274–88).

References

ALPERS, S. (1989). *The Art of Describing: Dutch Art in the Seventeenth Century*. Harmondsworth: Penguin Books.

BANN, S. (1989). *The True Vine: On Visual Representation and the Western Tradition*. Cambridge: Cambridge University Press.

BARNES, T., and DUNCAN, J. (eds.) (1992). *Writing Worlds: Discourse, Text and Metaphor in the Representation of Landscape*. London: Routledge.

BARRELL, J. (1972). *The Idea of Landscape and the Sense of Place 1730–1840: An Approach to the Poetry of John Clare*. Cambridge: Cambridge University Press.

—— (1980). *The Dark Side of the Landscape: The Rural Poor in English Painting 1730–1840*. Cambridge: Cambridge University Press.

BASSO, K. (1988). ' "Speaking with Names": Language and Landscape among the Western Apache', *Cultural Anthropology*, 3/2: 99–130.

BENDER, B. (1993). *Landscape: Politics and Perspectives*. Oxford: Berg.

BERGER, J. (1972). *Ways of Seeing*. Harmondsworth: Penguin Books.

BERLIN, I. (1969). 'A Note on Vico's Concept of Knowledge', in G. Tagliacozzo (ed.), *Giambattista Vico: An International Symposium*. Baltimore: The Johns Hopkins University Press.

BLOCH, M., and PARRY, J. (eds.) (1982). *Death and the Regeneration of Life*. Cambridge: Cambridge University Press.

BOURDIEU, P. (1977). *Outline of a Theory of Practice*. Cambridge: Cambridge University Press.

BRYSON, N. (1983). *Painting and Vision: The Logic of the Gaze*. London: Macmillan.

BURKE, P. (1990). *The French Historical Revolution: The Annales School 1929–1989*. Cambridge: Polity Press.

BUTTIMER, A. (1971). *Society and Milieu in the French Geographic Tradition*. Chicago: Association of American Geographers.

—— and SEAMON, D. (eds.) (1980). *The Human Experience of Space and Place*. New York: St Martin's Press.

CARTER, P. (1987). *The Road to Botany Bay: An Essay in Spatial History*. London: Faber & Faber.

COLLINGWOOD, R. (1960). *The Idea of Nature*. Oxford: Oxford University Press.

COSGROVE, D. (1984). *Social Formation and Symbolic Landscape*. London: Croom Helm.

—— (1985). 'Prospect, Perspective and the Evolution of the Landscape Idea', *Transactions of the Institute of British Geographers*, NS 10: 45–62.

—— (1993). *The Palladian Landscape: Geographical Change and its Cultural Representation in Sixteenth-Century Italy*. Leicester: Leicester University Press.

—— and DANIELS, S. (eds.) (1988). *The Iconography of Landscape: Essays on the Symbolic Representation, Design and Use of Past Environments*. Cambridge: Cambridge University Press.

CRARY, J. (1990). *Techniques of the Observer: On Vision and Modernity in the Nineteeth Century*. Cambridge, Mass.: MIT Press.

CRONON, W. (1983). *Changes in the Land: Indians, Colonialists and the Ecology of New England*. New York: Hill and Wang.

—— (1991). *Nature's Metropolis: Chicago and the Great West*. New York: W. W. Norton.

DANIELS, S., and COSGROVE, D. (1988). 'Introduction: Iconography and Landscape', in D. Cosgrove and S. Daniels (eds.), *The Iconography of Landscape: Essays on the Symbolic Representation, Design and Use of Past Environments*. Cambridge: Cambridge University Press.

DIRKS, N., ELEY, G., and ORTNER, S. (eds.) (1994). *Culture/ History/ Power: A Reader in Contemporary Social Theory*. Princeton, NJ: Princeton University Press.

DRESCH, P. (1988). 'Segmentation: Its Roots in Arabia and its Flowering Elsewhere', *Cultural Anthropology*, 3/1: 50–67.

DUNCAN, J. (1990). *The City as Text: The Politics of Landscape Interpretation in the Kandyan Kingdom*. Cambridge: Cambridge University Press.

DURKHEIM, E., and MAUSS, M. (1963). *Primitive Classification*. London: Cohen & West.

EDIE, J. (1969). 'Vico and Existential Philosophy', in G. Tagliacozzo (ed.), *Giambattista Vico: An International Symposium*. Baltimore: Johns Hopkins University Press.

FEUCHTWANG, S. (1974). *An Anthropological Analysis of Chinese Geomancy*. Laos: Vithagna.

FOUCAULT, M. (1970). *The Order of Things: An Archaeology of the Human Sciences*. London: Tavistock.

GELL, A. (1979). 'The Umeda Language Poem', *Canberra Anthropology*, 2/1: 44–62.

—— (1985). 'How to Read a Map: Remarks on the Practical Logic of Navigation', *Man*, NS 20: 271–86.

GOMBRICH, E. (1966). 'The Renaissance Theory of Art and the Rise of Landscape', in *Norm and Form: Studies in the Art of the Renaissance*. London: Phaidon Press.

GREEN, N. (1990). *The Spectacle of Nature: Landscape and Bourgeois Culture in Nineteenth-Century France*. Manchester: Manchester University Press.

HAMPSHIRE, S. (1969). 'Vico and the Contemporary Philosophy of Language', in G. Tagliacozzo (ed.), *Giambattista Vico: An International Symposium*. Baltimore: Johns Hopkins University Press.

HARLEY, J., and WOODWARD, D. (eds.) (1987). *The History of Cartography*, i. *Cartography in Prehistoric, Ancient and Medieval Europe and the Mediterranean*. Chicago: University of Chicago Press.

HARVEY, D. (1989). *The Condition of Postmodernity: An Enquiry into the Origins of Cultural Change*. Oxford: Basil Blackwell.

HARVEY, P. (1980). *The History of Topographical Maps: Symbols, Pictures and Surveys*. London: Thames & Hudson.

HIGUCHI, T. (1983). *The Visual and Spatial Structure of Landscapes*. Cambridge, Mass.: MIT Press.

INGOLD, T. (1993). 'The Temporality of Landscape', *World Archaeology*, 25: 152–74.

—— (1994). 'Introduction to Social Life', in T. Ingold (ed.), *Companion Encyclopedia of Anthropology: Humanity, Culture and Social Life*. London: Routledge.

JAMESON, F. (1991). *Postmodernism, or, the Cultural Logic of Late Capitalism*. London: Verso.

KEESING, R. (1982). *Kwaio Religion: The Living and the Dead in a Solomon Island Society*. New York: Columbia University Press.

LAQUEUR, T. (1994). 'Memory and Naming in the Great War', in J. Gillis (ed.), *Commemorations: The Politics of National Identity*. Princeton, NJ: Princeton University Press.

LAYTON, R. (1986). *Uluru, an Aboriginal History of Ayers Rock*. Canberra: Australian Institute of Aboriginal Studies.

LÉVI-STRAUSS, C. (1966). *The Savage Mind*. Chicago: University of Chicago Press.

LIVINGSTONE, D. (1992). *The Geographical Tradition. Episodes in the History of a Contested Enterprise*. Oxford: Basil Blackwell.

LOCK, M. (1993). 'Cultivating the Body: Anthropology and Epistemologies of Bodily Practice and Knowledge', in *Annual Review of Anthropology*, 22: 133–55.

LOVEJOY, A. (1964). *The Great Chain of Being: A Study of the History of an Idea*. Cambridge, Mass.: Harvard University Press.

LOWENTHAL, D. (1961). 'Geography, Experience and Imagination: Towards a Geographical Epistemology', *Annals of the Association of American Geographers*, 51: 241–60.

MALINOWSKI, B. (1922). *Argonauts of the Western Pacific. An Account of Native Enterprise and Adventure in the Archipelagos of Melanesian New Guinea*. London: Routledge & Kegan Paul.

MERLEAU-PONTY, M. (1962). *The Phenomenology of Perception*. London: Routledge & Kegan Paul.

MICHASIW, K. (1992). 'Nine Revisionist Theses on the Picturesque', *Representations*, 38: 76–100.

MOORE, H. (1986). *Space, Text and Gender: An Anthropological Study of the Marakwet of Kenya*. Cambridge: Cambridge University Press.

MORPHY, H. (1991). *Ancestral Connections: Art and an Aboriginal System of Knowledge*. Chicago: University of Chicago Press.

MUNN, N. (1973a). *Walbiri Iconography: Graphic Representation and Cultural Symbolism in a Central Australian Society*. Chicago: University of Chicago Press.

Munn, N. (1973b). 'The Spatial Presentation of Cosmic Order in Walbiri Iconography', in J. A. W. Forge (ed.), *Primitive Art and Society*. London: Oxford University Press.

—— (1986). *The Fame of Gawa: A Symbolic Study of Value Transformation in a Massim (Papua New Guinea) Society*. Cambridge: Cambridge University Press.

Noyes, J. (1992). *Colonial Space: Spatiality in the Discourse of German South West Africa 1884–1915*. Reading: Harwood Press.

Olwig, K. (1984). *Nature's Ideological Landscape: A Literary and Geographic Perspective on its Development and Preservation on Denmark's Jutland Heath*. London: George Allen & Unwin.

Parkin, D. (1991). *Sacred Void: Spatial Images of Work and Ritual Among the Giriama*. Cambridge: Cambridge University Press.

Relph, E. (1976). *Place and Placelessness*. London: Pion.

—— (1985). 'Geographical Experience and Being-in-the-World: The Phenomenological Origins of Geography', in D. Seamon and R. Mugerauer (eds.), *Dwelling, Place and Environment: Towards a Phenomenology of Person and World*. Dordrecht: Martinus Nijhoff.

Sauer, C. (1963). 'The Morphology of Landscape', in J. Leighly (ed.), *Land and Life: A Selection of the Writings of Carl Sauer*. Berkeley, Calif.: University of California Press.

Shotter, J. (1986). 'A Sense of Place: Vico and the Social Production of Social Identities', *British Journal of Social Psychology*, 25: 199–211.

Smith, B. (1985). *European Vision and the South Pacific*. New Haven, Conn.: Yale University Press.

Strathern, M. (1988). *The Gender of the Gift: Problems with Women and Problems with Society in Melanesia*. Berkeley, Calif.: University of California Press.

Thomas, K. (1984). *Man and the Natural World: Changing Attitudes in England 1500–1800*. Harmondsworth: Penguin Books.

Tillotson, G. (1990). 'The Indian Picturesque: Images of India in British Landscape Painting, 1780–1880', in C. Bayly (ed.), *The Raj: India and the British, 1600–1947*. London: National Portrait Gallery Publications.

Tuan, Y. (1977). *Space and Place: The Perspective of Experience*. Minneapolis: University of Minnesota Press.

Turner, J. (1979). *The Politics of Landscape: Rural Scenery and Society in English Poetry 1630–1660*. Cambridge, Mass.: Harvard University Press.

Weiner, J. (1991). *The Empty Place: Poetry, Space and Being among the Foi of Papua New Guinea*. Bloomington, Ind.: Indiana University Press.

Williams, R. (1972). 'Ideas of Nature', in J. Benthall (ed.), *Ecology, the Shaping Enquiry*. London: Longman.

—— (1973). *The Country and the City*. London: Chatto & Windus.

Yates, F. (1992). *The Art of Memory*. London: Pimlico.

1

Looking at the Landscape:
Class Formation and the Visual

NICHOLAS GREEN

What has the art historian to say to the anthropologist about landscape and the ways in which it is perceived? At first glance, quite a lot. Landscape has been classically constituted by the discipline of art history as one of the major genres through which the 'modern' (that is, Renaissance and post-Renaissance) Western tradition of art can be traced: from the early glimmerings of an emergent 'realism' in the panoramic vistas of a Van Eyck or a Leonardo to the classic, ordered compositions of Poussin and Claude, so often imitated by eighteenth-century landscape gardeners; from the fresh perceptions of Constable's sketches to the even more authentic perceptual 'truths' of the Impressionists. In charting this route, art history has crystallized a specific vocabulary for dealing with the bundle of issues—the representation of place or environment, the organization and categorization of space—condensed in the term 'landscape'.

At its best the strengths of this perspective are twofold. First, it recognizes the importance of talking about codes of vision in assessing landscape. That is, it brings into focus the question of how we perceive the external world—whether psychologically, historically, or socially—as an issue that cannot be taken for granted, but needs to be theorized, analysed, debated. This is the kind of terrain worked over, from the specific stance of perceptual psychology, by Ernst Gombrich in his seminal *Art and Illusion* (1960). It is no accident that Gombrich chooses a Constable landscape as one of the key images around which to orientate his argument. The second strength, represented admittedly only in the more socially directed strands of art history, is the awareness that Western responses to landscape, as encapsulated in pictures, are not necessarily natural or universal.[1] Rather, the pair perception/representation is historically shaped by particular material conditions and social pressures. The most familiar example is the double portrait with landscape of *Mr and Mrs Andrews* by Gainsborough, discussed by John Berger (1972: 106–8) among others. You do not have to be a doctrinaire Marxist to concur with the view that this charming prospect has something to do with the ownership of property and the celebration of early agricultural capitalism. Art history, then, could be said to

be useful in furnishing some of the conceptual protocols for a more inter-
disciplinary project concerned with a 'landscape concept'. On the one hand we
have the apprehension of spatial/perceptual relations in terms of a well-estab-
lished and self-assured repertoire: the debate about mimesis, the division of
space into foreground, middle-ground, and horizon, and the naming of different modes of perspective, aerial as well as linear. On the other hand we have the
commitment to historical specificity. The question is: how far do these techniques and strategies add up to a schema of general analytical value, whether for
art history itself or for disciplines, such as anthropology and geography, also
intimately concerned with the perception and interpretation of space?

For there are certain rather more problematical implications to the art-
historical paradigm which need to be addressed. Perhaps, again, they can be
divided into two areas. First, this paradigm, almost without exception, works
with a clear division between representation and 'reality', between the landscape image and its referent in the so-called real world. In other words, it treats
the raw material 'out there' of trees and fields and mountains and streams (it is
of course instantly more complex as soon as peasants are introduced!) as un-
questionable, unchallengeable: an objective stratum of reality preceding artistic
or social interpretation. Thus, while the image is up for grabs from a whole
spectrum of competing perspectives, the thing represented—the place or environment—is somehow rendered inviolable. This is clearly not the case with
other artistic genres, whether historical and allegorical material or depictions of
social and contemporary scenes. And it explains why the discussion of landscape has been located at the heart of a rather facile debate about realism as a
mode of representation, a debate which seeks to adjudicate the realistic nature
of an image on the basis of its supposed likeness to an objective world 'out
there'. The worst excesses of this approach are reached when the art historian
compares his or her own photographs of the scene (as if photographs themselves are a transparent guide to reality) with the interpretations by the artist,
whether Courbet, Monet, or Cézanne. Further, if according to such a logic the
most authentic or 'true' image is that which comes closest to that which it
purports to depict, then, paradoxically, pictures deemed 'realistic' can be used
to inform us of what the world 'out there' is really like—a fundamentally
circular argument.

The second area of difficulty relates to the way in which the visual codes
employed in the production and consumption of landscape imagery are understood. I am not referring just to those traditional formalist accounts that
pull the genre into an evolutionary history of *style* as retrospectively defined
by such art historians as Lord Clark (1949) of *Civilisation* fame. Rather, what I
am getting at is that any discussion of landscape framed in terms of picture-
making and picture appreciation tends ultimately to be underpinned by an
aesthetic agenda concerned with artistic values and interpretation. Crudely
speaking, the perception of landscape imagery—and to some extent, following

the argument about realism above, the very materiality of landscape itself—
are claimed for a particular version of 'high' or élite Western culture. It is as
if there were some fundamental or necessary relation between the two—an
equation which certainly reverberates through the current national heritage
industry.

In other words, the rhetoric of pictorial composition, views and panoramas,
closed and open perspectives never comes value-free. It always carries an
implicit bundle of aesthetic assumptions and implications. Now, it may well be
that it is this association with aesthetics, and with the topics of 'beauty' and
interpretation raised by aesthetics, which have a certain appeal for the anthropologist keen to explore analogies in non-Western cultures. But within art
history the aesthetic equation acts as a strait-jacket which inhibits possibilities
for a more effectively historical understanding of landscape.

We might push the argument further still. At a more abstract level the art-
historical paradigm brings to bear a fixed conception of how we should approach the visual. This is true even of those 'progressive' or 'radical'
developments which have taken on board the importance of questions of social
relations, ideology, and theories of representation. Methodologically, the procedure goes something like this. We move from a given set of texts (they are
usually visual but need not be) outwards to broader historical structures within
which these texts are seen to be produced and circulated. In so doing, the
'radical' version at any rate casts its net much wider than the received wisdom
of art history to draw in bourgeois cultural patterns, professional groupings, the
input of the State, gender relations, and so on. From there, armed with that
knowledge, a number of conclusions are drawn about the imagery we started
with. There is here an implicit circularity which takes us from text to social
conditions (which are thereby separated off) and back again, reproducing a
figure-on-ground relation between the visual and what may be termed history,
conditions of production, readers, and audiences. What follows from this
prioritization of text-based analysis (also familiar in other areas of the hu-
manities such as literary studies) is often unconscious backing for the traditional notion of the art image as a fixed and closed entity whose meaning is
self-contained within the four sides of its frame. Moreover, such a model works
with a one-to-one relationship between text and viewer, sealing off the process
from other circuits and readings. That is to say, the intense perceptual dialogue
rooted in the hermeneutic concept of empathy that is played out between art
and art historian (who is deployed as the 'ideal' reader) sets the terms for how
the perception/reception equation is thought historically.

What worries me about all this is not just that the artificial and arbitrary
fixing of certain privileged objects and images marginalizes all kinds of processes that cannot quite be caught or pinned down in a textual way. What
concerns me, in relation to landscape specifically, is that the text-based paradigm narrows dramatically the field of possibilities through which we might

envisage the visual. It excludes all those more popular or casual forms of spectatorship where looking cannot easily be singled out from an interlocking network of activities. And it has no means of exploring the different ways in which modes of representation actively work on audiences, past and present, shaping identities and experience. Let me take an example from another area. As Morley (1986: 27–9) has shown in his discussion of television viewing, a programme like *Coronation Street* is rarely read in isolation. The process involves multiple moments, multiple activities and the intersection of multiple subjectivities. *Coronation Street* is inscribed in a broader series of early evening rituals: putting the tea on, getting the kids to bed, renegotiating domestic relations. In other contexts—the pub, the workplace, the launderette—other stories are relayed, other texts are embroidered around the original programme to affirm camaraderie, to pass the time at school or work.

The drift of this critique indicates something of the direction in which this essay is heading. Drawing on structuralist and post-structuralist debates about the material operation of ideologies and the constructive power of systems of representation, the aim here is to disaggregate the landscape text as the beginning and end points of analysis, and to situate it within a wider cycle of cultural activities. This entails refusing the aesthetic angle on picture-making as the primary focus for interpretation in favour of a more discursive approach to historical definitions of landscape and landscape perception. And it means investigating the other end of the equation: how the structures and languages for perceiving the environment are implicated in moulding the experience of spectators. All this can have radical implications for a more general inter-disciplinary project of 'looking at landscape'. By turning briefly to the case study of early nineteenth-century France, I hope to demonstrate that while pictures of the countryside form one piece of the puzzle, the codes of perception/reception were largely not *aesthetically* defined according to the terms understood by art history.[2] Far from it.

If one takes an overview of early nineteenth-century France, what is immediately striking is simply the proliferation of prints and pictures of nature. These varied from descriptive topographical prints in picturesque guides to the provinces (a burgeoning publishing genre from the 1820s) to illustrations in novels or magazines like the comic *Charivari* or the arts review *L'Artiste* (started 1831). They ranged from the many small paintings marketed by a new and expanding generation of art dealers, to more ambitious canvases displayed in the annual or biennial Salon exhibition and written about by the growing body of art critics in newspapers and periodicals. How much of this material could be regarded as *art* is debatable. Contemporary evaluations, both official and unofficial (that is from freelance art reviewers), placed landscape low in the established hierarchy of artistic values, though the critics at least did delight in savouring the countryside depicted. In fact, rather than force the imagery into the strait-jacket of 'high' culture, it is more fruitful to locate it in the context of the equally striking growth of cultural practices involved with actually 'experiencing' the countryside.

Such moves were registered in a variety of ways—for example in the expansion of *maisons de campagne* in the *Départements* around Paris, from the very foot of the capital to the Loire and the Fontainebleau forest. Notaries' advertisements for such country houses—or perhaps houses in the country would be a more accurate description—indicate that they varied from small two- or three-room cottages, often purpose-built for the visitor or retirement couple, to large *châteaux* with extensive grounds.[3] Further, they were offered both for sale and for *rent*: the implication being that their use was to be temporary and transient. One medium-sized property south of Paris was sold jointly in 1847 to two Parisian businessmen, though it was clearly not large enough to cater for both of their establishments at the same time. In the previous twenty years the house had passed through the hands first of a Parisian doctor and then of a Parisian bar-keeper or dealer in soft drinks (*limonadier*).[4]

Also significant was the development of tourist guides, again mainly to areas within reach of the metropolis. Unlike their eighteenth-century precursors with their Rousseauesque reveries on nature, these later guides became increasingly functional. How to get there, where to stay, what to look out for; this kind of information was spliced with pictorial evocation of major 'spots' and panoramas. One prime site was the forest of Fontainebleau, some fifty kilometres south-west of Paris. With its mix of ancient trees, lush green glades, barren sandy screes, sudden vistas, and curious rock formations, it was well suited for the role of nature at its most 'natural' and 'primitive'. The opening up of part of the Paris–Lyons railway through Fontainebleau in 1849 gave the tourist trade a crucial boost. But the impetus was by no means all from the centre. At Fontainebleau local entrepreneurs and literateurs played a key role. Most important was the ex-soldier and self-made businessman Claude-François Denecourt, who built up a virtual monopoly of the local tourist-guide market.[5] Denecourt not only exploited his military experience to map a novel variety of routes through the forest linking its most scenic features but also obtained official permission to create new paths, blasting his way through rock and undergrowth, revealing unsuspected perspectives, and constructing belvederes and look-out points.

When we systematically survey all these 'texts', setting the visual representations of landscape alongside other cultural practices dealing in the countryside, three features stand out. The first is the pervasive presence of Paris. Accessibility to the capital—by coach, steam-boat, and, from the 1840s, by train—is the keynote of many tourist guides and country-house advertisements. Similarly, landscape prints and pictures were commodities predominantly produced and circulated through the economic and cultural circuits of the city, specifically through the most self-consciously 'modern' circuits: the newspapers, luxury dealers, exhibitions, and boulevard entertainments.

With one minor exception there was no equivalent proliferation of nature imagery and activity in the big regional centres or the rapidly industrializing towns beyond the capital. For a brief period under the Restoration, landed gentry and small town 'notables' in independent provinces like Brittany did lay claim to an alternative vision encoded through a picturesque rhetoric of ancient *châteaux* and local curiosities.[6] The landscape was read here in terms of a putative discourse on the nation, explicitly anti-metropolitan in stance and often, though not exclusively, linked to a right-wing legitimist politics. The correlatives of geography, history, and even economics were used to validate a cultural inheritance rooted in the land. But from the late 1830s this alternative vision was already fading under the impact both of changing political constituencies and vocabularies and of the increasing dominance of Parisian culture. A nationalism of the land was only effectively to re-emerge during the early Third Republic in the 1870s.

So, while acknowledging such exceptions and countercurrents, the material under discussion was by and large a metropolitan phenomenon, locked materially and symbolically into the cultural embrace of the capital. It addressed a metropolitan or metropolitan-identified clientele. Now, it is relatively standard to twin town and country in some oppositional relation (Williams 1973). But by the Parisian connection I mean something quite specific: that it was the material conditions and the cultural developments germane to the capital that generated those vocabularies of looking which were capable of bringing nature into visibility as a significant form of social experience.

This becomes clear when we turn to the other features shared by early nineteenth-century French landscape. The second element—again present as much in the newspaper reviews of paintings as in house advertisements and tourist guides—was a stress upon the pleasures and benefits to be gained from plunging into, becoming immersed—if only temporarily—in the sensations of the countryside. One art reviewer of the late 1830s invited his readers to step inside the picture, to sit beneath the painted trees, or dive into the limpid blue of the lake.[7] Similarly, the moderate republican politician Jules Simon (1890: 3–4) recalled wandering in the 1840s around the picturesque part of the Luxembourg, a modest landscape garden in the heart of the city. 'There was nothing', he mused, 'more delicious, after a wearying day, than to find yourself hidden amongst these great trees, to forget Paris in the centre of Paris, to smell the invigorating scents of earth and vegetation.' Again, a light-hearted journalistic account (Janin 1843: 241), evoked Sunday excursions to the valley of Montmorency, north of the city, where: 'The grand young men and the most unaffected girls are at once seized with the sweet folly of shouting, running, climbing, lying upon the grass, mounting on horseback and galloping through the hilly and venerable forest.'

The notion of sensual immersion in the sights and textures of nature can of course be interpreted in a variety of ways, for example in terms of contemporary definitions of poetic reverie or of a more philosophical tradition of Rousseauesque 'naturalism'. But crucially at this moment it fed off a powerful environmental language promoted and implemented in the Paris of the 1820s onwards. From official reports into sanitation, disease, crime, and prostitution (most notably Parent-Duchâtelet's major study of 1836), to the schemes of utopian planners and popular sociologies, there was registered a deep perceptual anxiety about the urban environment. Medical language was all-important, setting up a series of mutually reinforcing equations between dark, enclosed and fetid spaces and the incursions of disease, crime, and even sedition. In itself the discourse was not in any sense new. What was specific to this conjuncture was, first, the increased impact of medics as a professional pressure group within the State (especially within the police department) and, secondly, the way the potency of environmentalism was condensed in and through a number of perceived crises: the cholera epidemic of 1832, continued political unrest following the 1830 Revolution, and the dilapidation of the old, central quarters of the city. Most relevant for us is the expansive and flexible form of this discursive logic. In the context of the metropolitan topography the sensual perception of dark and claustrophobic spaces carried social and moral overtones. According to the same logic, the plunge into open space, fresh air and sunlight, lush vegetation—whether in an urban garden or outside the city's boundaries—was invested with connotations of health, wholesomeness, and security.

The third feature—and perhaps the most significant for the current discussion—is the recurrent reference to a vocabulary of views and panoramas, to an apparently pictorial mode of looking. Obviously that is evident in the materiality of the pictures themselves but also, I would argue, in artists' use of compositional formats and codes such as framing devices and recession effects that draw attention to the very process of viewing. In the 1840s' landscapes of Théodore Rousseau (at that time a rather mysterious figure due to official disapprobation but who was to become a leading landscape ideologue in the ensuing decades) the use of darkened foregrounds and focusing effects plays on the theatricality of popular ocular viewing machines as much as on traditional art-based perspective.[8] Equally, the pictorial emphasis comes through in the many visual descriptions in the tourist guides and in the play on situation and outlook which characterized notaries' advertisements. Turning to the Fontainebleau entrepreneur Denecourt again, his constructed paths were also richly pictorial, presenting an ever-changing kaleidoscope of shifting scenarios: now an open perspective, now a close-up of a dramatic rock formation, now a tantalizing glimpse through screens of silver birch. The metropolitan parks of such places as Boulogne and Vincennes, begun in the 1850s under the Second Empire, followed similar principles. Under the direction of the engineer Adolphe Alphand (1885) cement was cunningly piled up in picturesque compositions of rock and falling water. The grouping of trees and carefully modulated slopes were combined to present a sequence of 'natural' vistas, alternately intimate and grandiose.

Here, you may say, the pictorial—and in effect the artistic—defines the terms for the perception of landscape. Certainly, one reading would be to stress continuities with eighteenth-century modes of viewing associated with the landscape gardens of the landed gentry and early financial bourgeoisie. Another obvious response would be to look to the codes of art appreciation then circulating among art theorists, critics and, to some extent, among an élite audience of connoisseurs and collectors. But what comes across from the historical evidence is how marginal and ineffective were these élite traditions. The artistic response seems to have been largely overdetermined by more 'popular' modes of perception rooted in the culture of the modern city. This is the nub of my argument: that pictorial forms of viewing are not always what they seem to be. Remember that nature commodities were predominantly circulated through the dealers, exhibitions, and newspaper reports, all circuits focused within the most dynamic areas of the city. In that particular urban milieu 'looking at pictures' involved a quite different rhetoric. This was a culture of modernity which hinged on a distinctive principle of *spectatorship*.

Parisian modernity was shaped by a cluster of material conditions that came together in the 1820s and 1830s: the development of finance capital and land and building speculation, the application of new forms of urban technology often under the impulse of the State (bitumen pavements and gas lighting), the growth of luxury trades and consumption including art-dealing, and the rapid expansion of the Press. The coherence of all these developments was secured by their location within a particular topography of the city, the quarters north and west of the old city and centred on the Boulevard des Italiens and the Chaussée d'Antin. In these areas—associated as they were with modern building, dynamic financial speculation, and entertainment—modernity was projected through a pattern of intersecting appearances and activities: the spectacle of the theatre, boulevard promenade and cafés, the surface sheen of bitumen and gas with their connotations of novelty, the decorative fashions of promenaders both male and female, the almost erotic appeal of the shop window display. Witness in this respect the arcades, those elegant covered walkways lined with enticing boutiques, where the visual allure of window displays was intensified by strips of mirror set either side of the window. The strolling shopper or *flâneur* would catch the narcissistic reflection of his or her own appearance alongside the decorative commodities on offer in the boutiques.[9] The spatial and visual arrangement of the arcades encapsulated a series of linkages between promenading, looking, self-display, and consumption that was entirely characteristic of metropolitan culture.

So, what we are talking about is a structure of spectatorship which twinned the glamour of modern appearances and technology with the thrill of urban entertainments *and* the pleasure of a consuming gaze. Nature commodities were very much part of that metropolitan circuit, as is most graphically demon-strated by the diorama. A proto-cinematic entertainment invented by Louis Daguerre around 1821, the diorama deployed changing light effects on to and through a painted canvas to transform the scene displayed to the audience.[10] It was by all accounts a brief but 'magical' experience. Landscapes, especially with storms, earthquakes, and volcanoes, were very much to the fore in an event that seemed to combine the thrill of invention with authentic reality. I would suggest that when guides and advertisements luxuriated in sweeping panoramas and charming views they too, in part at least, were taking their cue from the same structures of spectatorship precipitated by the culture of the modern city. In other words, they were referencing less the picture as text than a way of seeing in which novelty, entertainment, and consumption were all implicated.

Landscape in early nineteenth-century France can be seen to signify a Paris-related phenomenon, whether we are talking about pictures or the countryside 'in the flesh'. In that context nature was visualized—or, rather, only became visible in any meaningful way—at the *intersection* of two distinct ideological axes: the sensual immersion in a healthy environment and the rhetoric of consuming spectacle. It was precisely that mix that made nature a potent force, not just the receptacle of forms of leisure and pleasure but active in framing the identities and experience of spectators. For though constructed as solitary, even private, this was a profoundly social relationship, shaped by conditions and languages which placed the participant in a very specific relation to existing categories of class and gender. That is to say, it primarily addressed those social constituencies who not only had the economic resources and leisure to make country trips and buy tourist guides, but who identified personally both with dynamic urban modernity and with environmental threat. In fact, it was at the level of *personal* experience and identity that the dialogue with nature was socially effective.

One example of this structure in action will have to suffice. Take the case of the historian Jules Michelet, a typical example of the new cadre of self-made and highly motivated metropolitan professionals. Listen to Michelet (1924: 179) deep in the countryside near Nantes where he had retreated into voluntary exile after the Napoleonic *coup d'état* of 1851:[11]

I am writing to you here . . . in a delightful study between the bright day of the sunlit orchard with its green lawns and the deep greens of the great tree-lined alley which through the other window comes right up to me! No noise apart from the sounds of several insects and the birds singing . . . it is a luxuriant wilderness rich with fruit trees and vegetables. I am suspended, suckling at the breasts of nature.

Written into the familiar imagery of the countryside is a distinctive structure of feeling: a sense of self projected on the one hand through immersion in tactile, aural, and visual perceptions (losing oneself in the sensual, indeed maternal environment), and on the other hand, through the assertion of personal control in ordering the scene into perspectives and tableaux. For Michelet nature precipitated a complex and relatively unstable form of subjectivity—a delicately poised sense of a centred ego—but one that complemented, feeding off and into, his more public personas played out in the city.

Although I would not argue for any direct or functional fit between such modes of subjectivity and class formation, it seems clear that the processes of 'being metropolitan' did, in the 1830s and 1840s, exert a cultural hegemony over key fractions within the emergent bourgeois power bloc: from 'progressive' aristocrats to financial notables, speculators, and some industrialists. In particular, this cultural repertoire had much to say to nascent groups of cultural professionals—journalists, historians (like Michelet), economists, writers, artists—who were often involved in their own work in the analysis and celebration of Paris. But it also exerted a more symbolic grip over many in the provinces who imaginatively identified with the metropolis at second hand through reading newspapers and novels (such as Flaubert's *Madame Bovary*) or through local cultural circles. At the same time, this was an ideological position shared neither by sections of the more traditional and right-wing aristocracy nor by the artisan and urban 'underclass' who were themselves defined in terms of threat. Further, the dialogue with nature did not express class identity in a reflective or static fashion. This was an active process that partially and unevenly reworked the subjective experience of participants, sharpening their sense of a centred ego—a certainty of individual purpose posed against older ruling class personas—and, in the case of men, intensifying their masculinity.

Let me briefly draw the threads together. Of necessity the historical argument has been radically foreshortened here to keep in focus the issues raised by the 'landscape concept'. At the most general level, the essay has staked out a polemic against those idealist tendencies, most evident in art history but perhaps also inflecting aspects of urban sociology and anthropology, that deal in the currency of universal or immanent meanings when it comes to talking about landscape. In particular the case has been put against any necessary tie-up between 'looking at landscape' and aesthetics. Any attempt to delineate a general 'landscape concept' applicable in an interdisciplinary fashion to different domains would have to address the problems inherent in such concepts as 'the aesthetic' and 'the pictorial'. Further, it has been suggested that in this specific historical instance, landscape cannot be adequately understood simply as a set of objects and themes that were ideologically loaded—that in fact it cannot be grasped as *text*. Rather, it involved a materially-located process of perception and identification, a two-way dialogue that worked to shape forms of social identity: which is to reverse the usual equation that reads pictures as expressive of social relations.

In attempting to unpick that historical formation it has been important to refuse some of the usual distinctions drawn between representation and something called 'reality', and to recognize that the organization of space is always already coded in the way it is experienced. The flip side of all this is the relativization of what we mean by pictorial vision. It is time to have done with a common sense that claims the visual as the primary property of pictures. Indeed, this is where art history has much to learn from anthropology with its much more flexible and relativist approach to modes of perception and reception. In breaking the chains of that particular restrictive practice we could turn our attention to all those other 'ways of seeing' that mould the experience of space and through which space moulds social relations.

Notes

1. See e.g. Barrell (1980).
2. The issues thrown up by this historical case study form the substance of Green (1990), from which much of the evidence for the current essay is derived.
3. See *Journal Général d'Affiches, annonces judiciaires, légales et avis divers*, throughout the 1840s.
4. *Archives Notariales, Archives Départementales*, Melun (Seine-et-Marne)—18 E 352—file of the notary Gravier, 7 Nov. 1847.
5. See Société des Amis de la Forêt de Fontainebleau, 1975.
6. See Delouche (1977) and Bertho (1980).
7. *L'Artiste* (1839), 2/2: 269.
8. See the catalogue *Théodore Rousseau* (Louvre, 1967) for a spectrum of the artist's pictures, many of them using both framing devices and deep perspectival effects. My reading here is partly based on the codes projected in contemporary landscape treatises, such as Laurens (1849).
9. On the importance of the arcades, see Benjamin (1973).
10. See Helmut and Alison Gernsheim (1968: 14–38).
11. Michelet refused the oath of allegiance to Napoleon III required of all state functionaries and consequently lost his prestigious position at the Collège de France.

References

ALPHAND, A. (1885). *L'Art des jardins*, 3rd edn. Paris: J. Rothschild.

BARRELL, J. (1980). *The Dark Side of the Landscape: The Rural Poor in English Painting, 1730–1840*. Cambridge: Cambridge University Press.

BENJAMIN, W. (1973). *Charles Baudelaire: A Lyric Poet in the High Era of Capitalism*, trans. H. Zohn. London: New Left Books.

BERGER, J. P. (1972). *Ways of Seeing*. London: BBC and Penguin Books.

BERTHO, C. (1980). 'L'Invention de la Bretagne: Genèse sociale d'un stéréotype', *Actes de la recherche en sciences sociales*, 35 (Nov.), 45–62.

CLARK, K. (1949). *Landscape into Art*. London: John Murray.

DELOUCHE, D. (1977). *Peintres de la Bretagne, découverte d'une province*. Paris: Librairie Klincksieck.

GERNSHEIM, H. and A. (1968). *L.-J.-M. Daguerre: The History of the Diorama and the Daguerrotype*. New York: Secker and Warburg.

GOMBRICH, E. (1960). *Art and Illusion: A Study in the Psychology of Pictorial Representation*. New York: Pantheon Books.

GREEN, N. (1990). *The Spectacle of Nature: Landscape and Bourgeois Culture in Nineteenth-Century France*. Manchester: Manchester University Press.

JANIN. J. (1843). *The American in Paris or Heath's Picturesque Annual for 1843*. Paris: Appleton & Son.

LAURENS, J.-B. (1849). *Théorie du beau pittoresque*. Montpellier: M. Sevalli.

LOUVRE (1967). *Théodore Rousseau, 1812–1867*. Paris: Musée du Louvre.

MICHELET, J. (1924). *Lettres inédites (1841–1871)*, ed. P. Sirven. Paris: Les Presses universitaires de France.

MORLEY, D. (1986). *Family Television: Cultural Power and Domestic Leisure*. London: Comedia.

PARENT-DUCHÂTELET, A. (1981). *De la prostitution dans la vie de Paris* [1836], ed. A. Corbin. Paris: J. B. Baillière.

SIMON, J. (1890). 'Souvenirs de jeunesse', *Faisons la chaîne*, ed. P. Audebrand. Paris: Levy.

Société des Amis de la Forêt de Fontainebleau (1975). *Claude-François Denecourt*. Fontainebleau.

WILLIAMS, R. (1973). *The Country and the City*. London: Chatto & Windus.

2

Land, People, and Paper in Western Amazonia

PETER GOW

It is hard to see Amazonia as landscape, in the sense this term has for people from temperate climes. The land does not recede away from a point of observation to the distant horizon, for everywhere vegetation occludes the view. In the forest, sight penetrates only a short distance into the mass of trees. Along the big rivers, you can see further, but even here there is no distant blue horizon. The sky starts abruptly from behind the screen of forest. Sight is hemmed in, and you would succumb to claustrophobia had not a plane journey or many days of travel let you know the scale of this land of big rivers and unending forests. To travel in most of Amazonia is to pass through an endless succession of small enclosed places, and to imagination itself is left the task of contructing out of these an immense extension of space. Only when an Amazonian landscape has been radically transformed by roads and deforestation is it revealed as visually extended space. A bright red road extends to the horizon, while buildings, fences, and isolated trees recede away into the distance. It looks more like a northern temperate landscape, with the wilderness forest no longer dominating the visual field, but simply a hazy transition between land and sky in the far distance.

Being able to see Amazonia has nothing to do with sight as naïve perceptual experience. The eyes that see the colonization frontiers as landscape are eyes structured by a particular kind of visual practice. As Ong has put it, 'Only after print and the extensive experience of maps that print implemented would human beings, when they thought about the cosmos or universe or "world", think primarily of something laid out before their eyes, as in a modern printed atlas, a vast surface or assemblage of surfaces (vision presents surfaces) ready to be "explored"' (1982: 73). It is not simply that we perceive the world as structured like a map or a landscape painting. Looking at a deforested Amazonian landscape, we are looking at a visual environment constructed from maps, and at a simulacrum of a northern temperate environment. Much of the recent colonization of Amazonia has proceeded along roads, which themselves had their first existence as lines drawn across the empty spaces on maps. And the most 'developed' form of this newly constructed landscape is based on cattle pasture, the only economic rationale of which is that it makes this land look 'civilized', that is, like the domesticated rural landscapes of Europe or

North America. In Brazil and in Peru, Amazonian cattle-ranching is possible only because of massive state subsidies (Hecht and Cockburn 1989). As with the roads, it is what is written on paper, not produced in the land, which makes the colonized and deforested parts of Amazonia look, to some people, like real landscapes.

Seen from an airplane, uncolonized Amazonia looks like uninhabited wilderness, but it is not. It is people's land. It is either currently inhabited or, if it is not, it shows constant evidence of recently having been so. Even the naïve viewer can see settlements from the air, while the more knowledgeable voyager can see the network of irregular patches of secondary vegetation that are the mark of slash-and-burn agriculture. The most knowledgeable, such as certain ecologists and Native Amazonian people themselves, see even more, and find the marks of human activity in what is apparently virgin forest. For the ecologists, this knowledge is essentially abstract, and produced by their own accumulation of records on paper in their scientific practice. For Native Amazonian people, this knowledge is part of lived experience in the sense of 'what is going on'. It is with the nature of this latter knowledge as lived experience that this essay deals. What does it mean that Native Amazonian people do not create representations of their land, and what implications does this have for their modes of experience?

I must make it quite clear from the outset that I do not argue that Native Amazonian people have some sort of immediate relationship to the land. As will become clear, particular people have densely mediated relationships to particular places: this is what makes Amazonia a lived human landscape. But I am arguing that these mediations do not, on the whole, take the form of *representations*. By 'representation' I mean something which stands for something else in its absence. To use Gibsonian terminology, a representation is that kind of visual display which presents a virtual surface to perception (Gibson 1986). What makes an object into a representation is both its mode of fabrication and an element of fantasy. A piece of paper with lines on it is a piece of paper with lines on it. It only becomes a map of the Bajo Urubamba when direct perception is denied, and the course of that great river is imagined in the lines on the surface of the sheet. The issue is not primarily one of perception, but one of social processes. What sort of processes produce and depend on representations, and what sorts do not? It is this question of the agency of representations that I address here.

I assume here that the engagements between people and land on the Bajo Urubamba river in Eastern Peru are meaningful actions, and that the ramifying results of such engagements are themselves meaningful to native people. There is as much meaning, for native people, in the process of forest regeneration in an old garden as there is in a mythic narrative or in a shamanic curing session. The focus must therefore be on the existential form of the symbolic process (see Munn 1986), for clearly forest regeneration, the narration of myths, and shamanic curing are not the same sorts of things. But an analysis of the existential forms of such symbolic processes cannot rely on the difference between representation and the thing represented. The issue is too serious to be modelled analytically on the relationship between the thing itself and the other thing that only stands for the thing itself. The empty spaces on maps of Amazonia have already allowed too many people to pretend that nobody lives there.

The View from Santa Clara

Santa Clara is a small native community on the right bank of the Bajo Urubamba river. It has a fluctuating population of about eighty to ninety people, most of whom are identifiable as Piro or Campa. When I first arrived on the Bajo Urubamba in 1980, I chose to study in Santa Clara rather than in any other nearby community because it closely approximated my image of what a beautiful Amazonian village should be. Most of the houses are arranged around a central square, and many are shaded by large mango trees. Even the dissonant note of the corrugated iron roofs can easily be forgiven as one gazes on the majestic silhouette of the *pifuayo* palms against the sky or the line of tall *ojé* trees marking the boundary of the forest in the background. You cannot see the mainstream of the Urubamba river from Santa Clara, or even from the port, which means you are screened from the constant to-and-fro of travellers. But you never lose awareness of the river, either in the dry season when you can hear the shingle rolling in its bed, or in the rainy season when it slowly escapes its channel and floods the village and the forest.

As I lived in Santa Clara, I began to learn that the river and the forest are not undifferentiated, to learn that each is a mosaic of different small zones. Learning the differentiation of the forest was relatively easy, preconditioned as I was by my reading to recognize gardens, secondary forest, and primary forest. Learning to differentiate the products of the complex interaction of river and forest was more difficult. It is easy, in the abstract, to know that landscapes are formed by flowing water, but difficult to understand in practice the dynamics of a large Amazonian river. Over the eight years I have known the Santa Clara area, the mouth of the Huau river has shifted upstream by half a mile while the height of Santa Clara has risen perceptibly. It has taken me this long not to be mystified by statements like, 'This is good land for making a plantain garden. It's new land, it used to be the main channel of the river.' Equally, all inhabited space, each settlement, took on a precise social meaning. I slowly learned the meanings of Huau, Nueva Italia, Kinkón, Bellavista, El Aguajal, etc. I learned that the inhabitants of Santa Clara were, on the whole, on fairly bad terms with the people of all these places. With some settlements, such as Huau or Nueva Italia, the hostility had to do with old fights between kinspeople. But in many cases, residents of Santa Clara had lived with these people in the past, and sometimes mentioned their desire to move in with them again. With other places such as Bellavista and El Aguajal, the hostility was based on ties between *patrones* and *peones*, bosses and workers. The settlements are small commercial plantations owned by non-native people, who employ men from Santa Clara as labourers. But here again, several people in Santa Clara had lived on these plantations in the past, and all older people had lived as slaves on the *haciendas* of the great *patrón*, Pancho Vargas.

As my knowledge grew, Santa Clara also began to lose its stability. It ceased to be a place with no beginning, and its inhabitants ceased to be a group of people inevitably linked to this site. I came to realize that the settlement of Santa Clara had a fairly precise and short history, and that its inhabitants had little more reason to live there than anywhere else. Had I arrived fifteen years earlier, Santa Clara would have looked as tenuous and new as the house Roberto was building on Mapchirga stream. I also realized that the movement of old Mauricio and his wife Clotilde into this house meant more than they said. They told me that they had moved to look after the house while their son Roberto was away on the coast. But by then I knew that Roberto had left Santa Clara largely because of his strained relationship with his older brother Artemio, the village headman. Old Mauricio and Clotilde were expressing their dissatisfaction with Artemio by living far from the village. Their youngest daughter Sara moved in with them, and she thereby added to the friction within the community. In Santa Clara, other people began to voice criticisms of Artemio's high-handed behaviour. His oldest sister and her husband announced their intention to shift residence to their new garden on Mapchirga stream, and their married son said the same. I was now aware that these minor shifts in residence were part of the infinitely subtle politics of a native community. Annoyed with Artemio's behaviour, his coresidents were moving out. Roberto's house on Mapchirga looked as though it would become a new community.

Seven years later, everyone was again living in Santa Clara. Although Artemio was less respected as headman than before, Roberto seemed to have disappeared for good, and his parents were now obviously too old to live far from their children. His niece Miriam had transformed from a feckless teenager into a young and competent mother, and she complained about the ever-increasing dryness of the river channel that flowed past Santa Clara. She told me, 'We're going to move the village to Mapchirga. The canoes can get that far when the river is low and there is clean water to drink. Santa Clara is no good any more, so we're going to move there.' Miriam and her husband Limber were young and active, but also mature enough to voice their opinions in public, and be listened to.

One day I walked past the rotting posts of Roberto's house with my godson Hermes trailing behind. Sara had given birth to him while she lived here with her parents. I pointed out the house site to him, saying that this was where he was born. He looked a little confused by my statement, but trotted on after me to bathe in the Mapchirga stream. As we washed, he told me that he was afraid to be in this place, for his mother had told him that jaguars walked about there. 'Don't be afraid,' I told him, 'there are no jaguars here.' But his fear made this once-lively place seem desolate, and I wondered if he spoke the truth.

Over the years, as my knowledge of the place called Santa Clara and its people has deepened, I have realized that this is not just a natural landscape in which people live and to which they give meaning. I have realized that their lives are intimately bound up in it. I learned about this landscape by moving around in it, but also through hearing it being described in a thousand different narratives told by native people. Anthropologists customarily analyse such narratives for the way in which they reveal the meanings people attribute to a landscape. But there is surely more to the issue than this. The native people of the Bajo Urubamba do not just impose meanings on the land, any more than I did when I told young Hermes that this site was where he was born. Something about our relationship was implicated in this particular place, and our being there together. Equally, his childish fear of jaguars would have been easy to dismiss had he not referred to his mother as an authority. Experience has made me a greater authority on the past than Hermes, but experience has made Sara a greater authority on the dangers of lonely spots in the forest than I.

In my case, perhaps telling Hermes that he was born in such-and-such a place reflects an anxiety to establish a deeper relationship with this young stranger. But for Hermes, a young boy growing up in a native community on the Bajo Urubamba, telling me that jaguars frequent this spot is part of his growing understanding of the landscape in which he lives. His knowledge of this landscape comes partly through moving through it, and partly through what older people tell him about it. Hermes is still a young child, but already he has learned from his mother to fear this place on Mapchirga stream, and to seek reassurance in it from his godfather. Hermes has already learned, if he ever needed to be taught, that the land is an aspect of kinship.

Kinship and Land

Elsewhere I have developed at length my analysis of kinship for the native people of the Bajo Urubamba (Gow 1991). I argued there that the term 'kinship', in this specific social context, must be understood in its widest possible sense. Kinship cannot be limited to the social implications of being born, procreating, and dying, for it must also include the wider conditions of those social implications. On the Bajo Urubamba, being born is not a sufficient cause of being a person, for one must also be grown through acts of feeding. Equally, sex is not a sufficient cause of procreation, for sex is predicated on the work of feeding another person, just as procreation is predicated on the work of re-peated sexual intercourse. Death is predicated on these relations too, for the old die because they have exhausted their vitality in creating others through work, and the newborn die because their parents' acts of production or consumption rebound on them as sickness. There are no pristine acts in the creation of kinship, for every kinship relation is predicated on former acts which created the people it binds together. Kinship is implicated in the whole social universe of the native people of the Bajo Urubamba, where any relationship which is not one of kinship receives its full meaning only in this opposition.

In truth, I did not learn of the centrality of kinship for native people through the classical anthropological techniques. I found the famous 'genealogical method' rather embarrassing to use, for my informants were either insulted or aggrieved by my objectification of their kinship relations. Nor was it easy simply to elicit the idioms of kinship, for my informants were acutely aware of my own presence among them, and thus of my potential as a kinsperson. I learned about kinship through what native people told me about the land, and through observing how they used the land in their relations with other people, including myself.

From the very start, my relationship with native people was focused on what I ate. Could I, or would I, eat what they call 'real food'? The first couple I stayed with, the schoolteacher of Huau and his wife, suggested that I pay them money and be cooked 'fine food', which is the food that white people eat. When I lived later with this woman's parents in Santa Clara, I was never asked to pay anything and was fed with 'real food', the food native people eat. I paid for nothing, as I was constantly reminded, but I was also constantly asked for 'help', in the form of an endless stream of shotgun shells, presents of store-bought food, small gifts, and large amounts of alcohol. I represented this help to myself as a slightly more expensive version of the earlier relationship of paying for food, but I was wrong. Native people endlessly told me that they fed me for free because they themselves paid nothing for the food. As one man put it, 'Here you do not have to pay for food. If you want to eat plantains, just clear a garden and plant it. Then you have plantains. If you want to eat fish, just go to the river. It is full of fish. Here you eat well, you don't need money.' For native people, 'real food' is free, but it is not defined strictly by the absence of payment. 'Real food' is produced locally, through human interaction with the land.

The native people of the Bajo Urubamba are slash-and-burn agriculturalists. Each year every married man, especially if he has children, is expected to clear a new garden in the forest for himself and his wife. The couple then plant this garden with a sequence of crops, depending on what they expect to need over the next few years. Gardens produce for more than a year, sometimes almost indefinitely, so each couple has a series of producing gardens scattered around the community. Further, various tree species and other cultigens are planted in gardens, and these will be harvested over many years. The exclusive control a couple have over a garden declines as a function of the work they put into it. As they stop weeding and replanting a garden, and as the secondary growth takes over, their exclusive control wanes. The products of an old garden (*purma*) are free for anyone who takes the trouble to harvest them, but the site will be referred as the *purma* of the original makers until the memory is totally lost.

In addition to the work of gardening, men, and to a lesser extent women, are producers of game. Forest game, particularly the animals of remote inland areas, are the most desired food items, but river fish are the most commonly eaten. Unlike garden crops, the game animals of the forest and river exist outside of human agency. Humans do not create them nor do they work to multiply them. They are produced and multiplied through the agency of forest and river spirits, the 'owners' and 'mothers' of their respective domains. The game is produced as food by locating and then catching it.

The major garden crops are plantains and manioc. Plantains are the daily staple and, served with fish or forest game, are *comida legítima*, the 'real food' which constitutes kinship relations. Manioc is processed by women into *masato*, the beer which is circulated to the maximal extension of kinship. The circulation of real food and manioc beer is continuous in native communities, in a process whereby kinship made in the past is remembered and kinship is created for the future. As I have discussed at length elsewhere (Gow 1991), kin ties, for native people, are generated by acts of being fed as children by adults: acts which are subsequently extended by productive adults in memory of care given as children. Kinship is predicated on the active work of men and women linked together in marriage. Through work, they make gardens, harvest plantains and manioc, cook and brew beer. The products of this work are then circulated. This is what I saw every day in Santa Clara, where 'life's dull round' is the ceaseless process of kinship.[1]

Landscape Implication

The production and circulation of food produces people, who respond with memory of these acts of caring. But equally, these productive activities create the mosaic of vegetation zones around the village. To use Sauer's terms (1963), these are modifications of the natural environment through human landscape agency. These zones are not however a useless by-product or detritus of native people's productive activities. They are at once important resources for local people, and loci of kinship. To understand this requires a short detour on some recent research on Native Amazonian ecology.

There are a number of studies on the impressive ecological knowledge of Native Amazonian peoples. Any anthropologist who is informed on natural history will have had experience of this. Many of the most arcane ecological relationships in neotropical rain forest, such as the symbiotic relationship between oropendolas (New World orioles) and a species of wasp, or the parasiticism of a vine species on a large ant, are the common knowledge of Native Amazonian people. But as ethno-ecologists have investigated Native Amazonian peoples in greater depth, it is becoming clear that these people do not simply know their environment, but that they have also been consciously manipulating it over extensive periods. I refer to Denevan's studies of the creation of grasslands by the Gran Pajonal Campa and of the long-term manipulation of forest regeneration by the Bora of north-eastern Peru, and Posey's work on the modification of forest and savannah by the Central-Brazilian Kayapó.[2] These studies are opening up a new temporal depth to Native Amazonian ecology, by revealing that these people interact with an environment which has already been formed by purposeful human agency.

My work on the native people of the Bajo Urubamba was not conducted with such issues in mind, but they have suggested a new importance for the information I did collect in the course of daily life in these communities. As I learned about the local landscape of Santa Clara, I became increasingly impressed by the way in which kinship, as a temporal process, was bound up in it. This can be illustrated by the following example:

Roberto wanted to make a pasture for cattle. He had no cattle, but intended to purchase some from one of the local *patrones*. He chose a site where the path leading from Santa Clara to El Aguajal crosses the Mapchirga stream. This was, to my eyes, an undifferentiated area of forest. But as the forest was cleared, even I could see that growing among them were species like *pifuayo* palm, which is a full domesticate, incapable of dispersal in the wild. I was helped in this perception by the fact that Roberto had left them standing proud. I asked Roberto's father Mauricio who had planted these trees, and he told me that his own brother-in-law Tiburcio had done so, some thirty years before. I knew that Tiburcio had lived on Mapchirga in the past, but was now able to locate his house site precisely. Meanwhile, nearby, the men of Santa Clara were helping Roberto's brother Artemio clear a new garden. In doing so, someone found a long straight log lying on the ground. After testing it with his machete, he commented that such a log would make an excellent house post. Old Mauricio came to look, announced that it was indeed good wood for a house post, and that this very tree had been felled twenty-five years previously by a Campa man, Julio Felipe, when he lived on Mapchirga. This information naturally excited me, for it provided both spatial and temporal locations for a narrative the old man had told me weeks before. He had told me that Tiburcio had lived on Mapchirga, and that he had been joined there by some Machiguenga people from the Alto Urubamba. Then Tiburcio had left, and Julio Felipe had immigrated from the Tambo to live at the site. Later the Machiguenga people left, moving back to the Alto Urubamba, as did Julio Felipe. I knew nothing of the Machiguenga, having never met them, but I did know Julio Felipe, for he had returned to the Mapchirga years later, and now lived some distance upstream from Roberto's new house.

There are several important points to be made about this series of incidents and stories. The first is that such processes first introduced me to the time depth of kinship for native people. I was endlessly told such stories, usually in order to relate an incident notable for its humour, tragedy, or mystic import. Each narrative embeds the focal incident in an apparently superfluous mass of information about who else was there, what they were eating, and what they were doing when the incident took place. Such a story, told in the physical setting of Santa Clara, would profoundly irritate me, providing a mass of the 'hard data' on kinship I had come to discover, but in a style marked by imprecision. If I asked, 'Where exactly were you living when this happened?', the reply would be a vague, 'Over there,' or, 'Just downstream from where old Julio Felipe is going to make his new garden.'

Such imprecision has a precise meaning. Once you already know where 'over there' is, or where old Julio Felipe is making his garden, you can locate the spatial meaning of the incident. If you do not know, how could it matter? You, as a listener, are not implicated in the landscape in which these things happened, so can only relate to them in the abstract. As you become implicated in the landscape, these stories take on new meanings. I say implicated in the landscape, rather than saying simply 'as you gain knowledge of the landscape'. In this context, knowledge would suggest a purely subjective experience. It is not such an experience, because implication depends on actively moving around in the landscape, and leaving traces in it.

The implication of the listener in the environment occurs through the agency of older people. Most of the men clearing Artemio's gardens did not live in the area when it was cleared for Julio Felipe, and of those few, most would have been too young to take part. So the prior event of garden-making was not part of their personal experience. But old Mauricio was there, and so was able to explain what had happened. This is the most important fact, for it implies a great deal about kinship. The garden was being cleared for Artemio and his wife Lilí, to feed their children. The products of the garden would also circulate as manioc beer to everyone else in Santa Clara, and to visitors from elsewhere. But in making this garden, with these projects in mind, they were re-clearing land which had once been old Julio Felipe's garden. The produce of this garden had fed old Mauricio and his wife Clotilde, who had often drunk beer with Julio Felipe. And the men working in the garden that day were the sons, sons-in-law, grandsons, and other younger kin of old Mauricio and Clotilde and of Julio Felipe. These younger men were co-operating to make Artemio's garden, just as they would co-operate to make everyone's gardens, because of the prior relationships between these old people who made them. And the relationship between old Mauricio and Clotilde and Julio Felipe was implicated in this ancient garden, and the network of settlement sites and gardens that had once radiated from it and which are now old secondary forest.

No one on the Bajo Urubamba would ever appeal to an abandoned garden as a basis for current social action. No one would say, 'I help him because we both ate food from that garden when we were children.' Native people say, 'I help him because we are kin' (see Gow 1991). The focus is always on an active relationship between two living people. But landscape is implicated in these relationships in two different ways: as active place-making and as narrative of places. The active relationships between kin implicate landscape because the help that kin give each other is landscape modification: kin help each other to transform forest into gardens. The most radical implication of kinship in landscape is the act of house-building. Kin help each other to build houses so that they may live together. Living together is the supreme act of kin, for it implies the ceaseless acts of generosity which constitute 'life's dull round'. The village is at once the scene of kinship and the product of kinship.

Native people are quite capable of specifying kin relations in the bald terms of a 'genealogical method'. Anyone can say, of any other, that 'He/she is my older sibling/parent/aunt or uncle/etc.', and follow out the links between them. A young native stranger to a community will be interrogated by older people in just this fashion, 'Where do you live/who is your father/who is your mother/who are your grandparents?' The interrogation continues until a familiar name is mentioned, at which point the older person will say, 'Haa, you are my younger brother's grandchild! Call me "grandfather".' But such situations are limiting cases, caused by long-distance travel. Normally, native people know their kin either because they grew up among them, or because they have heard them endlessly referred to in the stories of older kinspeople.

This is the force of the apparently extraneous information in native people's narration. The stories older people tell to the young are, as I have said, filled with details of place and of people. Often the locations are meaningless to the listener, as, for example, when old Jorge Manchinari told his grandson Pablo and me about, 'the time he was almost killed by the Brazilians on the Yuruá river'. Old Jorge detailed exactly where he and his companions ate and slept during their epic flight up the Yuruá river. Neither Pablo nor I have ever travelled on this river, so these locations meant nothing to us. But Jorge's companions were Pablo's older kin, and the ascendant kin of many people living in the Santa Clara area. The residential histories of these old people are the origins of the younger generations. Pablo's mother was born in Brazil, and Pablo sometimes jokingly calls himself a Brazilian. Pablo is implicated in a distant landscape he has never seen, but only a little bit. He is really implicated in the landscape of Huau and Santa Clara, to which old Jorge and all his kin returned to raise their children.

The details of these stories are not extraneous to kinship relations which are constituted elsewhere. They are not simply adventures that people had away from the serious business of living. They are stories whose heroes are the narrators themselves, and they are told to the younger kin of the narrators.

Elsewhere I have discussed how these narratives implicate kinship in their form, content, and place of narration (1990, 1991). They are only told to those who do not know, that is, to junior kin who cannot have personally experienced the events. Native people narrate these stories as evidence that they are, as they say in Piro, *kshinikanu/kshinikano*, 'those who remember, think about, care about', and younger people listen to show that they are willing to learn. These narratives are 'face-to-face' communication in a radical sense, for they imply the presence of older and younger kin together in one place. Living together is central to kinship, and to the ceaseless acts of generosity between kin. Narratives of personal experiences track the production of present coresidence, the here and now of a village, through other places and people. The act of narrating expands the spatial and temporal dimensions of the village outwards into a wider landscape, while simultaneously focusing these dimensions to the mutual co-presence of narrator and listener in this one place.

The Dead and Powerful Beings in Landscape

Implication within a landscape is central to native people's understanding of life. For any particular person, this implication occurs through being born, growing up, marrying, and working as an adult to raise children, and through dying. But native people are always implicated in particular landscapes which are always changing. A child grows up in a particular house in a specific village site, eating the food produced in particular gardens. But grown to adulthood, and working as an adult man or woman, the landscapes of childhood will have transformed. The house site will almost certainly be abandoned, the village site may have been abandoned, and the gardens will be regenerating as forest. This temporal process of landscape is not just a physical fact, it is constantly reiterated by native people. Younger people are constantly moving around, discussing shifts of house site and gardens, or even moves to other communities. Old people deny that they will move, and say, 'I am old now, I know where I want to die.' This is not some sort of romantic choice of a beautiful spot for death, for the place chosen is always the place in which one lives. It is a statement of resignation in the face of old age, for the old realize that their failing physical strength will preclude them from making gardens or building houses.

When an adult person dies on the Bajo Urubamba, the house in which he or she lived is abandoned. It is sometimes burned down, but more often it is dismantled and the reusable parts, like new thatching or a well-made door, are used in a new house. The reason is that the dead soul (Spanish: *alma*; Piro: *samenchi*) is potently attached to this place, and indeed to all the places it knew in life. It hangs around these places, weeping and begging its surviving kin to join it in death. The sorrow of the dead soul evokes a lethal nostalgia in the living, causing them to sicken and die if they succumb to it. The dead soul is an image of memory, incapable of any kinship action except evoking the pity of its kin. Native people stoically ignore such imprecations, and avoid the places where the dead soul is likely to be encountered. Over time, by this means, the landscape becomes punctuated with places avoided by the living because they are associated with dead souls.

The dead soul is an image of memory, and disappears as memory disappears. Native people have no fear of the souls of dead strangers, for with no link of memory, they are incapable of having relationships with them. For the same reason, they have no fear of the souls of remote ancestors, who are also strangers to them. But they do fear another aspect of the dead, which has no link to memory. This is the bone or corpse demon (Spanish: *difunto/muerto*; Piro: *gipnachri*). A dead soul is always the dead soul of someone in particular, met with in a particular place associated with that person. It is an image of memory, as I have said. The bone demon is also a dead person, but no particular dead person. It is not tied to particular places, but wanders freely around, even entering villages at night. It seeks to eat people or to kill them through violent sexual intercourse, and is the embodiment of desire.

The dead soul is relatively easy to avoid, provided one avoids places associated with it. But the bone demon is not, for it inhabits the same zones as humans and travels freely. It is consistently encountered in the known inhabited landscape, but in unpredictable ways. Bone demons inhabit the same zones as humans, but not particular places. Their cannibal and sexual desire for the living reflects the place of human desire in the creation of kinship, and the motor force of landscape modification. It is the oral and sexual desire of men and women related as husbands and wives which initiates the transformation of forest into gardens and houses. I do not think it would be too far-fetched to argue that the bone demons stand at the far end of that process, as once-used places are retransformed into undifferentiated forest. The bone demons are the 'agents' of forest regeneration, and are associated with those planted species which *no saben morrir*, 'do not know how to die'. In particular, they are associated with *ayahuasca*, 'corpse vine', the curing hallucinogen.[3] The bone demons are both the deep past of kinship (anonymous forgotten dead in secondary forest) and disembodied images of what makes kinship in the present and projects it into the future (oral and sexual desire).

Beyond the landscapes of living and dead humans, and encapsulating them, are the generalized worlds of the river and the forest as autonomous spaces. These spaces are generated by the supreme agents, the 'owners' and 'mothers' of the forest and river. These agents, variously described as giant anacondas and as beautiful tall white foreigners, create and maintain the forest and riverine domains. The forest is said to 'come from' (*venir de*) the giant forest anaconda *sachamama*, 'Forest Mother', just as rivers and lakes 'come from' *yacumama*, 'River Mother'. These domains are maintained and patrolled by *sacharuna*, 'Forest Person', and *yacuruna*, 'River Person', respectively. In shamanic discourse, they are called *gente*, 'people'. They are 'people' in this discourse because they are moral and knowledgeable agents, but they are not subject to birth or death. They generate and maintain space through their awesome knowledge (usually associated with their songs).

As immortal powerful beings, the 'owners' and 'mothers' of the forest and river do not depend on humans for their existence, and are usually indifferent to them. But in order to live, humans must invade these spaces in hunting, fishing, travel, and especially in the creation of specific landscapes of villages and gardens. In response, the powerful beings inflict humans with sickness and death. Although human sorcery is the commonest diagnosis for severe or fatal illness, killing power ultimately derives from these powerful beings, whether directly or through the medium of shamanic use of these powers. But equally, they are also the sources of curing power. Shamans take *ayahuasca*, and through the medium of *ícaros*, curing songs, tame the powerful beings into revealing themselves as people (see Gow 1991).

Taking drugs, shamans enter the forest and river, and perceive these directly as settlements filled with people. The landscape comes full circle, with the supreme antithesis of human activities, the depths of the river and the centre of the forest, revealed as human settlements. When shamans take hallucinogens, their souls leave their bodies and wander freely, and they see directly as the spirits see. The spirits call to them, inviting them into their houses to eat and drink. They live with the spirits as kin, eating their food and hearing their powerful and beautiful songs. The general categories of space, the forest and the river, which in everyday experience are the location of specific landscapes of implication of specific persons, are transformed into the specific houses and villages of powerful beings, the agents of space at its most general. This transformation of the general into the specific, and the specific into the general, is a hallmark of shamanic experience.[4]

Meaning and Representation

When shamans take hallucinogens, they see the forest or river as settlements full of people. One might argue that these shamans transpose a cultural image (human settlements) on to natural domains (forest and river), and proceed to say that shamans 'represent', in their discourse, the natural as cultural. But to do so would be to ignore all the other complex ways in which the landscape is implicated in people, and people in the landscape. When a shaman says he sees a forest tree as a house full of people when he takes *ayahuasca*, we cannot restrict analysis to that tree and to that image. We must take into account that houses are made out of forest trees, on ground where trees once stood, are abandoned to turn back into forest, and so on. The shaman's hallucination may strike us as particularly dramatic and exotic, but it can only be understood as one particular point in the complex processes by which people and landscape interact.

The statements shamans make about their drug experiences are perhaps not easy to understand, but at the very least shamans are saying that they see these things in a way that is closely connected to the everyday perception of kinship in the environment. Kinship, as I have argued, is directly perceived by native people in the environment because it is there. It is there because kinship is created out of human landscape agency. The position I have taken here may raise certain problems within the psychology of perception, although it should not. I suspect most psychologists would deny that people could perceive directly such a complex cultural category as kinship is for the native people of the Bajo Urubamba. But in so far as kinship is only about direct social relations, and in so far as these relations implicate direct landscape modifications, native people must be able to perceive kinship in the landscape. It is of course true that each native person must be socialized into so doing, but this is already given in the relations of kinship.[5]

In my analysis, I have sought to avoid any claim that the native people of the Bajo Urubamba 'read' kinship into their environment, or that they 'represent' it as an aspect of kinship. I will return to the issue of representation later. The metaphor of culture as a particular reading of the world is as popular as it is unanalysed. It models all human culture on a very restricted Western cultural practice. It implies encoding and decoding of information, senders and receivers of information. In the process I have described here, there are no senders and no encoding of information, and hence no receivers or decoding. To suggest that Tiburcio planted fruit trees around his house on Mapchirga as a kind of postcard to future generations has only to be stated to seem ridiculous. Logically, therefore, it is as ridiculous to suggest that I, or anyone else, read the history of his residence in the mature fruit trees revealed as Roberto cleared the site.

Writing and reading are interesting human cultural practices in their own right, but they should not serve us as unanalysed metaphors for either human culture or human thought. Writing and reading, properly understood, imply texts, which are fabricated forms of graphic representation. As such, they are material objects and hence parts of the material environment. To conclude my account, I will discuss one such object which is intimately bound up in the processes of landscape and kinship I have described here. The object is a text, consisting of both written words and a map, the land title of the *Comunidad Nativa de Santa Clara*.

According to the schoolteacher of Santa Clara, there are two copies of this text. One is kept in the Ministry of Agriculture in Lima, the capital of Peru, the other is kept by Don Mauricio Fasabi, in his capacity as most responsible person in the community. Most of the time, this document rests unseen in a box in old Mauricio's house. I have only seen it once, when the schoolteacher called for it to be produced at the height of the land dispute discussed below. I was interested in the map primarily to help me understand the lived landscape of Santa Clara. Even as maps go, this one is remarkably abstract. It includes no reference points other than certain abstractly defined orientation co-ordinates. Even the ecologically salient boundaries and sites, like the banks of the Urubamba or Mapchirga river, are sketchily represented. Its only interest, as a map, is that it shows that the village of Santa Clara, and hence much of the land gardened by its residents, technically lies outside the community territory.

Needless to say, nobody in Santa Clara uses this document to orientate them in their environment, and probably nobody could. It is not even used as knowledge about the environment. If people in or outside Santa Clara need to locate the precise boundaries of the community land, they do not do so with reference to this map, but by reference to the paths around the territory cut by the men of Santa Clara in the company of the agricultural engineers of SINAMOS when the land was first surveyed for titling. These paths were made in the landscape by known people at a known time, and hence define the community territory. They are there in the environment, the objectification of the act of demarcation of community land, and they are periodically cleared to emphasize their existence.

The land title document is used by no one in Santa Clara as knowledge of the environment, but it is used as a physical reference point in the ongoing struggle between the people of Santa Clara and their immediate neighbours over land ownership. The land immediately downriver from Santa Clara is the plantation of Eustaquio Ruis. This man was drowned in 1981, and his plantation was taken over by his son-in-law Manolo. Until 1975, when Santa Clara was legally constituted as a *Comunidad Nativa*, Ruis had claimed ownership of all its territory. The claim had no legal basis, but was backed by the entire power of the white *patrón* class in the area. Years before, when Tiburcio and his kin lived on Mapchirga, Ruis's pigs had regularly raided their gardens. In retaliation, the Piro people killed and ate one of these pigs. Ruis called the police, who took Tiburcio and his fellows to court in the local administrative centre of Atalaya. The judge, a friend of Ruis's, sentenced the men to a month's work for Ruis. He made them clear a large pasture, on which he installed cattle. It was to escape from Ruis, his pigs, and now his cattle, that Tiburcio and the rest left Mapchirga and moved far upriver. The current inhabitants of Santa Clara were not involved in this dispute, but its story is still narrated as an example of what a white *patrón* is capable. The land title document was used in fights with Ruis's son-in-law Manolo, as a sign that there was nothing arbitrary about the boundary between his land and that of Santa Clara. The boundary is present to perception as the path cut along the limit between the two areas. This path is a material reality, linked to the material reality of the title deed. In some mysterious way, it refers to the power of the state in Lima. The people of Santa Clara would have been extremely reluctant to appeal to the vague authority of

Lima in any fight with Manolo, but fortunately Manolo was equally reluctant to chance his luck.[6]

The land title of Santa Clara, as an object, thus does not represent the environment of Santa Clara to anyone in the area. At most it is a material token of another set of powers which native people have learned historically to use against their exploiters. The copy of the land title that sits in Don Mauricio's box thus has a particular efficacy as the material embodiment of a particular set of events in the political history of the Bajo Urubamba and of a particular configuration of power relations. The land title takes its small place within the complex of meaningful relationships between the inhabitants of Santa Clara and the local landscape. It does not stand for the totality of these relationships for native people, nor could it. For native people, there can be no such totality, as long as people need to clear land for gardens and houses, as children grow, and as narratives trace the past into the present.

The other copy of the land title, in Lima, is something else. It is part of a vast mass of texts and documents, laws and title deeds, and of the social relations these inhabit. That land title document defines the relationship between the people of Santa Clara and their land as a unidirectional relationship of possession. It links that relationship to a multiplicity of other relationships of similar or different order, such that the people and land of Santa Clara become enchained within a network of graphic representations and social relations about which they know little or nothing. By representing the ties between people and land in Santa Clara, the land title imposes potential limits to the meanings of those ties, and simultaneously imposes new meanings on it. Analytically, the complex circulation of multiplicities of relations between the people and the landscape of Santa Clara, as meaningful action, cannot be reduced to the unidirectional relationship between a collective subject (the *Comunidad Nativa* of Santa Clara) and an object (the territory of Santa Clara). But the land title implies that they can, and the power relations within which it operates suggest that they might well be.

Conclusion: A Landscape and a Land Title

I began this paper with the problems that people from the temperate North have with seeing Amazonia as a human landscape. I have argued that one small part of Amazonia, the Bajo Urubamba river, is lived as a human landscape by local native people through a multiplicity of engagements with the forest and river, with each other in acts of generosity and in narration, and in encounters with the dead and with spirits. Finally, I pointed out a little object which lies hidden within the landscape of one native community, the land title, which contains another vision of this landscape. In conclusion, I want to draw out some of the implications of this analysis.

For the native people of the Bajo Urubamba, the local environment is a lived space. It is known by means of movement through it, seeing the traces of other people's movements and agency, and through the narratives of yet other people's agency. The narratives, while apparently most distant from embodied experience, are in fact closely linked to it, for they depend on the simultaneous presence of speaker and hearer in one place. That which is indeed distant from embodied experience is the origin of the general spaces of landscape outside of human agency, which is revealed only through the medium of drugs. At this level, the major difference between this landscape and that embodied in the land title is the concreteness of the former and the abstraction of the latter. The land title might seem to be an airy representation of the concrete presence of people in the land. But it is not, for it is the concrete embodiment of certain very important social processes. Their effects were not too evident on the Bajo Urubamba at the time of my fieldwork, but their potential was definitely there.

It might be thought that I have given the little piece of paper which embodies the land title of Santa Clara a more portentous significance than it deserves. But one has only to look into the processes of struggle for land in Amazonia, or anywhere that indigenous tribal people are fighting for control of their country, to see just how important these little bits of paper are. The legal registration of indigenous people's land claims, and court battles surrounding it, is primarily an issue of the portentous significance of pieces of paper. We imagine such pieces of paper to embody abstract principles of ownership and control, but they can do so only because they *are* pieces of paper. It is not after all the land of Santa Clara that is held in the Ministry of Agriculture in Lima, but a paper representation of it. As many Native Amazonian people have found to their dire cost, it is these pieces of paper which determine who owns what, not their own complex relationships to their land.

In the ongoing social processes of Santa Clara, it is the path cleared around the community territory which matters, not the abstract representation of this boundary as the ink line on the land title map. The boundary path is the direct embodiment of native people in the landscape of Santa Clara. But the little inky line on the piece of paper is the direct physical embodiment of someone else. This someone else, unknown to the people of Santa Clara and to myself, is the one who embodied the laws of the Peruvian State in the process of registering the *Comunidad Nativa de Santa Clara*. The land title of Santa Clara is not a representation of Santa Clara primarily because it looks like Santa Clara, but because its 'standing for' that landscape has the potential to be effected as concrete social action.

Ethnography itself, as writing about culture, is also engaged with pieces of paper. It is, as we all now recognize, a mode of representation. But this does not mean that what ethnographers are writing about, 'culture' or 'society', is itself a form of representation. Unfortunately, however, certain of our most important and pervasive models of culture are based on this metaphor: Durkheim's 'collective representations' and Boas' 'seeing eye of tradition' (see Sperber 1985 and Sahlins 1976 for powerful recent restatements of these respective positions). In both cases, cultural processes are modelled on the classic order of representation. In the Durkheimian case, bodily-interior states are modelled as materially fabricated objects of a specific type, while in the Boasian case, culture is modelled on the aesthetic contemplation which constitutes the viewer's place in relationship to representation (see Foucault 1970 on classical representation). It is like the two aspects of a classic Western landscape painting: the fabricated painting and the viewing aesthete.

As Foucault has shown so clearly in his analysis of Velasquez's *Las Meninas*, subject, object, and world are held together in a specific mode in the order of representation.[7] But Foucault's work, however enlightening about the interior construction of Western modes of knowledge, provides ethnographers with no guide to reflection on the modes of experience with which they seek to engage. The relationship between the people of Santa Clara and their land cannot be decanted from a critical reflection on Western philosophy, for it must be sought out in active engagement with these people, with all the problems that involves. But equally, we must avoid clutching at the fantasy of 'immediate presence', the mystical participation with other peoples in other countries. We must not model the experiences of the people of Santa Clara as the inverse or spectral images of our own.

This is why I have placed such stress on the specific forms of lived experience of landscape of the Bajo Urubamba. As Munn has shown in her study of Gawa (1986), specific practices create the world, or spacetime, in which they occur, and which thereby constitutes the immediate experience of the agents who produce it. In so far as it is the specific practices which constitute both world and subjective experience, it is to variations in specific practices that we must apply our attention. In this light, the creation and use of little bits of paper with their inky lines, as a specific practice, can be seen to generate a very different spacetime from the oral narratives of older kin on the Bajo Urubamba. Indeed, Latour (1987) has argued that it is the production and amassing of marks on paper that is the central practice of science, rather than any mode of thought or contemplation of objective reality. The spacetime generated by these marks on paper, or representations, is what we call 'the real world'. It is this spacetime which is then lived by us, as the abstract order is imposed on other spacetimes: in other words, as a line drawn on a map is effected as a road cut across part of Amazonia.

In his study of the changing ecological relations in colonial New England, Cronon writes, 'Our project must be to locate a nature that is within rather than without history, for only by so doing can we find human communities which are inside rather than outside nature' (1983: 15). But we must be careful not to reduce history to one aspect of human material-making, the production of texts, representations. We must begin to think of other possible histories inside nature, of the meanings of patterns of deflection in vegetation, of making paths through the forest, of abandoning old gardens, and of telling stories in a particular place and at a particular time. And we must begin to think of the implications of those other histories as modes of lived experience.

Notes

The field research on which this article is based was carried out between 1980 and 1988, and funded by the Social Science Research Council of Great Britain and the Nuffield Foundation. I thank Tim Ingold, Eric Hirsch, Michael O'Hanlon, Cecilia McCallum, Alfred Gell, Christina Toren, and Maria Phylactou for their comments on an earlier version. The formulation of the problem benefited greatly from discussions with Nicholas Green.

1. I borrow this apt phrase from Rivière (1969).
2. Denevan (1971), Denevan *et al.* (1986), and Posey (1987).
3. In Piro, *ayahuasca* is called *kamalampi*, which seems to be closely related to the root *kama-*, 'to have supernatural power', and 'to kill'. The term *kamchi* refers to any supernatural being, but is also used of the bone demon. A similar relationship holds in Campa.
4. My analysis of the dead and of spirits draws on Munn (1970). Cf. also Myers (1986).
5. But see Toren (in Ingold (1990)) for a critique of the concept of 'socialization' with implications for the analysis presented here.
6. See Gow (1991) for a more detailed account of land ownership and disputation on the Bajo Urubamba.
7. See Green (1990) for an analysis of this tripartite system in the representation of landscape, as well as his reflections on landscape as personal experience.

References

CRONON, WILLIAM (1983). *Changes in the Land: Indians, Colonists, and the Ecology of New England*. New York: Hill & Wang.

DENEVAN, W. (1971). 'Campa Subsistence in the Gran Pajonal, Eastern Peru', *The Geographical Review*, 61/4: 496–518.

——TREACY, J. M., ALCORN, J. B., PADOCH, C., DENSLOW, J., and FLORES, S. (1986). 'Agricultura Forestal Indígena en la Amazonía Peruana: mantenimiento Bora de los Cultivos', *Amazonía Peruana*, 13: 9–33.

FOUCAULT, MICHEL (1970). *The Order of Things*. London: Tavistock.

GIBSON, JAMES (1986). *The Ecological Approach to Visual Perception*. London: Lawrence Erlbaum Associates.

GOW, PETER (1990). ' "Aprendiendo a defenderse": la historia oral y el parentesco en el Bajo Urubamba', *Amazonía Indígena*, 11: 10–16.

——(1991). *Of Mixed Blood: Kinship and History in Peruvian Amazonia*. Oxford: Clarendon Press.

GREEN, N. (1990). *The Spectacle of Nature*. Manchester: Manchester University Press.

HECHT, SUSANNA, and COCKBURN, ALEXANDER (1989). *The Fate of the Forest: Developers, Destroyers and Defenders of the Amazon*. London: Verso.

INGOLD, TIM (ed.) (1990). *The Concept of Society is Theoretically Obsolete*. Manchester: Group for Debates in Anthropological Theory, University of Manchester.

LATOUR, BRUNO (1987). *Science in Action*. Milton Keynes: Open University Press.

MUNN, N. (1970). 'Transformation of Subjects into Objects in Pitjantjatjara and Walbiri Myth', in R. Berndt (ed.), *Australian Aboriginal Anthropology*. Nedlands: University of Western Australia Press.

—— (1986). *The Fame of Gawa*. Cambridge: Cambridge University Press.

MYERS, F. (1986). *Pintupi Country, Pintupi Self*. Washington: Smithsonian Institution Press.

ONG, WALTER (1982). *Orality and Literacy: The Technologizing of the Word*. London: Methuen & Co.

POSEY, D. (1987). *A Ciência dos Mẽbêngôkre: Alternativas contra a Destruição*. Belém, Pará: Museu Paraense Emílio Goeldi.

RIVIÈRE, PETER (1969). *Marriage among the Trio*. Oxford: Clarendon Press.

SAHLINS, M. (1976). *Culture and Practical Reason*. Chicago: University of Chicago Press.

SAUER, CARL (1963). *Land and Life*. Berkeley, Calif.: University of California Press.

SPERBER, D. (1985). *On Anthropological Knowledge*. Cambridge: Cambridge University Press.

3

People into Places:
Zafimaniry Concepts of Clarity

MAURICE BLOCH

The Landscape

The Zafimaniry are a group of shifting cultivators living in eastern Madagascar who traditionally rely mainly on maize, beans, and taro. They number approximately 20,000. They are one of many such groups which are sometimes called Tanala and sometimes called Betsimisaraka but they differ from any of these because of the very specific environment in which they live. They inhabit a narrow band of montane forest found on a step of the sharp north–south escarpment which runs almost the whole length of Madagascar. This is an area at an altitude of approximately 1,400 m. which is very different in terms of climate and vegetation from almost anywhere else in Madagascar. To the west, lies the drier and treeless central plateau of Madagascar where the most important agricultural activity is irrigated rice cultivation. The neighbours of the Zafimaniry on this plateau are the Betsileo who are similar in many ways to the Merina who occupy the northern part.[1] To the east, at the foot of the escarpment, the forest is very different since the climate is much hotter. On that side the neighbours of the Zafimaniry are people usually referred to by the term Betsimisaraka who practise a different type of shifting cultivation and who mainly grow dry rice and sugar cane, two crops which the Zafimaniry cannot grow.[2]

Daniel Coulaud in his excellent geographical study of the Zafimaniry (1973) rightly characterizes their country as being cold, foggy, and damp. In the same book he also chooses to stress the fact that the Zafimaniry are running out of forest as a result of overswiddening which itself is caused by a rapid rise in population. As do many Europeans who have known Madagascar since the nineteenth century, he somewhat exaggerates the speed of deforestation and sees it in purely negative terms; nonetheless there is no doubt that this process is taking place. The deforestation, which is indeed due to overswiddening (itself in part due to the creation of nature reserves as well as to the growth in population), leads to people having to adopt a new kind of agriculture and so they turn to irrigated rice cultivation, which is possible in the valley areas of the deforested land. When I first studied the village—which I shall call Mamolena —in 1971, there were only two households out of a total of thirty-three which owned irrigated rice fields, but now, out of a total of fifty households only eight do not have such fields.

In fact most of these rice fields have only been created in the last three years, and this rapid change has been made possible by the irrigation work undertaken at the instigation of a local Catholic missionary and because of a general warming of the climate which enables the rice to ripen, and which the Zafimaniry, probably correctly, attribute to the retreat of the forest.

The Zafimaniry are therefore faced by two linked changes in the landscape as this would be understood by the outside observer. One is the gradual disappearance of the forest. This means that there are some areas where secondary forest has given way to steppe-like grassland, and that, more generally, primary forest is rarer and further away than it used to be. The second is that there are now wide, levelled valleys, terraced for irrigated rice fields, which in some cases are very extensive.

The Zafimaniry primarily interpret this process of change in ethnic terms. For them, people who live *an patrana*—that is, in the treeless land where irrigated rice cultivation is possible—are Betsileo; and, because their own land is becoming *an patrana*, they say that they too are becoming Betsileo. Similarly they will often say that the people who live to the west of them, in lands where the forest has practically completely disappeared, were once Zafimaniry, but that they have, by now, become fully Betsileo as a result of the environmental change. In some way this might seem strange to those unused to Malagasy notions of ethnicity but, as Astuti (forthcoming) points out, Malagasy notions of ethnicity depend much more on the type of life one leads than on who one's parents were. Thus, in a case such as this, where the geographical change makes one adopt the way of life of another group, one becomes a member of that group.[3]

Rather surprisingly, the Zafimaniry do not seem to mind this de-ethnicization, though they find the process very interesting and are continually talking about it. They neither regret it or attempt to resist it.[4] This ethnic indifference is also reflected in the way they see the retreat of the forest and the growth of the steppe-like areas. When in the field, with my post-Rousseau, post-Sibelius sensitivities, strengthened every evening by the BBC World Service's lachrymose accounts of the disappearance of the world's rain forest, I tried as hard as I could to get my co-villagers to tell me how much they deplored the change in their environment and the extinction of all the biological species which goes with it. I failed to get the slightest response, though people occasionally, and without much interest, noted a few minor inconveniences which deforestation causes.

One evening, sitting on a rock side-by-side with an older woman I knew well, indulging in the somewhat sentimental conversations which she much enjoyed, looking from the village to the forest lit up in the reds of the setting sun (one of the rare days when it was not raining), I thought the moment had come to make her say how much she liked the forest and regretted its passing, and so I asked her once more . . . After long reflection she said wistfully that, yes, she liked the forest. 'Why?', I asked eagerly. 'Because you can cut it down,' she replied.

Ideas concerning the environment are thus in many ways the very opposite of those which characterize the recent 'ecological panic' of the West. The Zafimaniry's concern with the environment is not with how not to damage it but with how to succeed with making a mark on it. This chapter is about what this means. My first reaction and interpretation of this total inversion of conventional modern European aesthetics was to assume that the landscape was apprehended by the Zafimaniry in a purely utilitarian manner. I soon became aware, however, that this was quite wrong. This realization was again and again forced on me by the one area of correspondence between my (modern, European) sensibilities and theirs. The Zafimaniry are as enthusiastic as are the *Guide Michelin* and municipal authorities about good views.

Good Views

On the path to the village where I lived there is a place where, before plunging into the valley which has to be crossed to reach it, one can view the houses and the hill on which the village is perched. Whenever people pass this spot, however foul the weather, and however much they are in a hurry to get back from a hard day's work, they will stop for a moment, or longer, and view the village from this vantage point. When the gangs of young men who have gone off for several months' waged work in other parts of Madagascar return home, they too will stop at this spot and sit there, singing songs for an hour or more, looking at the village, sometimes with tears in their eyes.

This almost institutionalized liking for good views and the places from which they can be seen is not exceptional. On expeditions to other villages with co-villagers, whenever we emerged from the forest on to a hilltop where one could see afar, we would also stop for a considerable time to enthuse about the clarity, to point out to each other this and that spot, to bask in the sunshine, to discuss the general topic of the beauty and value of good views and to feel sympathetically each other's euphoria at looking at such elating sights. This praise for good views emphasizes the 'spaciousness' (*malalaka*) and, above all, the 'clarity' (*mazava*), of the view: two words which seem to echo whenever people are commenting on viewed landscapes. This viewing takes on a very specific form. It consists in listing the hills and mountains in sight and the villages and towns which have been or still are on them. The further the mountains one can see, and some are very far, well beyond Zafimaniry country, the more the view is praised. Indeed my companions had much pleasure in demonstrating how many of these hills and villages they could name, in teaching and testing me, and occasionally showing me off to a friend who could not believe that a foreigner could know such things.

Above all it is the fact that one can see *clearly* that is endlessly stressed. The full impact of this evaluation can only be appreciated when one remembers two facts about the geographical environment of Zafimaniry country which explain how little clarity there normally is. First, the countryside is both mountainous and wooded so that it is usually very difficult to see far. The forest which has to be crossed to go from one village to another, or to go to a swidden, is often oppressively and menacingly enveloping, to the extent that Zafimaniry may easily become lost, something which often happens, occasionally with fatal consequences. Secondly the countryside is, for much of the time, shrouded in mists, rain, and clouds which cling to the forest most of the day and reduce the visibility to a few yards. Not surprisingly, the Zafimaniry much dislike and fear this cold lack of distance and are continually grumbling about it as they realize that they must go into the forest once again for their daily search for firewood or some other reason, shivering in their thin and permeable clothes.

Clarity is thus for the Zafimaniry a central value. It is both aesthetically valued and associated with pleasant living conditions. However, the notion of clarity is extended well beyond the visual in Zafimaniry culture. Thus, when one wants to show respect and admiration to a speaker who speaks in the authoritative ancestral code one should interject, every two sentences or so, the

Fig. 3.1. The Zafimaniry village emerging into clarity from the forest below.

exclamation *Mazava!*, which means 'Clear!' Yet another insight into the Zafimaniry valuation of clarity is that their most powerful medicine against most diseases is a wood called *fanazava*, a word which literally means 'that which renders clear'.

It is thus by understanding the central value of clarity and what lies behind the enthusiasm for viewing panoramas which display clarity that I feel we can share Zafimaniry ethical and aesthetic concepts about the landscape as well as understanding their equanimity towards the geographical changes occurring around them, whether these have been produced by them or not.

People into Places

The most commonly quoted Zafimaniry proverb is: *Ny tany tsy miova fa ny olombelona no miova.*[5] It is best translated as: 'While the land[6] does not change the living people[7] change.'

This proverb, and many others like it, can serve as a very useful introduction to Zafimaniry concepts of the relation of human beings and their environment. It reflects a constant awareness of the fragility and impermanence of human life in a world which is not concerned with their problems and which therefore affects them randomly. The way of talking about this uncaring environment—the forest, the sky, and the weather—is to refer to *Andriamanitra* or *Zanahary*, words which the missionaries have chosen to translate as 'God' but which for the Zafimaniry refer to a force somewhat different from the European version of the Christian God. This is because 'God' is not associated with a moral purpose but manifests itself as a destiny which is neither reward nor punishment, simply a state of affairs which affects you and which you cannot resist.[8] 'God', in this sense, is the external, unchangeable parameters of one's life, including the topography, which affect people in ways beyond explanation.

The countryside, a manifestation of God, is therefore a permanent but uncaring environment within which impermanent and weak human beings must live. However, things are not quite as bad as might appear because, although the land does not care and remains the same, human beings have the *potential* to transcend their impermanent nature and in this way become a part of the land.

Marriages into Houses

This potential becomes realized when human reproductive success comes close to immortalizing the producers. Every pregnancy brought to fruition, every child reaching adulthood, every adult producing living offspring, are outcomes

of enterprises which one hardly dares to expect will succeed but which sometimes do.[9] However, when these uncertain projects succeed and cumulate in
spite of the unconcern of the cosmic environment, then human life begins
to take on an aspect which is not intrinsic to it, but which it can sometimes
attain. It gains the potential for permanence, something which is characteristic
of the unchangeability of land. Or rather, in these cases, through its reproductive success, which becomes a social success, human life becomes something lasting which can be *attached* to the land and thereby attempt to
participate in its stasis.

This is because a successful growing family—or rather a successful 'growing'
marriage, since that is the true Zafimaniry focus—is realized in a material thing
attached to the land: their house (see Bloch 1993 and forthcoming). Social
achievement is to make a marriage a lasting feature of society and to make the
house, which is the material manifestation of this success, an enduring feature
of the unchanging earth. This intimate association of marriage and houses
exists because marriage is primarily thought of in terms of houses, thus the
beginning of a marriage is referred to as 'obtaining a house place for a hearth'.
Then, as a marriage stabilizes and produces children, grandchildren, etc., so
the house of the couple becomes more permanent. This happens as the woven
bamboo of which, at first, much of the house consists is gradually replaced by
heavy hardwood beams which, ultimately, will be decorated with carvings
which are said to 'celebrate' the durability and hardness of the wood.[10] This
transformation will all be due to the hard work of the couple, their relatives and
descendants over many decades.

Even the death of the founding couple does not mark the end of this
evolution. In a successful marriage, although the individuals die and disappear
as flesh and bones, the couple survives in another form, as the material house
itself. This continues to 'harden' and beautify as children, grandchildren,
great-grandchildren, and so on, contribute to the building by increasing the
proportion of hard wood to soft material and continue to cover the surface of
the wood with ever more decorative engravings. Such a 'hardening, stabilizing,
lasting'[11] house is what attaches itself to the land and gains permanence.

In fact, the continuing presence of the couple after their death in the house
is, in some contexts, even more specific. Two parts of the house are more
particularly seen as the material continuation of the original pair and these
become the object of many cults to the ancestors (Bloch: forthcoming). One is
the carved central post of the house made of the hardest part of the hardest
wood known to the Zafimaniry. This is associated with the man of the original
marriage and remains the focus of all meetings of his descendants. The other
focus is the three stones of the hearth which, together with a cooking pot (or in
some cases a wooden plate) and a large wooden cooking spoon, are associated
with the woman of the original marriage. It is really the conjunction of these
artefacts which initially makes a marriage evident. And, after the death of the

Fig. 3.2. A carved central post and a hearth from a Zafimaniry holy house.

couple, it is the remaining linked presence of the central post and the hearth which represents the continuing productive existence of the couple. However this is only so because they are *conjoined* in a single enduring entity: the house as a whole which is their fertile union made manifest.

A house which is the material objectification of the continuing fecundity of a marriage which took place a long time in the past continues to become ever harder and more beautiful. This is because the descendants have an absolute duty to continue to look after it, to increase the proportion of its hardwood content and to magnify its growing durability by decorating its wood. The very appearance of such a house thus bears witness to the number of descendants that the original couple have produced and to their piety towards their ancestors. Such a house gradually becomes referred to as a 'holy house': that is, a place where the descendants will obtain blessing from their ancestors. Significantly, there is a central rite that should occur at dawn when the rising sun makes the village 'clear'. At such times the descendants of the original couple congregate inside the holy house, they gather around the central post and eat food cooked on its hearth. Then they may address the central post and hearth as if they were the original man and woman respectively.

When, in this way, the house of the original couple has become a 'holy house' it has usually also become the essential centre of a village. This is because the descendants of the original couple will gradually build less permanent houses around the holy house but in positions which mark their junior status, since these 'children houses' will be to the south and lower from the summit than is the 'holy house'.[12]

The process of transformation from soft house to holy house, from single house to village, is always uncertain and takes a long time, but every existing village is evidence of the fact that it is possible. When the process has occurred it demonstrates not only that the original founders have had success as reproducers of impermanent human beings but that they have been able to transform this mutable living flow into a permanent, stable, material feature of the land: a village, perched on a hill, firmly resting on the hard rock of which these hilltops consist. This is the successful attachment of active mobile living people on to the uncaring land to which the Zafimaniry dare to aspire.

In order fully to understand the visual impact of this success we must also take into account another Zafimaniry notion concerning the landscape: altitude. Every Zafimaniry village should be on the summit of a hill and one of the words for village also means hill.[13] Zafimaniry villages rise up out of the surrounding forest since they are placed on high rocky outcrops partly for defence but also so that they may be 'in the clear'. In the morning and sometimes during the day the villages are actually above the clouds which swirl past in dark greens and whites through the forest below, turning different villages into so many islands of clarity and definition above a chaotic and indistinct sea of vegetative growth and transformation. Clarity, altitude, and the pleasure of warm sunshine in a cold climate are thus inseparable in this region as this was continually pointed out to me.[14]

However, neither clarity nor altitude are absolutes; both are a matter of more or less since not all summits are equally high. In fact the difference in height and therefore clarity is of great importance in Zafimaniry thought because the differential altitude of villages is seen to illustrate differential seniority and legitimate political authority, two concepts which are inseparable throughout Madagascar. Thus, just as the houses within a village stand in a genealogical relationship to each other which can be seen at a glance in terms of which house is nearer the summit, so too with Zafimaniry villages. The village from which a couple set out to form a new one by establishing a house becomes the 'parent' village which 'gave birth' to the subsequent locality and should be higher than the 'child' village. When this is so, this is pointed out as an illustration of the rule and, when it is not so, an *ad hoc* explanation is sought (Bloch 1975).[15]

The same principle is applied to explain the political order even beyond Zafimaniry country. Very high hills and mountains emerging from the mists of the lowlands, either within their boundaries or beyond, are always talked of admiringly as the past abodes of kings, even though the Zafimaniry never had their own kings, and have historically spent a great deal of their energies resisting the pretensions of various rulers. Similarly the Zafimaniry talk of Ambositra, the administrative centre of their region, as being above them and they will say they go 'up' to Ambositra or to Antananarivo, the capital of Madagascar, in spite of the fact that both towns are far below them in altitude.

In fact, altitude, clarity, permanence, legitimate political power, and genealogical seniority are to them facets of the same thing, all different aspects of the
successful couples, now ancestors, who, by transforming the uncertain turmoil
of life and youth into houses and villages and making 'places' which remain,
have achieved a victory over time since, unlike living humans, 'the land does
not change'.

Here, however, we must be aware of another aspect which makes this possible success of human beings much more ambiguous, almost ironic. An aspect
of the transformation of a marriage into a house and then a village is that, as
people become fixed to place, they are at the same time losing their much-
valued 'lively' and sensuous character as *olombelona*: living people, since they
are becoming immobile 'places'.

The spatial aspect of people is apparent from the first. The Zafimaniry have
a tendency to refer to anybody from outside their own village simply by the
name of the locality. Thus, when I was confronted with a new face, which led
me to ask who we had just crossed on our path, I would simply be told the name
of a village. Similarly, as noted above, genealogy in terms of people is rapidly
replaced by genealogies in terms of villages.[16]

The merging of people and places in this way is, however, little more than a
celebration of the success of the ancestors who have *established* their marriage so
that it has become a house, although a celebration already tinged with the
sadness of the loss of the joy of being truly alive, since we must not forget that
for the Zafimaniry, as for other Malagasy, youth, strength, and movement,
although antithetical to the success of the establishment of the house, are
nonetheless greatly but differently valued.[17]

But, in Zafimaniry culture, there exists a further stage in the process of the
mutation of people into localized, permanent things, and then the loss implied
in becoming an object and a place becomes much more apparent. In this other
mode the very success of living beings transformed into permanent features of
the land seems, ultimately, to undermine the point of the exercise.

Megalithic Monuments

A good while after death megalithic stone monuments to commemorate a
parent[18] are sometimes built in prominent places. If the person commemorated
is a woman, the monument takes the form of three stones, like a hearth, covered
by a large flat stone by way of cooking pot. If the person commemorated is a
man, the monument recalls the central post of the house and looks a little like
a menhir.[19]

The differences in commemoration by means of a standing-stone as opposed
to a holy house are revealing. First such commemoration by stone is an
even greater success in inscribing the living person in the unchanging land

FIG. 3.3. Male and female standing-stones on site of a Zafimaniry village.

since stone is, and is perceived to be, even more permanent than the hardest wood. However, commemorative stones, unlike holy houses, do not link the person with their descendants, while the house does so through the mechanism of blessing. First, this difference is reflected in the fact that such stones are erected *outside* the villages where their descendants live. Secondly, the stones commemorate individuals, not, like the houses, couples. This is true even if a number of standing-stones are, as is usual, all in one place. These groupings do not join couples or lines of parents and children in the way that houses do.

What unites the people who are commemorated together in a gathering of standing-stones is that they stand in a relationship of siblingship. Precisely for this reason, the stones represent the opposite to the married couples unified in houses. In Zafimaniry thought, sexual relations between brothers and sisters are highly incestuous and cannot produce normal offspring. Marriage and human reproduction necessarily require the spatial separation of cross-sex siblings as a necessary first step before the hearth and the central post can be united in a fruitful marriage and house. Thus, the postmortem rejoining of the central posts and the hearth of brothers and sisters implies the negation of growth through sexual reproduction and the destruction of the conjugal units to which the siblings belonged in life. The megalithic groupings of hearth and central post convey, above all, broken houses.

People, therefore, are made into places twice, as houses and as megaliths. These two ways celebrate, however, two completely different and opposed aspects of the social person. In one case, people are immortalized as successful and therefore lasting parts of the productive and reproductive side of life, as unified married couples. In the other case, they are immortalized as part of an unchanging unity which has refused the reproductive process in order to gain the permanence which comes from staying put as an undivided sibling group. The contradiction between these two states is particularly clear in the case of women, since it is they who normally move at marriage, and it is dramatically illustrated at their funerals. Then, a veritable tug-of-war occurs over the body, with the woman's natal family pulling at one end and her husband's family pulling at the other. The contradiction, however, also exists for men since they too are considered by the Zafimaniry to have become at marriage a part of their wife's family. All Zafimaniry are therefore pulled between the two poles of siblingship and marriage and when siblingship wins it is at the expense of the engagement in growth and reproduction which a successful house celebrates.

This means that the permanence gained by the construction of megalithic monuments is absolute but it is in opposition to the relative, but 'growing', permanence of successful human life in houses and villages. Absolute stasis is thus gained at the expense of human reproduction.

Here the symbolic difference between wood and stone comes to the fore. What fascinates the Zafimaniry about wood is that it originates in a living thing which, nonetheless, ultimately gains far greater permanence than human beings. It is because of this fact that they use hard wood to make the houses and villages into which the living become transformed. Wood demonstrates a familial and metaphysical success in its passage from life to lasting object. It would seem however that, because it originates in a living thing, it is, although very hard and permanent, not eternal. Stone is seen as eternal but, on the other hand, it is not, nor has ever been, in any way alive. To become wood, as do the successful couple in the house, is therefore to succeed in transforming life as far as it will go towards stasis, but this cannot be all the way. To become stone, however, as do the groupings of siblings, is a way of becoming immortal but at the cost of the total abandonment of life and of marital reproduction and parent–child relationships.

Admittedly, the setting up of these standing-stones involves a great ritual organized principally by the descendants of the dead and therefore they might be thought to link the descendants to their parents in a permanent way. This is not so, however, since once set up, the stones do not remain the concern of any specific group and the name of the person for which they were set up is soon forgotten even by their direct descendants. Rather, the standing-stones are seen as places for offerings made by anyone who disturbs or profits from the land in which they are situated, irrespective of their connection to the dead. Thus the person who gathers honey from a nearby tree will leave a little on the stone, and so will the person who clears a swidden near one of these stones. In making these offerings the giver is usually totally ignorant of the one for whom the stone was raised. If, therefore, the stones are centres of cults, these are merely cults of placation of the environment or of God, since the environment is a manifestation of his power.

It is as if in achieving greatest permanence by attaching themselves most totally to the unchanging land by means of stone the living human has in fact become merely a feature of this land and not any more an ancestor of 'living people'. The extreme success of attaching people to places through standing-stones ironically renders its outcome pointless on a human scale. Perhaps nothing shows this better than the fact that people often say of the ancestors for whom these stones have been made, as they do of all very remote ancestors who have stopped being directly concerned with sanctioning the activities of their descendants according to moral rules, that they have become that uncaring power: *Zanahary*, that is, god/s.[20]

This assimilation of ancestors so commemorated and God can be seen in yet another way. When there is no such commemorative standing-stone nearby, the honey-gatherer or the maker of a new swidden will leave the offering he would have left on the artificially raised stone simply on a prominent natural rock in exactly the same way. They will do just as well. The Zafimaniry say of such prominent rocks that they are 'standing-stones made by God' and the difference of authorship makes no difference to their function.

In making standing-stones people have been turned into places, but at the cost of losing all aspects of human vitality. The significance of houses and standing-stones, of God and of the ancestors as embodied in the central post and in the hearth, enable us to see a part of the meaning which the Zafimaniry attribute to the landscape when they look at it from a hill and praise the clarity of the view. They are looking at summits, many of which have villages on them and the others, it is presumed, once had such villages. These summits represent their history, the achievement of their ancestors who have inscribed themselves on to the unchanging land, especially on those points which rise out of the chaos of the forest and the mist and stand clear and certain in the sunshine. Their pleasure is a celebration of this achievement and they are quite explicit about this, but they are not so forthcoming in explaining the melancholy which is also palpably present and is so often expressed in the songs which are sung from places where there is a good view. What I felt this was about was that they also are aware that, seen from afar, this achievement is slight, many of the 'villages' have returned to forest, the viewed landscape and especially its contours seem, in the end, unaffected by human activity, and the ultimate fruit of human efforts at immortality are nothing but rocks, largely indistinguishable from the many other rocks placed there by God, that power, which for the Zafimaniry, is the source of accidents beyond human control.

Clarity and the Two Kinds of Landscape

If I am right in interpreting Zafimaniry's emotions and understanding about the landscape in this way we can now understand the Zafimaniry's apparent indifference to the passing of the forest and the creation of the new irrigated rice terraces.

Apart from their practical evaluation of the process—which on the whole is more positive than negative—the Zafimaniry, to my surprise, often praised this new type of deforested land by using that same charged term *mazava* which they use for good views. On one level the reason is obvious. Cleared forests are indeed clearer, and so are terraced rice valleys. Not only do they enable you to see further, but they do not catch the mist and the clouds as the forest does. However, they also represent something else (though I must admit that I have never been told this in so many words). The cleared rice valleys are also a sign of living humans having finally successfully made their mark and attached themselves to the unchanging land. They represent an even greater success than villages in achieving what the ancestors sought to achieve, and they do this in a way which appears, at least viewed from the end of a newly made rice valley, as less pyrrhic than turning people into rocks.

Notes

Fieldwork among the Zafimaniry was carried out in 1971 with the help of a grant from the Social Science Research Council and in 1988–9 with help from a grant from the Spencer Foundation.

1. For accounts of the Betsileo in English see Kottak (1980). On the Merina see Bloch (1971) and (1986).
2. Recently new varieties of dry rice have been grown in Zafimaniry country on an experimental basis, but this is not yet significant economically.
3. This is made particularly easy by the fact that the Zafimaniry and the Betsileo speak an almost identical dialect of Malagasy.
4. They see the climate and the environment as directly affecting people. Thus they stress how hard they have to work and how this makes them strong. They say that if you live long in the hotter parts of Madagascar you become weak and that if you do not have to carry the heavy loads which they do, for example because you have carts like the Betsileo, you will also become weaker.
5. The proverb occurs in a number of variants but the meaning is constant. The version I have chosen is given because it is the simplest.
6. The Malagasy word *tany* has a very similar range of meanings to the English word 'land'.
7. The normal Malagasy word for people, *olombelona*, literally means 'living people'. I have kept the rather pedantic form in full as it seems to me most revealing. R. Dubois, partly rightly and partly wrongly, elaborates this point (Dubois 1978).

8. This notion is often referred to by the word *anjara* which is translated in the standard dictionary as part, lot, destiny, turn (Abinal and Malzac 1988: 49).
9. This statement is based on a wide range of ethnographic data which cannot be discussed here.
10. The part of the wood used for making such a house is the dark core of the tree which the Zafimaniry call *teza* which also means 'lasting' (see Bloch 1993). The carvings on the house, which have often been described (e.g. Verin 1964), are seen by the Zafimaniry as a celebration of this 'durability'.
11. The words all attempt to translate the Malagasy verb *mateza* derived from *teza* (see n. 10).
12. These houses too may be referred to as 'holy houses' but they are less 'holy' than the houses of the founding couple. The holiness of a house is a matter of degree. Practical problems of topography mean that the rule which places houses in rank order is not always fully followed.
13. *Vohitra*: the word is also used in Merina and Betsileo in the same way.
14. Slaves in the past were obliged to build their villages on low ground and the first thing they did when they were freed, in the area where I worked, was to move their village to a summit.
15. For example, the explanation continually given for the fact that the very senior village of Ambohimanzaka was very low was that the inhabitants had been forced by the French to move its location. This had indeed been so.
16. There is an exception to this when people are actually in the presence of tombs, when they, or rather the senior people, do make an effort to remember individual names.
17. The conflict between the value of ancestralization and of vitality is extensively discussed for the Merina in Bloch 1986.
18. Because of the opposition of the Catholic church this has only rarely been done in the last few years though alternatives with similar meanings are being developed.
19. The monument for men was sometimes first of all of wood and identical in its carvings to the central post of a house. I believe the erection of such wooden posts was a first stage in the erection of a stone monument but I am not all that clear as these wooden posts have not been erected for a long time. Rather bewilderingly they are called 'wooden male stones'.
20. The ambiguity comes from the fact that the plural is not marked in Malagasy words.

References

ABINAL, R. P., and MALZAC, R. P. (1988: 1st edn. 1888). *Dictionnaire Français-Malgache*. Paris: Éditions Maritimes et d'Outre-Mer.

ASTUTI, R. (forthcoming). 'The Vezo Are Not a Kind of People: Identity, Difference, and "Ethnicity" among the Vezo of Western Madagascar', *American Ethnologist*.

BLOCH, M. (1971). *Placing the Dead: Tombs, Ancestral Villages and Social Organisation among the Merina of Madagascar*. London: Seminar Press.

——(1975). 'Property and the End of Affinity', in M. Bloch (ed.), *Marxist Analyses and Social Anthropology*. London: Malaby Press.

—— (1986). *From Blessing to Violence: History and Ideology in the Circumcision Ritual of the Merina of Madagascar.* Cambridge: Cambridge University Press.

—— (1993). 'What Goes Without Saying: The Conceptualisation of Zafimaniry Society', in A. Kuper (ed.), *Conceptualising Societies.* London: Routledge.

—— (forthcoming). 'The Resurrection of the House', in J. Carsten and S. Hugh-Jones (eds.), *About the House: Buildings, Groups and Categories in Holistic Perspectives.* Cambridge: Cambridge University Press.

DUBOIS, R. (1978). *Olombelona: Essai sur l'existence personnelle et collective à Madagascar.* Paris: L'Harmattan.

COULAUD, D. (1973). *Les Zafimaniry: Un groupe ethnique de Madagascar à la poursuite de la forêt.* Antananarivo: F.B.M.

KOTTACK, C. (1980). *The Past and the Present: History, Ecology, and Cultural Variation in Highland Madagascar.* Ann Arbor, Mich.: University of Michigan Press.

VERIN, P. (1964). 'Les Zafimaniry et leur art. Un groupe continuateur d'une tradition esthétique Malgache méconnue', *Revue de Madagascar*, 27: 1–76.

4

Moral Topophilia: The Significations of Landscape in Indian Oleographs

CHRISTOPHER PINNEY

This chapter is concerned with the depiction of landscape in a genre of popular Indian art. These landscapes are represented through a stylized aesthetic which expresses a historical and moral topophilia.[1] They frequently give visible form to the intersection and conflict of, on the one hand, a folk model of historical decay and, on the other, a nationalist political language of modernity. I refer to these mass-produced depictions as 'oleographs'[2] while others refer to them as 'calendar art' or 'bazaar art'. Although this artform is 'now sedimented as an authentic Indian "kitsch"' (P. Uberoi 1990: 43), it is a product of a colonial hybridity in which Indian and European styles were mixed. Patricia Uberoi has argued that the Indianization of this hybrid form of representation should be understood within the context of a rising cultural nationalism which sought to construct an appropriate past through a new traditionalizing Hinduism. This was recognized by nationalists of the time: the printing press established in Bombay in 1892 by Ravi Varma (who 'perfected' the style and ensured its mass reproduction and India-wide penetration)[3] was patronized by moderate nation-alists such as Gokhale, Ranade, and Dadabhai Naoroji (Guha-Thakurta 1986: 188), and Surendranath Banerjea claimed that these images 'were working towards a re-instatement of national culture in the same way as their nationalist speeches were' (ibid.). Uberoi is particularly concerned with the articulation of feminine identity with this new 'national ethos'; here I will argue that the limited appearance of 'landscape' can be read for similar clues. It has often been noted that within Indian art there has been remarkably little that could properly be described as 'landscape' as understood in the Western tradition. However, both the presence and absence of 'landscape' in oleographs and the relationship between 'place' and 'space' reveal much about the construction of this new national Hinduized identity (inflected through landscape as 'the land' or 'the nation') and its continuing negotiation.

I will argue that 'place'—the supposed site of a 'being-in-the-world',[4] on which personal and national identities are grounded, can never exist in itself. In the context of oleographs, it is only when confronted with a disenchanted hodological[5] 'space' that this 'place'[6]—retrospectively, and at the point of its disappearance—acquires absolute 'presence'. Identity (national or otherwise) can only exist as the 'other of others' (Dumont 1972: 78).[7] This chapter will examine how in contemporary oleographs this 'other' is invoked in various forms.

This is a process I will trace in both popular visual representations and villagers' perceptions of rural and urban landscapes in central India. My analysis will thus be both art-historical and anthropological. In both these sets of evidence it will become apparent that both terms of the dichotomy of 'place' and 'space' form part of an indivisible semantic field. In formal pictorial terms, I will argue, 'place' is connoted by the foreground which exists in a state of mutual dependence with a 'space' connoted by the horizon.

My analysis will focus on two sets of evidence. The first of these is art-historical: an ideologically inflected Western tradition of landscape depiction which contrasts with its intermittent appearance within Indian representations. The second of these is ethnographic: the industrial environment of the town of Nagda in central India in which most of the images discussed here were collected and where the largely formal analyses presented here assume a phenomenological reality.[8]

Tradition, Modernity, and the 'Loss of Self'

Some of the oppositions (both historical and spatial) which will be discussed in this paper are apparent in product number 3399 (Fig. 4.1) of Jain Picture Publishers (Bombay), a still from a popular Bombay film. Within this film-set re-creation of metropolitan opulence, mahogany side-tables are set either side of a rear-wall window whose curtains waft open in a gentle breeze. Above these tables, set within old frames and gilded buff mounts are what appear to be two aquatints, probably from Thomas and William Daniell's *Oriental Scenery* (published 1795–1816). At the centre of this enclosure of decorum and bourgeois restraint is a central figure which sets up a radical discontinuity between backdrop and foreground. Sonam, an actress, is seated on some unseen object and clad minimally, in yellow. Before her, in a candytwist brass pot, is a display of white calla lilies, red gladioli, and ornamental grasses. From this arrangement she has plucked a single stem of gladiolus and strokes this blood-red floral blade, connoting desire, across her chin as she fixes the camera in her languid vision. This image exemplifies very clearly two critical features of 'landscape' on which I will dwell.

A formal reading might stress the manner in which the Dionysian foreground of '3399' with its vivid colours expresses proximal immediacy, and its form encodes fecundity and desire. The foreground suggests being-in-place and the parochialism of the senses. Further out in the distance is the horizon, indicated by the white space of nothingness which causes the curtain to drift

FIG. 4.1. Product number '3399' (colour photographic postcard, Jain Picture Publishers, *c*.1990). Courtesy of Jain Picture Publishers.

back into the foreground. This horizon is literally pictured within the aquatints as a dividing line between earth and sky. The foregrounded wielder of gladiolus suggests an unavoidable now-ness, a capitulation to the senses. The background suggests distance and history—a temporal cartography that speaks of epochs and kingdoms. The Indian consumer of this image would read it within an 'inter-ocular field' (Appadurai and Breckenridge 1992: 52) within which Daniell prints, and other Raj landscapes, are frequently used to signify classical elegance and sobriety. They are, for instance, a common trope in cigarette advertisements in which they connote wealth and discernment.[9]

A contextualized reading—located more explicitly in the understandings of Nagda people, and of pan-Indian iconographic decipherings—might point out that the red gladioli in this picture may be taken as a substitute for blood, the offering of which the fierce goddess Kali demands.[10] The offering of red hibiscus—substituting here for blood—to the image of the goddess in the Kalighat temple (Calcutta) is a favourite theme of Bengali oleographs. Film heroines, or indeed anyone who is able to lounge scantily dressed within the cosmopolitan arena of '3399', can be taken as exemplifying the generally destructive power of women's barren eroticism, and this image is clearly a mediation of fear and prurience. What is also clear, however, is the distinction between a cartographic distance and an Indian foreground of self-possession and placedness; and further that the foreground—together with all it signifies through its placedness—does so only as the other of hodological space.

Whereas the Daniell prints by their very nature are constituted as pictures and set themselves up as objects to be seen by a centred viewing subject,[11] the flowers in the foreground are de-centred objects of desire. They are organized only in a partially perspectival manner. They inhabit an existential three-dimensional space, they have perfumes, scatter pollen at will, and can be plucked out and used for purposes that have an intensified meaning for others inhabiting this intersubjective place. They manifest all those qualities which cannot be trapped behind glass.

Product number '3399' is a perfect landscape of power and desire. The distal is represented through the cold abstract gaze of the Daniell prints. For all the soft gradations of the aquatint technique and the desires of early landscape artists to possess the body of the newly subjugated India, within '3399' the prints are actors in the service of 'a reifying male gaze that turned its targets into stone' (Jay 1988: 8) and that de-eroticized the visual order. They create a polarity, a principle of difference, in which the desires of the foreground can be brought into play in the form of this Bombay Olympia who fixes the viewer's gaze.

'Our Whole Domain': Landscape and Possession

Although King Edward VII is reported to have muttered, halfway through his tour of the White City exhibition in 1908, 'Too fatiguing! Too fatiguing! Merely a bird's eye view' (Newman 1937: 279), this aerial vantage point was more commonly and positively used in the Western discourse of other places to denote the lofty and encompassing perspective that was able to fit all life below into the framework of a picture or view (see Pinney 1992a: 43–4).[12] Clearly such effects of power are apparent in certain individual images which through their point of view suggest this encompassment of a domain, but it can also be argued that the archive of landscape representations—the collectivity of attempts to 'know the country'—can work in the same way (Pal and Dehejia 1986: 16).[13]

In South Asia this archive was amassed through the media of cartography, land surveys, and landscape paintings. The sheer quantity of these, particularly between 1780 and 1880, supports the claim that 'at no other time has one country been so extensively and minutely observed by artists from another' (Tillotson 1990: 141). The most articulate analysis of the relationship between 'view' and 'land survey' is Rosalind Krauss's study of American nineteenth-century cabinets of stereographic landscape photographs. They constituted a 'complete topographical atlas' (Krauss 1985: 141), 'in whose drawers were catalogued and stored a whole geographical system' (ibid.). Within this 'compound representation of geographic space' were individual views which could be plucked from the drawers and used to verify the whole encompassing schema. These 'unique images', perhaps like the Daniell aquatints, were 'views' embodying an 'insistent penetration', a centred space that recast the landscape as territory. Often this was merely for the lingering gaze of the viewer, but just as often in the American case it was the gaze of the State. In this case, Krauss notes 'view and land survey are interdetermined and interrelated' (1985: 141).

In India too, the British visual representation of the landscape can be seen frequently to operate with similar effects. Despite the early efforts of travellers and missionaries, early cartography in India was largely the product of army route surveyors (National Archives 1982: iii), during the eighteenth century. Later, landscape art became as much an adjunct to military conquest as did the map and the survey and the military associations of landscape are also apparent in much early photographic work. For instance Linnaeus Tripe (in *Photographic Views of Madura*) photographed the south-east angles of the Tirambar pagoda in Madurai in 1858 in order to show where the British had earlier attempted to burn it down.

John Berger, in a famous argument, suggested that of the various Western genres of painting, landscape was least permeable to the expression of property interests. Almost as an exception to the rule he cited Gainsborough's *Mr and Mrs Andrews*, arguing that 'their proprietary attitude towards what surrounds them is visible in their stance and their expressions' (1972a: 107). A picture produced in India at a similar time suggests interesting comparisons (Welch 1978: pl. 2).[14] *A Company Official Surveys the River* is a watercolour in the Company style from *c*.1770 and was probably painted in Murshidabad or Kasimbazar. As in *Mr and Mrs Andrews* the central figure(s) hold sway over the landscape within which they are situated. The Andrews are depicted under a tree growing on their land; the Company official is gazing at what is probably the Bhagirathi River, the principal trade-route through upper India throughout the mid-eighteenth to nineteenth centuries. It was upon such routes that the fortunes of the East India Company and the private trade and bribery of its officials depended (Welch 1978: 28). In both pictures the central figures span the foreground and horizon; in both there is a contrast between the encompassing horizon (rolling fields and woods in Gainsborough, sparsely wooded hills in the Company watercolour) and a foreground in which there are signs of personal ownership and possession (sheaves of wheat, and a dog and a servant, respectively). The proprietorial presence is expressed here not simply in a linear movement from near to far, but in the establishment of a middle ground where the rational imperatives and futurology of the horizon are synthesized with a field of personal meaning and immediacy in the foreground. Finally we may note that in both these images 'ownership' is implied by a physical presence *within* the picture frame, but as we shall see in an alternative strategy of viewer-spectatorship 'physical ownership of the painting [guarantees an] immanent presence within it' (Berger 1972b: 216; see also Pinney 1992a: 45).

The historical and political context within which the work of those such as the Daniells came to be created is overturned in 3399, for the framed aquatints are not immediately accessible to the viewer except through the foregrounded figure who we may suppose possesses these images (or who is owned by the possessor of these images). But this is a partial inversion, an incomplete appropriation, in which the visual ideology of these landscape views is not challenged. If the Daniell prints in 3399 represent the world as 'picture' (see below), the starlet is encompassed by the same gaze, for she takes possession of them as pictures, not as part of a continuous terrain which proposes any new relationship between image and viewer. Additionally, it is only through a further process of what Ashis Nandy has termed 'the loss of self'[15]— a fresh invasion by the West of the Indian psyche—that she has come into proximity with these early icons of the start of that process within colonial India. The starlet's alienation from the ideal Indian woman is mirrored by the historical reference to this earlier, more profound, alienation.

The foreground here is then the terrain upon which a continuing colonization is played out, suggesting a unity between foreground (starlet) and horizon (Daniell prints). From the point of view of Indian cultural nationalism, however, this is a regrettable homology. It will not be until the final images in this chapter (Figs. 12, 13, and 14) that we will encounter the synthesis between place and space for which such a cultural nationalism yearns. To get to that point, however, we must first consider the antitheses upon which such a synthesis rests and the growth of a 'nationalist' popular art which defined the visual form in which this solution became possible.

Similar spatial juxtapositions to those discussed above are apparent in Fig. 4.2, a calendar print which depicts the hugely popular movie heroine Hema Malini in an example of a long-standing genre of women with bicycles.[16] Here the opposition between an 'Indian' foreground and a 'foreign' horizon apparent in Fig. 4.1 persists, but the temporal and moral polarity is reversed. In the foreground the sari-clad film actress Hema Malini pushes her bicycle towards the bottom right of the picture. She wears a red *bindi* and bangles— signs of married (and thus constrained) respectability—and assumes a sedate posture.[17] In the distance, facing in the opposite direction—with her hand on her hip—is a representative of the new woman. She is dressed in Western clothing and stands astride a scooter, an inappropriate mount for a woman of propriety.[18] No doubt most people who purchase this calendar are happy to have confirmed their suspicion that inside every proper bicycle-pusher there lies this distant and half-imagined scooter-riding *id*, but the image demonstrates a complex temporal disjunction between traditional foreground and modern distance.

The juxtaposition of the bicycle and the scooter suggests a complementary technological narrative since many Nagda Hindus represent past and future time in terms of an opposition between rural and urban, cold and hot, craft and machine which these two devices epitomize rather well. The trusty Atlas bicycle in the foreground connotes, like the village, harmony and self-sufficiency. The scooter, probably produced with imported Italian technology,

Fig. 4.2. Calendar print with the actress Hema Malini in the foreground (publisher unknown, *c*.1985).

connotes the loss and destruction to be seen everywhere in the present *kaliyug*, often glossed in Nagda as the 'age (*yug*) of machines (*kal*)'. *Kali* in *kaliyug* refers specifically to the demon Kali, but in everyday use *kaliyug* is said to be the *yug* of both machines (*kal*) and the goddess Kali (*Kālī*) of whom the Western-dressed scooter-rider may also be seen as a representative. The polarity of a cool and pure (*sattvik*) ruralness and a heating and destructive modernity is enacted within the much more complex framework of the four *yugs*—*sat* (or *satya*), *treta*, *dvapar*, and *kali*. For our brief purposes we need only note that history as lived through in these *yugs* is a process of degeneration— a fall from an age of truth when everyone knew their duty and lived harmoniously together in idyllic villages taking only what fruit and nuts they required, to a period in which everyone is motivated only by greed, where castes jostle antagonistically and the old *sattvik* rural order disintegrates in the pandemonium of urban and industrial routines. In an elaborate series of oppositions— the spiritual (*atmik*) versus the physical (*bhautik*), peace (*shanti*) versus hubbub (*hallagulla*), truth (*satya*) versus the actions of the dissembler (*bagula bhagat*[19]) —a retrospective and threatened embodiment of presence is created in the face of a threatening modernity.

The Ethnographic Context

This is an appropriate point at which to introduce another landscape, a terrain which provides the ethnographic context of the arguments advanced here. The town of Nagda is located in Madhya Pradesh and has a population of 79,000,[20] and it is here that most of the images discussed were purchased. Nagda plays the role of the scooter-riding woman to many of the inhabitants of Bhatisuda, a nearby village which prides itself on its bicycle-riding tranquillity. In this central-Indian context Nagda—an industrial centre and location of Asia's largest viscose rayon factory—represents modernity and its neighbouring villages have become bulwarks of a contrary traditionalism in which earlier, foregrounded values are privileged.

Nagda is divided into two sections dissected by the main Bombay–Delhi railway line. On the north side is the mandi, *or bazaar area, a mixture of shops, cinemas, and houses that spreads in a ramshackle manner over a large area. South of the railway track lies Birlagram—'Birla's village'. The late G. D. Birla was one of India's greatest industrialists and Nagda is one of the many townships throughout India which bears his name. In contrast to the generally cramped and hastily constructed dwellings that surround the bustling bazaar area, in Birlagram there are well-maintained roads leading to comparatively luxurious management quarters, sports and social clubs, and gardens. There are also the more spartan areas of the* mazdur basti, *the labour colony, where manual workers live in regimented semi-comfort, and squalid slum areas of* jhompris *which house those workers whose needs the factory building programme has failed to meet. Beyond the* mazdur basti *are three factories which merge together into a vast industrial complex, a tangle of vents, towers, and chimneys. The oldest of the plants is part of the Gwalior Rayon and Silk Manufacturing (Weaving) Company Ltd. This dominates the industrial skyline with a lofty chimney surmounting the powerhouse and two squat stacks on which are emblazoned the initials of the Company, GRASIM Industries Ltd., by which acronym the plant is popularly known. It is this factory which is built on disputed land and which is located as the major source of pollution, the issue around which most political and social lines are drawn in this area.*

Approaching the factories from the railway station a large sign can be seen opposite the Grasim Balmandir—the Hindi medium school—which says (in English) 'GRASIM Industries Welcomes You'. As one enters the factory area proper one passes the Rural Development Centre and the UCO Bank, both housed in low buildings to the south of the main factory General Office which stands opposite the east gate to the Viscose Rayon Division. The smell of chemicals is very noticeable here. All the buildings are in characteristic pastels edged with brighter colours and there are many small lawns edged with canna plants and marigolds. What this exemplary carpentered universe exemplifies is elaborated in two painted wall reliefs which can be seen here. The first, measuring about 4 feet by 7 feet is on the nearside of the General Office building and locates Nagda as a centre of progress, a modernist propellant reaching for the stars (Fig. 4.3). Modernity is here represented in the form of clusters of grey skyscrapers which reach from the yellow base of the relief up into the sky, towards a large sun which dominates the centre of the picture. But this progress is not simply the covering of the world with more and more tall buildings, but is also, as the dramatic intervention of red from the bottom left of the relief towards the sun suggests, imbued with eschatological significances which offer even Nagda a transcendent potentiality.

A further 100 yards up by the side of the east gate to the Viscose Division is another similar depiction (Fig. 4.4). Though more pleasing, it shares the abstract and totalitarian resonances of the earlier image. It also suggests progress as a separation from the foreground, as an ever-upward movement beyond mortality and the constraints of the picture space. Measuring approximately eight feet by fifteen feet, the image leads the viewer's eye along a winding road. At the start of its journey the road is flanked by trees, but such arboreal signifiers of the traditional soon give way to minimalist red-and-white street lights which in turn are discarded as progress gains momentum.

In the village of Bhatisuda, this evaluation is offered by few people. In my attempts to discuss these two murals I repeatedly encountered villagers' unwillingness or inability to respond to this factory propaganda. Whereas the contents of mass-produced oleographs were always rendered transparent (e.g. 'This is our Visnu Bhagvan in the *satyug*'; 'This is Siva Bhagvan in the Himalayas'), these images were always described in terms of the hypothetical intentions of an artist employed by the company, or some important official in the company who would be able to explain it all to me. To the extent

FIG. 4.3. GRASIM mural (General Office building), Nagda. Photograph by Chris Pinney.

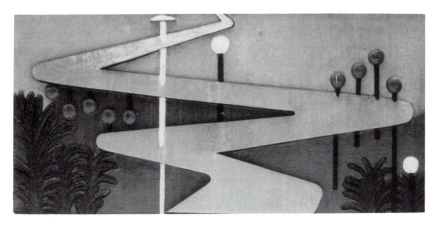

FIG. 4.4. GRASIM mural (near Viscose Division), Nagda. Photograph by Chris Pinney.

that villagers were unable to give any reading of the image, or to feel that these were images that related to their own individual concerns, the propaganda had failed.

Six kilometres upstream on the river Chambal lies Bhatisuda, where members of the dominant caste of Jains[21] have been engaged since the 1950s in an ongoing struggle with the owners and managers of the industrial complex.

On the south side of the railway station in Nagda there is a metalled road which traverses the outer boundary of the factory labour colony before running parallel to the main factory complex for a few hundred yards. Here a dusty track branches to the east passing over an open drain of factory effluent that trickles through the old boilers and furnaces which lie scattered round. This route arrives two kilometres later at the small village of Azimabad Pardhi where the traveller has to ford a small stream and from where, after scrambling up a slight rocky incline, lies a direct path to the village of Bhatisuda.

About three kilometres further on from this, at the crest of a gentle ridge, the village can be seen among a cluster of nim *and* pipal *trees. In the other direction the towers and outline of the factory can still be seen in the dusty haze that cloaks the billowing effluent from the various chimneys. Near the village slow-moving bullock carts return from the fields, their heavy wooden wheels crunching over the undulating track. Groups of cattle urged on by small boys stroll back to the milking sheds and village milkmen with heavily laden bicycles trundle past on their way to the teashops in Nagda.*

The complaints of the Jains, and many other higher castes is that the industrial complex was built on land unjustly appropriated from the Jain ex-*zamindar*, that the various factories produce excessive airborne and waterborne pollution in the river Chambal, and that the industrial complex has acted as an agent of moral degeneration in the local area and continues to threaten the stability and tranquillity of village society.[22]

In Nagda, the symptoms of modernity are everywhere. Passing the petrol station by the GRASIM airstrip the rickshaw-driver's friend dismounts and the driver turns down the blaring cassette of Juma Chumma, *the hit song from the film* Hum *which in Nagda—as elsewhere in India—is breaking box-office records. We come to a halt beneath the 'GRASIM Industries Welcomes You' sign where a security guard produces a whimsical salute as I make my way further along the road into the GRASIM complex by foot, for rickshaws are not allowed up these private roads.*

'K' is one of the most important men in Nagda, the person at the apex of the desires and grievances of most GRASIM employees. When I saw him on that occasion I shivered in his air-conditioned office as we both drank chilled mango juice through straws beneath a small photograph of G. D. Birla, the deceased magnate responsible for the foundation of this industrial township. He clearly prides himself on being a mediator, smoothing the conflict between metropolitan demands and rural expectations. Every direct question is annulled, turned around, and made harmless. Enquiries about the origins of workers are confounded by poetic confabulation—'Birlagram is also a village'; 'Of course our first aim is to employ local people . . .'

'K' once quizzed me sternly about my liking for the village of Bhatisuda, and especially about my relationship with 'B'—'the man who had caused more trouble for the factory than anyone else'.

The romantic vision of an idyllic rural society associated with the *satyug* being threatened by the evil materialism of the industrial *kaliyug* is part of a cross-culturally familiar paradigm in which 'history' and 'tradition' are negotiated. What needs to be stressed for the purposes of this chapter, however, is that the tensions and oppositions apparent in many oleographs and calendar illus-trations are lived out by the people of the Nagda area in their daily lives, in their journeys between village and town, between field and factory, in terms of this powerful historical paradigm of decay.

Both the historical framework and the moral and ontological trajectories traced within this framework echo Heidegger's critique of modernity, and indeed both can be seen to serve similarly conservative ends. The *satyug* encodes a time and a landscape intermittently realizable in the present in the same way that poetry as understood by Heidegger does: 'through poetry one glimpses the possibility of an unforced, authentic being-in-the-world that en-ables man to experience once again that sense of rootedness in time and place that is lost through the will to subjugate nature to the purposes of human technological control' (Norris 1988: 164–5). I hope to show that the rural

landscapes within many oleographs suggest, and are read as suggesting, a
particular placed-ness. This is a placed-ness whose rightness reflects longing
and yearning, rather than the specific locations of modernity. This placed-ness
can only be conjured up through an opposition with its inversion and denial: it
only achieves a clarity and potency at the moment of its threatened disappearance. I hope also to demonstrate at the conclusion of this paper that such
strategies of contrast and opposition are also used to conjure up the dreams of
an ideal future coded in a united, prosperous, and militarily secure India.[23]

Oleographs, Chromolithographs, and Calendars

In the Nagda area, evaluations of the rural and the urban cannot be disen-
tangled. They exist as each other's necessary antitheses. Similarly, in
oleographs, 'space' and 'place' always exist as part of a semantic field in which
each pole is defined through the possibility of its own negation. Each pole 'is
not some thing but only the other of others, thanks to which it signifies
something' (Dumont 1972: 78).

Semantic fields are sometimes visible within a single image but they also
operate across the archive of oleographic representations such that the presence
of the distal or the proximal in one image serves to mark only its absence in
another. What then of the 'field' within which this semantic flux operates?
What is its history and its contemporary dimensions?

Although 'oleographs' now bear the weight of being stylistically peculiarly
'Indian' they are, as Patricia Uberoi has recently stressed, the product of a
cultural 'coming and going' during the nineteenth century. Although chiefly
concerned with Hindu religious themes, stylistically oleographs are a manifestation of the 'Romanization' advocated by Sir Charles Trevelyan and Lord
Napier in the mid-nineteenth century.[24] From the late 1870s onwards, the
activities of the Calcutta Art Studio, the Chitrashala Press in Pune and the Ravi
Varma Press in Bombay led to a growing saturation of urban and rural India
with 'realist' mass-produced chromolithographs and oleographs. The hybrid
and colonial nature of this work was recognized by contemporary commentators although this recognition has subsequently been effaced.

As Tapati Guha-Thakurta (1986: 166) has argued, Ravi Varma 'represented
not so much a break as a culmination of the Europeanisation of taste, technique
and convention' which had penetrated South Indian court painting throughout
the nineteenth century. Important among these was the impact of 'Company'[25]
style painting on artists resident in Tanjore. Attracted by British patronage, the
Deccani miniature style was imported by artists from Hyderabad, adding to the
cultural mix. British patrons required sets of gouache paintings on paper of
'native castes and occupations' which were 'marked by naturalistic scenic backdrops of sky, clouds, fields and a distant horizon line of trees, where the English

water-colour landscape was emulated with thick and opaque colours and a naive juxtaposition of strokes of dark and light tone' (ibid. 168). By the mid-nineteenth century, the centres of court painting and the clearest Western influences had shifted from Tanjore to the courts of Puddukotah and Travancore in which Ravi Varma was to start his career.[26]

Ravi Varma learnt oil techniques from an itinerant European artist in Travancore court. He proceeded to win numerous prizes at exhibitions in Madras, Vienna and elsewhere from the 1870s onwards. Such was the demand for his works that in 1884[27] he was encouraged to have them mass-produced as oleographs and chromolithographs and in 1892 founded his own Ravi Varma Press in Bombay. Some contemporary images are lineal descendants of Ravi Varma oleographs.[28]

Among the images reproduced here, Ravi Varma's influence is perhaps most directly visible in Figs. 4.5 & 4.14 ('Shiv Shankar' and 'Agricultural Beauty'), for it was Varma who first gave form to some of the gods in their currently recognizable physiognomy and iconography, and produced a series of images of Indian women in which eroticism was closely allied to a nationalist identity.[29] More generally one may trace a line from contemporary 'calendar art' back to Ravi Varma oleographs and the products of other early presses. In both these we find the same 'paintings of backdrops, the loudness of colours, and the crude, heavily-shaded naturalism of the divine figures' (ibid. 189).

Fig. 4.5. Shiv Shankar (oleograph published by Sharma Picture Publication. A 1980s colour oleograph from a 1950s gouache). Courtesy of B. G. Sharma.

In both Ravi Varma and the contemporary examples discussed in this chapter we find the same symmetrically centred subjects—religious icons rendered in a formulaic photo–illusionism, and the same kinds of landscape backgrounds which mix the conventions of Victorian photographic portraiture with the hybrid Company style (and more recently Nathdvara[30] school) backdrop.

Ravi Varma's importance also lay significantly in his ability to bridge the market from the traditional patrons of court art to the wider market of the metropolitan middle-class élite: 'while their images and themes were ostensibly Indian, these paintings matched up to the growing familiarity of middle class, literate Indians with the "history" and "allegory" paintings of the European Academy artists' (ibid. 175). Following Ravi Varma's venture into mass lithography in 1892 and the later pirating of his works by other publishers in the early part of this century, Ravi Varma's works spread throughout the country. A catalogue of his pictures published in 1911 noted that 'From the Himalayas to the Cape Comorin there is now hardly a middle class house-hold in the country which does not possess one or two of the cheap reprints of Ravi Varma's original pictures' (Joshi 1911: 5).

The sociology of contemporary oleograph consumption presents a very different picture, for these images are now clearly disavowed by the élite. In Nagda, which is, as we have seen, a small provincial town, they are still likely to be found in almost all homes, business premises, and Government offices although they are more likely to be found in larger numbers in the homes of lower castes and Untouchables than among wealthy higher castes.[31] In Bhatisuda village they are popular across all castes and classes, but again it is lower castes and Untouchables who collect these with particular avidity.

Patricia Uberoi (1990: 43) has convincingly argued that Ravi Varma helped to define an 'Aryanized' past which served to exclude folk genres and lower caste paradigms. It is clearly the case that popular art has been a vehicle of 'sanskritization' and of the establishment of something approaching a canonical Hinduism, but contemporary oleograph production has also permitted what might be termed a 'democracy of the image'. One important consequence of the portability of the image in its mass-produced form is that it can be situated in contexts previously denied to it.[32] Thus Untouchables, who in Bhatisuda are still prohibited from entering the precincts of the central village temples, are able to control images of the deities in their own homes. This they often do in elaborate shrines which mix oleographs, firework packaging (often depicting deities) with other ephemera, and three-dimensional plaster or plastic images of the gods. Contemporary oleograph production has also been sensitive to 'non-sanskritic' desires—some of the best-selling images are of Ravidas and Ramdevji,[33] figures who have a following chiefly among Untouchable Chamars (tanners), and companies such as Sharma Picture Publication and S. S. Brijbasi produce a large number of images of regional 'folk' deities (e.g. Tejaji, Gogaji).[34]

Mangilal is 60 years old. He previously worked as a contracted worker in GRASIM and is now plagued by ill health. His kacca house lies on the southern flank of the village together with other Chamars (tanners) who prefer to be named as Ravidasi after the saint Ravidas. Inside the hut, to the left of the granary, are about fifteen images of deities. The largest of these is a framed portrait of Ravidas working at his shoes in front of a thatched hut. There is a printed mirror icon of Samvaliyaji[35] and a framed oleograph depicting the twelve jyotirlingas of Siva radiating round their central form. A stunning image of Siva, garlanded with snakes has been ripped from the front of a box of 'Ganga' incense sticks and pinned to the wall.

Hariram Ravidas has about a dozen images arranged above a wooden shelf on the wall opposite the front entrance to his small dwelling. They are a mixture of framed and unframed oleographs; subjects include the Rajasthani deity Ramdevji with a predominantly Chamar following, Hanuman bringing restorative herbs for the wounded Laksman, and Shiv Shankar (reproduced here as Fig. 4.5). To the left of the display is a large publicity calendar for GRASIM Industries depicting Laksmi, and a mirrored chrome-framed image of Samvaliyaji.

At the time of writing there are four large companies producing oleographs. Hem Chander Bhargava (Delhi) is the oldest of these having been founded in 1900. S. S. Brijbasi and Sons[36] which was founded in Karachi in 1922 and relocated to Delhi, Bombay, and Mathura at the time of Partition currently has many hundreds of designs available. B. G. Sharma, one of the most widely reproduced and interesting artists, previously produced designs for Brijbasi before setting up his own company (Sharma Picture Publication) to market his designs in the 1950s. The fourth company, J. B. Khanna, has been commissioning and printing oleographs in Madras since 1957. In addition to these concerns there are several dozen smaller companies—many located in the printing centre of Sivakasi in Tamil Nadu[37]—producing oleographs, posters, and calendars.

Constructing a history, a stylistic genealogy, is one way of understanding the nature of oleograph and calendar images but it leaves unresolved the nature of the relationship between images and their local context of consumption. If it is the case that the landscape elements which do occur in Hindu oleographs can be understood as part of the forging of a new 'nationalist' ideology of identity, how does this 'ideology' function in a contemporary context? I hope to show how many images in the Nagda region are engaged in a political praxis that attempts to negotiate the divides of tradition and modernity and in so doing define the nature of an ideal India. This is an India whose ideal is 'rural' and foregrounded in a 'place' suffused with benign divinity. But it is also recognized that elements of a technological order which appears to lie outside the traditional one are necessary and beneficial if incorporated and validated in terms of the older, purer order.

There are certain Indian oleographs which have the same practical navigational intentions as the Indian Ordnance Survey map described by Gell (1985: 276–8), but the point I wish to make here is that the majority of images depict large central figures (usually deities) who claustrophobically invade the space around them, who collapse 'space' into 'place' in these 'environmental portraits'. Among the former type—those which have a map-like utility—are pilgrim maps of Kashi (Benares/Varanasi) and Gaya (there are two similar examples produced by Chandra Art Cards and Shree Vijay Lakshmi Art Int.) in which perspectival drawings and photographs are superimposed upon a grid of roads. Others, for instance composite pilgrimage prints, share this map-like utility but combine the general framework of a map with perspectival images located within that encompassing schema. Thus the *tirth yatra chardham*[38] (versions by both Sharma Picture Publication and Brijbasi) is a grid-like pictorial structure comprising between ten and seventeen separate scenes centred on the court of Badrinathji. The frames depict (token-indexically) pilgrimage sites and deities from all over India together with various remarkable natural and man-made features. Vaishno Devi, who appears in one of the frames of Sharma Picture Publication's version, is also the subject of individual oleographs which organize the pilgrims' *pradaksina* (circumambulation) around the large central image of the tiger-mounted Devi. The print traces the journey from the bus station at the bottom left through a series of shrines, temples, *dharmsalas*, and sacred tanks to a row of shops opposite the point from where the trail started.[39]

Looking at the range of oleographs available in Nagda and widely throughout India it is clear that, as earlier noted, although there is remarkably little which could properly be called 'landscape' as understood in Western art history,[40] particular deities are associated with particular environments. Landscape is clearly present but rarely as an object of detached scrutiny. Many images distributed throughout houses and shops in the area constitute a visual hierophany that abruptly marks off spaces that are discontinuous from the wider experiential context. Most frequently the idiom through which this occurs is temporal so that, for instance, the avatars of Visnu are shown in landscapes that connote the epoch in which they were incarnated, or more commonly, deities are shown within a place which connotes the *satyug*, the earliest age of truth before the process of historical decay set in. Like the space of a church in a modern city which 'for a believer . . . shares in a different space from the street in which it stands' (Eliade 1959: 25), the place and the divine landscape that the oleograph embodies is not contiguous with the surrounding reality (the space and epoch within which the oleograph image appears):

Every sacred space implies a hierophany, an irruption of the sacred that results in detaching a territory from the surrounding cosmic milieu and making it qualitatively different . . . the theophany that occurs in a place consecrates it by the very fact that it makes it open above—that is, in communication with heaven, the paradoxical point of passage from one mode of being to another. (ibid. 26)

These hierophanic 'irruptions' (the occurrence of oleographs within the spaces of Nagda and Bhatisuda) point to the absence around them of what they depict. The floral luxuriance of many of the images, their colour-saturated fecundity, contrast starkly with the frequent barrenness and austerity of their surroundings. In Nagda, the ideal (the landscape of the *satyug* to be glimpsed around the gods) is more keenly felt in the ever-present reality of an everyday landscape created by the *kaliyug*.

The Places of the Gods in the 'Gas Chamber on the Chambal'

Siva, the powerful ascetic figure, is commonly depicted as the source of the Ganges. In some oleographs he is part of a family group together with Uma and Ganesh (Sharma Picture Publication's 'Shiv Uma Ganesh') who are situated in the midst of the icy Himalayas. When depicted with Parvati and his mount, the bull Nandi, clouds and waterfalls swirl all around (Brijbasi's 'Parvati Parmeshwar'). In Sharma Picture Publication's 'Shiv Shankar' (Fig. 4.5) he is seated on a tiger-skin beside a garlanded trident. The top of the pictorial frame is filled with the over-hanging bough of a banyan tree among which birds and squirrels play, and in the middle distance lie the Himalayas rendered in a chilly blue. Through his matted ascetic's hair spurts the same river Ganges whose descent to earth he had broken by catching it on his head.[41] From its new source in Siva the river then flows through the Himalayas before cascading over beautiful waterfalls and moving through the lily-bedecked quieter waters that flow by Siva's left side. Here landscape is little more than an aquatic extrusion of the being of this foregrounded deity.

By contrast, Saraswati—wife of Brahma and the goddess of learning—inhabits the lower foothills. In one widely available print (Fig. 4.6) whose iconography can be traced back to Ravi Varma and the Calcutta Art Studio, she is seated on a riverside rock adorned with jasmine flowers and her left foot is perched on an iridescent lotus around which swans paddle contentedly. Behind her, peacocks adorn verdant foliage, a small Ganges waterfall tumbles attractively, and distant mountains are imbued with a rich rosy hue from a setting sun.

[T]he Chambal was the main life-line for the entire Malwa tract, people depended on it for their very existence. Not any more. Today, the river is a killer, carrying with it tons of muck and dirt, [much of it] highly toxic to human, animal and plant life. For an entire stretch of 30 Kms. [downstream from GRASIM at Nagda], the Chambal has become an aquatic desert, with no fishes or other animals. (Padmanabhan 1983: 18)

As with the 'Shiv Shankar' image, in the Saraswati image the possibility of a horizon practically disappears in this irradiated and condensed being-in-place. Though there is clearly geographic distance, nothing here is distal: an entire environment is subsumed to a single divine propriocentrism. We have seen

Fig. 4.6. Saraswati (colour
oleograph, publisher unknown,
c.1990).

how in Siva's case this landscape is created by the subject of the portrait but
placed-ness is created also by the iconographic embedding of divine figures.
Thus Siva is at the centre of iconographic figures which in establishing his
identity also guarantee the impossibility of his displacement. Shiv is of necessity represented with his mount (*vahan*), the bull Nandi, and in this form sits
on a tiger-skin, has the Ganges flowing from his head, and so on. The sugges-
tion, made to me by Archana Srivastava, that Hindus cannot think of or
visualize deities without a chain of associated signifiers, suggests an
interconnectedness and embeddedness which precludes their association with
an abstract space.

Moving further through the imaginary geographic continuum that connects
many contemporary oleographs we encounter the goddess Laksmi perched on
a lotus in the midst of what is now a wide and more slowly flowing Ganges.

*The Chambal has been impounded by the Respondents to meet their water requirements. In
dry seasons the impoundment almost absorbs the entire flow of the river. The waste water of
the factory is discharged through Kachcha Nala . . . The quantity of waste water is very high
in comparison to the flow available in the river. Thus practically no dilution is available to
the waste in the river, as a result, the river down stream of Nagda is practically a drain of
stinking factory waste. (Revision Petition by Babulal Bharatiya dated 23 Feb. 1982 in the
High Court of Madhya Pradesh at Indore.)*

In Brijbasi's 'Diwali Poojan' two hands hold blossoming lotuses: from the
others fall streams of gold coins. The Himalayas are more distant here and a
mellow light falls on the gently sloping grassed banks of the river. Conifers are

here replaced by a few banana trees. Above them macaws frolic in the lofty trees and below them beautifully caparisoned elephants triumphantly hold up garlands.

Looking upstream from the gardens of the Birla House in Nagda I see what I assume are some of the lands belonging to Bhatisuda farmers; the banks are thickly shrouded with dense trees broken by the occasional taller eucalyptus. It is here that security guards are reputed to patrol during the summer assaulting those cultivators who attempt to use 'the factory's' water for their own fields. Downstream is the water intake pump, an elegant terracotta arched structure drinking in so many million cubic feet of water. The scorching sun drops further behind the horizon and for a moment the crows stop their incessant clatter. The noise of the powerhouse returns to fill the gap.

In Braj where Krsna as Gopal stands beside the banks of the river playing his flute surrounded by cows, peacocks, and doves (Sharma Picture Publication's 'Gopal Krisna'[42]) the mountains are not visible and the viewer can only glimpse small verdant hills in the distance. The goddess Kali epitomizes in many respects the opposite qualities of Krsna and she is often represented on a battle ground trampling Siva. Wearing a necklace of skulls and holding a decapitated head she stands amidst the carnage of war usually depicted in a ghostly red which obliterates the horizon.

The story takes us back to early 1954, when Nagda, then a small village with less than 500 people, was poised to become one of India's premier Industrial Centres . . . Hard working peasants who used to cultivate cotton in the black Malwa cotton soil lost their lands to the factory for a pittance . . .

The wheels of industry kept on moving, with ever increasing speed. Production and profits climbed new heights. Cartographers translated them into the language of lines on graph sheets, to be proudly displayed in air-conditioned rooms. Managers smiled, Trade Unions bargained for bonus. And the men who worked in the shop floor containing deadly gases vegetated and marched slowly towards their graves. (Padmanabhan 1983: 20, 4)

Prints of the Chamar saint Ravidas,[43] which are very popular among the Bhatisuda Ravidasis (Chamars) from whom they take their (new) name, locate him in a verdant, flower-filled setting among simple straw-thatched village buildings. Similarly, depictions of Rama (who is more popular with higher-caste Hindus) in exile in the forest of Dandaka place him among fronds of flowering plants. In the background his horse waits contentedly under a tree and Rama, Sita, and Laksmana's elementary straw dwelling is visible.

The one time prosperous and picturesque villages with a healthy population now present a pathetic picture of filth, stench, disease and slow death. (Padmanabhan 1983: vii)

This foregrounding in a floral luxuriance seems to express a complete harmony with their natural setting and acceptance of the path of *dharma* (duty) and *satya* (truth). In all these images, a human or divine figure dominates the centre and foreground and landscape details appear as physically extraneous although clearly homologous with the character depicted.

This describes only a part of the repertoire of the main picture-publishing companies in India but it is apparent that deities are represented in formulaic and restricted modes in which 'landscape' is employed as an iconographic attribute of the figure who dominates the picture space. As in Robert Howlett's well-known photograph 'Portrait of Isambard Kingdom Brunel Standing before the Launching Chains of the "Leviathan" (the "Great Eastern")' taken in 1857, we are confronted with what has been called 'environmental portraiture'. Writing about this portrait, Richard Brilliant (1991: 99) has argued that the backdrop is a 'part'—'a permanent aspect of his being, of his identity, from which he cannot and, if properly portrayed, should not be parted'. We might also observe that this 'part' similarly has no equivalent existence in the absence of its creator.

Such environmental portraiture also extends to ritually important personages who have also incontestably endured a life as a mortal such as Bhimrao Ranji Ambedkar (1893–1956), one-time student of the LSE, champion of India's Untouchables and principal author of the Indian Constitution. It is in this latter role that one oleograph (Fig. 4.7) depicts him, Constitution in hand,

Fig. 4.7. Ambedkar (colour oleograph, publisher unknown, *c*.1990).

standing before Herbert Baker's circular Parliament building (now *Lok Sabha*) in New Delhi. The flag of India flies on top of this and on Ambedkar's right the Buddha appears to give his blessing.[44] While there is no doubt that Herbert Baker's building does have an independent physical existence in Delhi and one can establish its location solely with the aid of maps, as presented here in this oleograph it is no more than an emanation of Ambedkar, a mere iconographic signifier of *his* identity. Just as the Ganges depicted in 'Shiv Shankar' flows from Siva's head, here the Parliament building is represented as Ambedkar's creation—in a landscape of political placed-ness. The Parliament building connoting the political ethos of independent India is as much his creation as the Constitution which he holds in his left hand. The building embodies his placed-ness just as the flag of an independent India and the Buddha signify his faith.

This same Parliament building appears in a very different guise in another oleograph (Fig. 4.8) where it is a distal object of other people's ambitions. The oleograph depicts Subhas Chandra Bose (1895–1945) the freedom fighter and commander of the Indian National Army which sought with the help of the Japanese to rid India of British imperialists during the last war. Bose is shown in the uniform of the INA astride a horse in a manner similar to older depictions of the Mahratta hero Sivaji. His right hand is raised in a clenched fist salute and with his other hand he points towards the Parliament building.

FIG. 4.8. Subhas Chandra Bose (colour oleograph, publisher unknown, *c*.1990).

Above this appears the slogan, *chalo dilli* ('Forward to Delhi!') echoing a chant of the 1857 insurrectionists (Bayly 1990: 409). The building here symbolizing the seat of political power is both spatially and temporally distanced—it is an object beyond Bose's own placed-ness, existing in a future time and place over which he hopes to have power.

The World as Picture

These two contrasting uses of the Parliament building illustrate with reasonable accuracy two types of relationship with the world which Heidegger placed within an evolutionary framework in his essay 'The Age of the World Picture'. He provides a framework which matches in an interesting manner the theory of decay and disenchantment traced by the *yugs*. Heidegger traces a scientific alienation predicated on Cartesian dualism and the rise of science, which allowed the world to be seen as 'picture'. Science, concerned with a mathematical knowing in advance (Heidegger 1977: 118) is concerned with the projection of objects within a spatio-temporal field of certainty (p. 119): 'We first arrive at science as research when the Being of whatever is, is sought in such objectiveness' (1977: 127). The 'certainty of representation' on which this all depends is all the fault of Descartes according to Heidegger (ibid.). The possibility of viewing the world as picture is a peculiarly modern capability (p. 130).

The benign surveillance of Birlagram always harbours the possibility of punishment. This is revealed at its most surreal, most unbelievable, when cycling on a hot summer day from Birla House to the village of Mehtwas. A metalled road about twenty feet wide snakes between the lavish gardens of the Guest House and the vineyard on the east flank of the Birla Gardens on the banks of the Chambal. Dawdling through here, over the patches of sunlight that fall on the ground through the cascades of bougainvillea, it is hard to believe that only one mile away are the noise and fumes of the H2SO4 division. More distant still are the traces of the events of 27 April 1975 when members of the factory security force shot dead two villagers from Mehtwas right here in this beautiful lane. Both Rami Bai, aged 60, and Shivlal, aged 13, had been protesting about the erection of a large security gate at the end of this lane. Despite recent attempts to reimpose this barrier and the survival of two shafts of steel sunk in the concrete road from the original structure, when I photographed this area in 1991 I remained unsure that this could really be the place that figured so large in local political folklore. Seldom had I been in a place which achieved such a denial of its history. As I paced around, confused, passing cyclists turned to stare, the wobble of their cycles as unsure as my perplexed camera searching for evidence. A communist (CITU) leaflet publicizing the management's attempts to re-erect the barrier declaimed nigrani mem sab kam hota hai *('everything is done under surveillance').*

For Heidegger (1977: 131), a Parmenidean elision of 'thought' and 'being' has been ousted by what Martin Jay (1988: 4) terms 'Cartesian perspectivalism'.[45] Although Plato defined beingness as *eidos* ('aspect'/'view'), the Greek view differed from the later Cartesian perspectivalism inasmuch as 'that which is, does not come into being at all through the fact that man first looks upon it, in a sense of representing that has the character of subjective perception. Rather, man is the one who is looked upon by that which is' (Heidegger 1977: 131). In the Middle Ages too the world is not brought before society as a picture. It is only the modern epoch that has a world picture in which the world is placed 'in the realm of man's knowing and his having disposal' (p. 130): 'There begins that way of being human that mans [*sic*] the realm of human quality as a domain given over to measuring and executing, for the purpose of gaining mastery over that which is as a whole' (p. 132). Heidegger's evolutionary lament—as indeed that of Nagda Hindus who have recourse to the explanatory paradigms of the *yugs*—might be recast as a fall from 'place' to 'space'. 'Place' is foregrounded and impresses itself existentially on man whereas 'space' is set apart in such a manner that man is able to have power over it and in the process lose sight of his own true identity.

Subhas Chandra Bose's gesture towards the world as picture—his attempt to gain mastery over the distal Parliament building, is legitimated by his huge popularity throughout India but it is a rare pictorial feature in the oleographs and prints displayed in Nagda and Bhatisuda. Indeed we might read the Bose oleograph as an example of 'strategic mastery', an expedient, parallel to the 'strategic essentialism' called for by Gayatri Spivak (1987). Bose is recognized as an expedient actor in time of great calamity and anguish and his portrait is able to bridge the proximal and the distal.

This is most unusual, for other images which lead the eye primarily towards the distal horizon do so to introduce those forces which can fracture the contented being-in-place-ness of the foreground. Perhaps the key image here is that of Sita glimpsing the demon Maricha disguised as a golden deer during her exile in the forest of Dandaka (see Pinney 1992*b*). The deer functions here as a symbol of *maya*, illusion, produced by Sita's own materialistic desire and yearning. Later in the story, after much tribulation, the foregrounded Sita is proved to have retained her purity despite the abduction by Ravana the King of Lanka.

Similar tropes and an identical use of pictorial space were evident in Fig. 4.2. In that image, the contrast of two visions of femininity (traditional and modern) plays, as do the *Sita haran* images, upon a temporal continuum from fore-ground to horizon. In the case of the scene from the *Ramayana* the sighting of the deer and Rama and Laksmana's chase of it pull the narrative dramatically along. Fig. 4.2 also initially suggests a progression from foreground tradition (the bicycle) to distal modernity (the scooter) but the positioning of the vehicles and the gaze of the women suggests a reversal of this—the return to the foregrounded tradition from modernity, the recapturing of an Indian identity, the reattainment of self.

But such a resolution is not always proposed. There is a genre of cityscape, represented here by Fig. 4.9, which often depicts cities such as Hong Kong, Singapore, or Sydney, and a common striking feature of their depictions is the absence of a foreground. The beholder of Fig. 4.9 looks out over an expanse of sea. In a similar image the Hongkong and Shanghai Bank building is viewed from across a road junction. Like nineteenth-century photographic representations of the Yosemite, these structures rise out of nothing, and no people are visible, as if to emphasize the vast inhuman dimension of it all. Equivalent ruralscapes are usually busily populated. Fig. 4.10, entitled 'Village Scenery', presents an imaginary view of rural life which accentuates a picturesque rusticity of decaying temples and crumbling walls. Women fill their earthenware pots from the river in the foreground while a mother and son purchase clay toys from a trader seated beneath a banyan tree. A devout woman salutes a homely Siva temple and cattle wait peacefully beside their carts while their masters attend to their spiritual duties. In another similar picture three children play with spinning tops, the infantile perpetual-motion machine, while white doves coo contentedly among the jack-fruit and banana trees in a pleasantly well-worn enclosure.

The cityscapes by contrast present a world—like that of the female scooter-rider—which partly fascinates but mostly repels the average buyer of these

Fig. 4.9. Hong Kong (photographic calendar illustration, publisher unknown, *c*.1985).

Fig. 4.10. Calendar print entitled 'Village Scenery' (publisher unknown, *c*.1985).

oleographs: a world which is often seen at a distance without any foregrounding so as to mark its divorce from the *dharmik* life of India. These images were purchased in Nagda—all the various vendors stock numerous examples—but I have rarely seen these displayed except in barber's shops where they are often juxtaposed with rural landscapes. In these images are depicted the spiralling discontent of the *kaliyug*—the desire for higher and higher buildings at the cost of spiritual impoverishment articulated so clearly by a Bhatisuda Jain.[46]

Both Heideggerian and Nagda perspectives imply similar readings of these images. The new Hindu identity that developed under colonialism, and which was to be defined in crucial visual terms, laid great stress on the sanctity of the past and we have seen the power of this past within Nagda and Bhatisuda. This, however, has not been an inflexible past, and in many respects Indian popular art suggests a more adaptive vision than Heidegger's. In particular it is apparent that mastery over the world as picture is tolerable if it is validated by the values of an Indian identity. We have already seen this in the case of Subash Chandra Bose. It is perhaps more strikingly present in an image of Mahatma Gandhi standing upon India (Fig. 4.11). As one would expect he is dressed only in a *dhoti* and sandals and holds in one hand a staff and in the other a copy of the *Bhagavad Gita*. His lean frame fills the whole length of the image and his gait suggests that starting from India (which he almost completely covers with his

FIG. 4.11. Mahatma Gandhi (colour oleograph, publisher unknown, *c*.1990).

sandals) he will walk around the world. In the deep blue background of astronomic space a slogan reads, *Satyamev jayte* ('The way of truth triumphs'), confirming that the figure of Gandhi here metaphorizes the principles of non-violent resistance and the principles of 'truth' with which Gandhi experimented during his life. This image of complete domination thus starts to look rather different once we grasp that the triumph is spiritual: the possession is no more than the adherence of a society to certain spiritual truths founded on a renunciation of all that possessive individualism described by Berger (1972*a*: 105–8). The triumph is not the conquest of the world by man, but the triumph of abnegation.

This image suggests some of the conditions under which 'space' can be conquered by this new Indian identity and also prepares the way for the final examples in my analysis which precisely resolve all the tensions we identified in '3399' at the start of this chapter. These are a series of calendar prints which depict foregrounded figures of various types set against a fecund agricultural background. These are the only images which completely resolve the tension of the foreground and the horizon, of 'place' and 'space' and which resolve the opposition we discovered in the image '3399' discussed at the beginning of this chapter. The genre encompasses two different forms—*jay javan/jay kisan* (Fig. 4.12) and 'Agricultural Baby'/'Agricultural Beauty' (Figs. 4.13 and 4.14). The former has its roots in Lal Bahadur Sastri's slogan *jay javan, jay kisan* ('victory to the soldier, victory to the farmer') and a series of films which developed this heroic pairing. These show twins—aged perhaps 5—one of whom is a soldier and the other a farmer. They stand in a wheat field whose verdant foliage and grain reaches their waists. The soldier wears military fatigues and a machine gun or rifle; the farmer wears a turban and holds a plough. It is likely that this image evokes Mehboob Khan's classic 1957 film *Mother India*,[47] but its primary reference is to the 1965 and 1971 wars with Pakistan, crucial moments in the definition of post-Independence India. In this pictorial assertion of India's military security there is also a dialectical validation of technology; military hardware is necessary to preserve Indian agriculture; the changes associated with the Green Revolution are the necessary productive basis for the consolidation of the nation-state.

The farmer's domain is present in the form of rectilinear fields through which run irrigation channels supplied by burbling diesel pumps. The fields are scenes of great activity—tractors are ploughing, fertilizers are being applied, pesticides are being sprayed. The soldier is shown protecting his brother's (his fellow Indian's) agricultural terrain. In one image an artillery unit is blasting its shells out into the distance, in another three MiG jets zoom up and across etching vapour trails over the sky. The ideological message of such images is very clear—the Indian soldier repulsing the Pakistan Army and the

Fig. 4.12. Calendar print of young soldier and farmer (publisher unknown, *c.*1985).

Fig. 4.13. Calendar print entitled 'Agricultural Baby'
(publisher unknown, *c*.1985).

farmer battling with nature are engaged in two complementary endeavours.
The increasing productivity of the Green Revolution (based on mechanization
and the chemicalization of the land as shown here) is as vital for the nation as
its military security.

A further sphere of this genre—usually entitled 'Agricultural Baby'—
depicts a single baby, sometimes with a slightly older girl in a similar context
(Fig. 4.13). Here the warfare is eliminated and replaced by baskets of fruit
and vegetables and pieces of sugar-cane. What remain are the tractors, the
perfectly regular fields, the pumps bringing forth water from various tanks and
wells, the mechanical threshers shooting out wheat and other grains, the bags of
fertilizer waiting to be showered upon the land. All these signs of agricultural
modernity are situated within the receding lines of the perspectively represented fields that recall Heidegger's (1977: 118–19) 'mathematical knowing
in advance' in which objects are projected within a spatio-temporal field of
certainty. Here, however, the landscape is no mere epiphenomenon of the
central image for the eye is also led away towards the horizon that signifies
'our' India, 'our' Bharat, 'our' Hindustan. Again, the relationship of figure to
landscape is very different to that described by Berger in the case of
Gainsborough's *Mr and Mrs Andrews*, for the land does not appear as an
individual's property, but rather as the environmental terrain of a suprain-
dividual identity. This is reminiscent of Emerson's conclusion reached in
nineteenth-century America:

Fɪɢ. 4.14. Calendar print entitled 'Agricultural Beauty' (publisher unknown, *c*.1985).

The charming landscape which I saw this morning is indubitably made up of some twenty or thirty farms. Miller owns this field, Locke that, and Manning the woodland beyond. But none of them owns the landscape. There is a property in the horizon which no man has but he whose eye can integrate all the parts, that is, the poet. This is the best part of these men's farms, yet to this their warranty deeds give no title (1894: 14).

We might substitute here for 'poet' that other eye which is able to integrate all the parts, the mythic identity of the nation.

The iconography of 'Agricultural Baby' is transferred almost wholesale in a series usually entitled 'Agricultural Beauty' or 'Agricultural Lady'. Here the central figure is an adult female, usually tightly attired in an attractive sari. Once again there are tractors, pumps, bags of fertilizer. In Fig. 4.14 the 'Agricultural Beauty' sits beside a pump and bags of fertilizer in the middle of an enormous field at the far reaches of which a tractor can be seen involved in its geometricized work. The picture composition is very similar to Jain Picture Publishers' '3399' (Fig. 4.1) with which I began this chapter. The foreground is dominated by a seated woman who stares straight at the viewer. Like the yellow-clad *masala* star of '3399', the figure in 'Agricultural Beauty' returns an erotic gaze, but whereas '3399' held a red gladiolus in her left hand, the 'Agricultural Beauty' holds a spray of sorghum in hers (sometimes the central figure holds a piece of sugar cane and in one case a bunch of grapes). In front of her, rather than a display of cut flowers, she has two bags of fertilizer and instead of the perspectival regularities of the Daniell aquatints on the horizon, the 'Agricultural Beauty' sits before the precisely delineated plot of agricultural land which a tractor is traversing. Whereas '3399' embodied conflicting and ultimately destructive demands, 'Agricultural Beauty' is safely ensconced within a unified, fecund, and self-possessed nation. It is in this political fiction of the nation that horizon and foreground, space and place, coalesce momentarily.

From the perspective of peasants and Jains in the village of Bhatisuda there are no such convincing resolutions on offer in the ethnographic context that has run as a subtext throughout this chapter. The rationalizations and modernity of the *kaliyug* are rarely able to signify the fecundity and productivity that the fields of the Green Revolution signify in 'Agricultural Beauty'.

But, within this village framework of an everlasting loss is an admission that all human time is lived in the *kaliyug* and that the presence incarnated in the *satyug* can only be the dream of a disappeared or yet-to-come world. The foreground—like the horizon—can never exist on its own and in itself. It will always figure 'the loss of what has never taken place, of a self-presence which has never been given but only dreamed of and always already split, repeated, incapable of appearing to itself except in its own disappearance' (Derrida 1976: 112).

Notes

I am indebted to Eric Hirsch, Manoj Khandelwal, Michael O'Hanlon, Archana Srivastava, and Giles Tillotson for many useful comments on this paper.

1. The term is of course taken from Yi-Fu Tuan (1974) and denotes 'all of the human being's affective ties with the material environment' (ibid. 93).
2. The term 'oleograph' (a varnished chromolithograph imitating an oil painting) was the one used at the moment of their inception in the late nineteenth century and is used (rather than 'chromolithograph', 'calendar art', or 'bazaar art') because it captures something of their historical and cultural specificity.
3. There were several earlier presses (such as Calcutta Art Studio and Chitrashala Press, Pune) whose output was more regionally disseminated.
4. I take this phrase from Norris's (1988: 165–9) gloss on Heidegger (see also Blackham 1961: 90ff.). The parallelism between Nagda high-caste views and aspects of Heidegger's diagnosis of modernity is striking and is explicated below.
5. 'Hodological' denotes a space that is homogenous, measured, and regular—in other words 'disenchanted'. I take the term from Littlejohn (1967: 333). Hodological is used throughout this chapter to denote the inverse of what Eliade describes as 'sacred space' (1959: 20), a non-homogenous space marked by interruptions, breaks, and qualitative differences.
6. In Hindi the concept of 'place' and 'space' are not clearly lexically marked (as indeed they are not within common English usage). The terms *sthan* and *jagah* can be used interchangeably, although *sthan* perhaps has more connotations of

placedness. The term *kshetra* (variously 'field', 'country', 'sacred site') has perhaps more connotations of 'space'.

7. Dumont is here referring to caste hierarchy as a semantic field.

8. I have strived for 'an informed re-assembling' (O'Hanlon 1989: 18) of the 'read-ings' and 'meanings' of these images in the context of the political and moral arguments evinced in the context of Nagda. However, I acknowledge the difficulty of completely banishing formal or 'physiognomic' readings (see Ginzburg 1989: 35).

9. I am grateful to Giles Tillotson for drawing my attention to this.

10. This paragraph, in contrast to my own formal deductions in the previous para-graph, records interpretations which people in Nagda bring to such images. Red flowers—as in the case of the Bengali Kali oleographs—are commonly used as substitutes for blood offerings to meat-eating deities and the film-makers clearly drew upon this pan-Indian symbolism to denote the actress in '3399' as symbolic of the goddess Kali.

11. I refer to an 'incarnated' viewer (Bryson 1983: 106; cited by Rotman 1987: 14) whose eye is at the apex of a triangle that mirrors the triangle within the image whose apex is the horizon or vanishing point.

12. That the hypothetical perspective of the bird can, in the modern epoch, become the actual perspective of the viewing subject is acknowledged by F. Deaville Walker (1925: 19) at the end of a written tour of 'The Land of the Hindus': 'we have now taken a bird's-eye view—may we say 'an aeroplane view'? of India'. Perhaps the politically most notorious example of the use of such a perspective is the opening sequence of Leni Riefenstahl's *Triumph of the Will* (1934) in which Nuremberg is first seen from the air as Hitler's plane descends from the clouds to the strains of Wagner.

13. In making this point I am anxious that the complexity of the painterly represen-tation of the Indian landscape should not be simplified. It should be noted that many of the artists of the period worked against such 'effects of power'. William Hodges (who after Cook's second voyage became the first professional British landscape painter to work in India) 'urged a cultural pluralism that would open [his] campatriots' eyes to the wealth of India's artistic and intellectual heritage' (Tillotson 1990: 146). Similarly, Tillotson observes the tension between the in-formative intention of much landscape painting and the picturesque aesthetic within which it was presented.

14. Giles Tillotson (pers. comm.) has pointed to a further, and more precise, Indian parallel to *Mr and Mrs Andrews*. This is Zoffany's *Mr and Mrs Warren Hastings* painted in Calcutta (1783–7). See Mildred Archer (1979: 140–1).

15. Nandy (1988: xi) argues that there is a form of colonialism which 'colonized minds in addition to bodies [. . .] it helps generalize the concept of a modern West from a geographical and temporal entity to a psychological category. The West is now everywhere, within the West and outside; in structures and in minds.'

16. There are extant prints in this genre dating from the 1940s.

17. Like the red flowers in Fig. 4.1 these are readily decodable iconographic symbols with meaning for all Indian consumers of this picture.

18. On the stereotype of the 'Western woman' within Hindi film see Rosie Thomas (1985: 126): 'Evil or decadence is broadly categorised as "non-traditional" and

"Western", although the West is not so much a place, or even a culture, as an emblem of exotic decadent otherness, signified by whisky, bikinis, and uncontrolled sexuality'.

19. The slippage between appearance and reality—the *maya* of classical texts—is most frequently voiced in Bhatisuda through the aphorism *bagula bhagat*—'egret saint'. In Bhatisuda, as throughout all the plains and lower hills, the cattle egret, elegantly and motionlessly perched on some perambulating or ruminating cow or buffalo, is a common and pleasing sight. But its exterior tranquillity is periodically broken as it snatches at passing creatures that can fulfil its appetite.

20. The 1991 Census recorded the population at 79,405. In 1950—prior to the development of the industrial complex—Nagda was a small village with about 2,000 inhabitants.

21. They are Svetambara followers of the reformist *acharya* Rajendra Sureshi.

22. There are other, divergent views as well. The model described here is that articulated most clearly by high-caste village employers. However, whereas these village employers stress the decline of history through the *yugs*, existence for local Untouchables has always been more of a plateau of misery. The *kaliyug* is a black age of declining morality, they agree, but it also has benefits such as access to relatively highly paid industrial work which has allowed them to break the shackles of the village economy. These other views are explicated in Pinney (1987).

23. I am extremely grateful to Archana Srivastava for enabling me to see the link between a threatened past and a desired future.

24. The causal link between the Art School movement and Ravi Varma's work has been questioned by Guha-Thakurta (1986: 183).

25. A term denoting a hybrid style of Anglo-Indian painting. See Mildred Archer (1972).

26. Guha-Thakurta (1986: 174) notes: 'Ravi Varma's evolution as a painter was integrally a part of this stream of development of Indian court painting—an alternative stream of Westernisation, quite distinct from that associated with the Schools of Art and its training of Indian artists and craftsmen.'

27. Sir T. Madhava Rao suggested that his 'popular epic paintings be sent to Europe to be oleographed' (Guha-Thakurta 1986: 186).

28. I hope to show in a forthcoming publication that both Ravi Varma's originality and influence have been somewhat exaggerated. See Joshi (1911) for the fullest early listing and illustration of Ravi Varma's works.

29. Uberoi (1990: 44) observes that the ten paintings for which Ravi Varma won awards at the 1892–3 International Exhibition in Chicago were depictions of women from different regions of India. Venniyoor notes that there is a long tradition within Indian art of the celebration of 'robust, full-grown, sensuous female[s] . . . The Manipravala poets of Malayalam, on whom Ravi Varma was nurtured, were in a way obsessed with female anatomy, and they have not spared even goddesses' (1981: 50).

30. Nathdvara is an important Pushti Marg pilgrimage centre in Rajasthan with its own tradition of Brahman temple painters. A large number of major 20th-c. oleograph artists have been Nathdvara Brahmans.

31. This I understand to be true throughout India. Ravi Varma's work, and in particu-

lar the oleographs, was later to be much vilified even by those who had previously supported him (see Venniyoor 1981: 66–82 and Guha-Thakurta 1986: 189).

32. This is a point that has been made in different cultural contexts by Benjamin (1970), Berger (1972*a*), and Malraux (1978).

33. On whom see Pinney 1992*b*.

34. One can trace a similarly democratizing trend in film production for there have been several Rajasthani films dramatizing Ramdev, Gogaji, and Tejaji.

35. A popular southern Rajasthani deity associated with Krsna.

36. Ravi Agrawal, personal communication, April 1991. It was not until 1928 that they started picture publishing, having dealt only in picture frames for the first seven years of their existence.

37. Situated in a very dry area of Tamil Nadu, Sivakasi developed as a centre for the manufacture of matches and fireworks. The large number of printing presses to be found in the town originally developed to supply packaging for the fireworks. Sivakasi is now the largest printing centre in India, producing most of the calendars that are sold throughout the country.

38. 'Pilgrimage to the Four Dham': this shows the four pilgrimage centres of Dvarkanath, Srinathji (Nathdvara), Puri, and Rameshvar.

39. This structure—in which narrative and space is organized around a central icon, is a common feature of much oleographic art. See Pinney 1992*b*.

40. I mean here 'landscape' as the portrayal of specific locations. Coomaraswamy's comments on the absence of 'portraiture' within the Indian tradition suggest useful clues for an understanding of the parallel absence of 'landscape'. Coomaraswamy observed that even where recognition of individual likeness was desired in the representation of living persons in traditional Indian art, 'it is the concept of the type discovered in the individual that really governs the representation' (1977: 90). Traditional artists (professional *silpins*) produced ancestral 'effigies' which strove for 'archetypal meaning' (1977: 89). The relevance of this lack of concern with the chronotope of the individual for understanding the absence of landscape is suggested by Stella Kramrisch's perceptive observation that 'portraiture belongs to civilizations that fear death' (cited by Coomaraswamy 1977: 89 n. 67). One might hypothesize that this chronotope also extends to the time-space in which the subjects of portraiture do (or do not) appear.

41. See Vitsaxis (1977: 73).

42. This is but one of a huge number of nearly identical images which can be traced back to Narottam Narayan Sharma's *Murli Manohar* published by Brijbasi in the early 1930s.

43. See Briggs (1920) and Khare (1984).

44. Ambedkar converted to Buddhism shortly before his death. This is also an extremely popular subject for oleographs.

45. 'In the Cartesian model the intellect *inspects* entities modeled on retinal images . . . In Descartes' conception—the one that became the basis of 'modern' epistemology—it is *representations* which are in the "mind" ' (Rorty 1979: 45; cited by Jay 1988: 5)

46. Bombay emerges as the central motif of this, in which buildings become higher and higher as speculators and residents pursue an illusory happiness (see Pinney 1987: 447–9).

47. The two sons of the impoverished heroine Radha (played by Nargis) pull a plough with their mother in order to preserve her honour from the local moneylender. See Rosie Thomas's brilliant analysis of this (1990).

References

APPADURAI, ARJUN, and BRECKENRIDGE, CAROL A. (1992). 'Museums are Good to Think: Heritage on View in India', in I. Karp *et al.* (eds.), *Museums and Communities: The Politics of Public Culture*. Washington: Smithsonian Institute.

ARCHER, MILDRED (1972). *Company Drawings in the India Office Library*. London: HMSO.

——(1979). *India and British Portraiture 1770–1825*. London: Sotheby Parke Bernet and Oxford University Press.

BAYLY, C. A. (1990). *The Raj: India and the British, 1600–1947*. London: National Portrait Gallery.

BENJAMIN, WALTER (1970). 'The Work of Art in the Age of Mechanical Reproduction', in his *Illuminations*. London: Cape.

BERGER, JOHN (1972a). *Ways of Seeing*. London: BBC.

——(1972b). 'Past Seen from a Possible Future', in his *Selected Essays and Articles: The Look of Things*. Harmondsworth: Penguin.

BLACKHAM, H. J. (1961). *Six Existential Thinkers*. London: Routledge & Kegan Paul.

BRIGGS, G. W. (1920). *The Chamars*. Calcutta: Association Press.

BRILLIANT, RICHARD (1991). *Portraiture*. London: Reaktion Books.

BRYSON, NORMAN (1983). *Vision and Painting: The Logic of the Gaze*. London: Macmillan.

COOMARASWAMY, A. K. (1977). 'The Part of Art in Indian Life', in Roger Lipsey (ed.) *Coomaraswamy, Selected Papers:* i. *Traditional Art and Symbolism*. Princeton, NJ: Princeton University Press.

DERRIDA, JACQUES (1976). *Of Grammatology*. Baltimore: Johns Hopkins University Press.

DUMONT, LOUIS (1972). *Homo Hierarchicus: The Caste System and its Implications*. London: Paladin.

ELIADE, MIRCEA (1959). *The Sacred and the Profane: The Nature of Religion*. New York: Harcourt Brace Jovanovich.

EMERSON, R. W. (1894). *Nature, Addresses, and Lectures*. London: Routledge.

GELL, ALFRED (1985). 'How to Read a Map: Remarks on the Practical Logic of Navigation', *Man*, 20/2: 271–86.

GINZBURG, CARLO (1989). 'From Aby Warburg to E. H. Gombrich: A Problem of Method', in his *Clues, Myths and the Historical Record*. Baltimore: Johns Hopkins University Press.

GUHA-THAKURTA, TAPATI (1986). 'Westernisation and Tradition in South Indian Painting: The Case of Raja Ravi Varma, 1848–1906', *Studies in History*, July–Dec.

HEIDEGGER, MARTIN (1977). 'The Age of the World Picture', in his *The Question Concerning Technology and Other Essays*. New York: Harper Torchbooks.

JAY, MARTIN (1988). 'The Scopic Regimes of Modernity', in Hal Foster (ed.), *Vision and Visuality*. Seattle: Dia Press.

JOSHI, S. N. (1911). *Half-Tone Reprints of the Renowned Pictures of the Late Raja Ravi Varma*. Poona: Chitrashala Steam Press.

KHARE, R. S. (1984). *The Untouchable as Himself: Ideology, Identity and Pragmatism among the Lucknow Chamars*. Cambridge: Cambridge University Press.

KRAUSS, ROSALIND (1985). 'Photography's Discursive Spaces', in her *Originality of the Avant-Garde and Other Modernist Myths*. Cambridge, Mass.: MIT Press.

LANNOY, RICHARD (1971). *The Speaking Tree*. Oxford: Oxford University Press.

LITTLEJOHN, KENNETH (1967). 'The Temne House', in J. Middleton (ed.), *Myth and Cosmos*. New York: Natural History Press.

MALRAUX, ANDRÉ (1978). *The Voices of Silence*. Princeton, NJ: Bolingen.

NANDY, ASHIS (1988). *The Intimate Enemy: Loss and Recovery of Self under Colonialism*. Delhi: Oxford University Press.

National Archives (1982). *Catalogue of the MRIO-Miscellaneous Maps of the Survey of India* (1742–1872). New Delhi: National Archives of India.

NEWMAN, HENRY (1937). *Indian Peepshow*. London: G. Bell.

NORRIS, CHRISTOPHER (1988). *Paul De Man: Deconstruction and the End of Aesthetic Ideology*. London: Routledge.

O'HANLON, MICHAEL (1989). *Reading the Skin: Adornment, Display and Society among the Wahgi*. London: British Museum.

PADMANABHAN, V. T. (1983). *The Gas Chamber on the Chambal: A Study of Job Health Hazards and Environmental Pollution at Nagda, Madhya Pradesh*. Ujjain: People's Union for Civil Liberties.

PAL, P., and DEHEJIA, V. (1986). *From Merchants to Emperors: British Artists and India, 1757–1930*. Ithaca, NY: Cornell University Press.

PAUL, ASIT (ed.) (1983). *Woodcut Prints of Nineteenth-century Calcutta*. Calcutta: Seagull Books.

PINNEY, CHRISTOPHER (1987). 'Time, Work and the Gods: Temporal Strategies and Industrialization in Central India'. Unpublished Ph.D. thesis, London University.

——(1992*a*). 'Future Travel: Anthropology and Cultural Distance in an Age of Virtual Reality; Or, a Past Seen from a Possible Future', *Visual Anthropology Review* 8/1: 38–55.

——(1992*b*). 'The Iconology of Hindu Oleographs: Linear and Mythic Narrative in Popular Indian Art', *Res*, 22: 33–61.

RORTY, RICHARD (1979). *Philosophy and the Mirror of Nature*. Oxford: Blackwell.

ROTMAN, BRIAN (1987). *Signifying Nothing: The Semiotics of Zero*. London: Macmillan.

SPIVAK, GAYATRI (1987). 'Subaltern Studies: Deconstructing Historiography', in her *In Other Worlds: Essays in Cultural Politics*. London: Methuen.

THOMAS, ROSIE (1985). 'Indian Cinema—Pleasures and Popularity', *Screen*, 26/3–4: 116–32.

——(1990). 'Sanctity and Scandal in Mother India', *Quarterly Review of Film and Video*.

TILLOTSON, G. H. R. (1990). 'The Indian Picturesque: Images of India in British Landscape Painting, 1780–1880', in C. A. Bayly (ed.), *The Raj: India and the British, 1600–1947*. London: National Portrait Gallery.

TUAN, YI-FU (1974). *Topophilia: A Study of Environmental Perception, Attitudes and Values*. Englewood Cliffs, NJ: Prentice-Hall.

UBEROI, PATRICIA (1990). 'Feminine Identity and National Ethos in Indian Calendar Art', *Economic and Political Weekly*, 28 April: 41–8.

VENNIYOOR, E. M. J. (1981). *Raja Ravi Varma*. Trivandrum: Government of Kerala.

VITSAXIS, V. G. (1977). *Hindu Epics, Myths, and Legends in Popular Illustrations*. Delhi: Oxford University Press.

WALKER, F. DEAVILLE (1925). *India and Her Peoples*. London: Edinburgh House Press.

WELCH, STUART CARY (1978). *Room for Wonder: Indian Painting during the British Period 1760–1880*. New York: The American Federation of Arts.

5

Landscapes of Liberation and Imprisonment: Towards an Anthropology of the Israeli Landscape

Tom Selwyn

Introduction

For several generations of Israelis, ideas about landscape have supplied some of the most potent metaphors sustaining the will to establish and maintain the modern State of Israel. While, assuredly, these have helped to shape attitudes and policies towards the land itself, their scope has always been more extensive, and the purpose of the present chapter is to consider ideas about landscape in relation to those ideological processes associated with the construction and formation of national identity. Contemporary events in the region lend the exercise a particular political piquancy.

I start out by considering the attitudes towards the land and the landscape of Jewish settlers in Palestine at the beginning of this century. To a large extent these were based on notions of 'liberation' and 'redemption', and I explore the meaning of these terms in this context. Their expression was accompanied by a set of ambivalent ideas about Arabs, and some of these are also examined. The second section of the chapter opens with a discussion of 'nature tours' and other aspects of the work of *The Society for the Protection of Nature in Israel* (*SPNI*). There are three short case studies which illustrate some of the key features of the activities of this important organization. These are complemented by a consideration of how the contemporary landscape has continued to play a part in the development of ideas about the 'bad' (mostly, but not exclusively, Arab) 'Other'. In the final section, I reflect upon the way in which the language of the conservation and defence of 'nature' and the language of the conservation and defence of the State interlock and interpenetrate one another. In the light of this, I raise the question of whether the same landscape which once promised 'liberation' has provided the seeds for a kind of contemporary cognitive 'imprisonment'.

1. Context

Labour Zionism

If, as Shaul Katz's (1985) authoritative article on 'nature tours' (*tiyulim*) in Israel makes clear, Israeli attitudes towards the landscape derive from a number of sources, including nineteenth-century Christian tours to the Holy Land and the German *Wandervogel* movement, the principal source is the collection of ideas and values associated with Labour Zionism. It was these which underscored the decisive years of Jewish settlement in Palestine and the birth of the Israeli State, and it is thus necessary to begin the present discussion with a brief consideration of some of their main aspects.

The term 'Zionism' gives misleading coherence to a disparate set of political ideas and political tendencies which emerged in Europe at the end of the nineteenth and the beginning of the twentieth centuries. It was formally initiated as the Jewish national movement, whose purpose was to create a Jewish national presence in Palestine, by Theodore Herzl at the first Zionist Congress in Basle in 1897. It was not a 'religious' movement, except in the very broad sense that part of the legitimacy for a modern Jewish settlement in Palestine obviously lay in ancient Hebrew culture as described in the Bible. In fact, Zionism was in many ways a modern and distinctively European political movement whose inspiration lay as much, if not more, in the ideas of the Enlightenment than in the ideas of the Bible, and was, moreover, as Walter Lacquer (1972) makes clear, fundamentally secular and unequivocally socialist in orientation.

Thus two of the main sources of inspiration for Zionist thought were Marxism and European socialism, and two of the movement's ideological founders, Bir Borochov and A. D. Gordon, emphasized the central role in Zionism not of a 'religious' but of a socialist redemptive process grounded in physical life and work on the land. For Borochov (1881–1917) Zionism was part of a global class struggle in which Bolsheviks confronted the Russian Tsar while the Zionist movement in Palestine carried the struggle to its Ottoman rulers. For Gordon (1856–1922) the central inspiration of the Zionist transformation of Jewish life in Palestine was to be a new and 'normal' relationship between men, women, nature, and work on the land.

Land, Liberation and Redemption

The stress placed by Borochov on class was echoed by others who emphasized the importance of the liberation of women, the young, and, of course, the individual person. Thus ideas of class, gender, age, and individual 'liberation' were each encompassed within the overarching goal of national 'liberation', and many of these ideas were placed within an idiom of the new relationship settlers were to have with the land and landscape of Palestine.

To illustrate the expression of these notions we may start with the case of women's liberation and refer to the writings of a Russian immigrant to Palestine in the 1920s, Rachel Janaith. Janaith felt herself to be part of a movement of women workers, and wrote of herself and her comrades that they wished to 'break into the naked soil of the wilderness in order to slake their thirst for work on the land and satisfy their passion for a partnership with mother earth'. They were, she continued, 'enslaved by one idea . . . not war, but liberation' (Katznelson-Shazar 1975: 139). Janaith was part of a wave of immigrants from Russia and other parts of Eastern Europe who came to Palestine between 1919 and 1923. Another member of the same cohort contrasted the situation of Jews in general and of Jewish women in particular, in the pogrom-blighted Poland and Ukraine of the time, with those newly migrated to Palestine and wrote of 'The spiritual renaissance of the women in Palestine' as 'part of the spring movement of the entire people . . . having to do with pioneering and with work on the earth, with the rediscovery of the old-new land and the old-new language, with socialist ideals' (ibid. 215). For these two women, then, and many of their fellow immigrants, sex roles in Palestine were to take a new form.

Age roles, exemplified in customary relations of authority by those of the elder over the younger generation, came under critical scrutiny too. The development of Jewish hiking traditions, associated as they were with European youth movements, was part of a Zionist agenda in which 'the revolt of the youth' played a decisive role.[1]

These liberationist sentiments were grounded in the idea that the processes of liberation were also redemptive. Thus, for Borochov, as well as being part of the global class struggle, Zionism stood for 'the redemption of the Jewish people, the renaissance of Jewish culture, and the return to the ancestral homeland'. For Martin Buber (Friedman 1982: 44) national redemption went together with the redemption of the individual person: Jews, in their European ghetto communities, had become spiritually fettered by a life determined by hollow commercialism and mechanically followed tradition. Zionism promised a 'renaissance' by which was meant not so much a 'return but rebirth: a renewal of the whole person' (ibid.).

The Jewish national renaissance was conceived by the early Zionists, therefore, not just as the establishment of a State but something altogether more ambitious. For A. D. Gordon (Mendes-Flohr 1983) 'returning to the land of Israel, Jewry will be transformed into an *Am Adam*; a "human people"'. Buber himself was actively hostile to the idea of nationalism as mere State building. For him (Friedman 1982: 49) the aim was to become established as a people, 'as a new organic order growing out of the natural forms of the life of the people'. And, as he went on to say (Mendes-Flohr 1983: 58), 'the rescue of our people . . . is not aimed at the capitalist exploitation of the region, nor does it serve any imperialistic aims whatsoever—its significance is the productive work of free individuals upon a commonly owned soil'. Gordon (*EZI*: 402) echoed this vision of a redemptive socialist life through work on the land: 'Man must return to nature and give expression to his closeness to nature by physical labour . . . by tilling the land . . . which must become the property not of individuals but of the community as a whole.'

Weinstock (1989: 37) explains the political and social context of the essentially secular and socialist underpinnings of Labour Zionism in terms of the break up of feudalism and advance of capitalism in Eastern Europe at the end of the nineteenth century, which led to 'the disintegration of Jewish trade and cottage industry and the formation of a large Jewish proletariat in Eastern Europe'. Coupled with the anti-Semitism of the Eastern European bourgeoisie it was natural that a Jewish national movement was perceived as part of a wider class struggle which involved Jews as workers.

In summary, then, the ideas of liberation and redemption which the early Zionist settlers brought with them to Palestine included the following elements. First, there was the idea of establishing a direct and working partnership both with the land, and more broadly, with the landscape as a whole, in order to express a human nature that had become cramped and partial in the ghetto. Secondly, there was the comparable notion of cognitively associating land, landscape, and the 'nature' therein with the resurgent nation. Thirdly, subsuming both of these, was a strongly holistic ethic in which the 'whole person' was realized only within the encompassing framework of the nation organized on a basis of collective ownership and collective agricultural work: ideologically, this was not an individualistic revolution, but an essentially socialist one. Fourthly, there was the idea of building and releasing an 'old-new' Jewish culture (to borrow from Herzl) based on farming rather than commerce: rediscovering, in some senses, a way of life which was widely believed to have ended for Jews with the sacking of the Second Temple. Fifthly, there was the idea of the 'pioneer' (*chalutz*) who was associated with a particular and recognizable set of dispositions towards the landscape and who went out into the land and countryside to discover its most intimate pathways, characteristics, and secrets in order to settle on and in it. Radically connected with these dispositions and practices were views about social relations which challenged established ideas and values about hierarchies of sex, age, and (in a more problematic sense) class. Indeed the significance of the term *chalutz* was, precisely, that it combined these elements. Finally, the whole project was conceived of as a redemptive process from which, as Liebman and Don-Yehiya (1984: 49) put it 'God was excised, and nature . . . emphasised'.

Ambivalent Others

How did these ideas relate to the Arabs? From the beginning of the twentieth century there was a view, later to be shared by Ben-Gurion and others, that the Arab *fellah* and the Bedouin were 'authentic residents of the land of the Bible—

perhaps descendants of the biblical patriarchs' (Rubenstein 1984: 53).[2]
Weinstock (1989: 69) records the claim of one of the first *Aliyah* settlers, I.
Belkind, that he felt closer to the *fellahin* than to the Jewish immigrants because
'being the descendants of the Jews of Palestine the *fellahin* have preserved the
ancient Hebrew way of life'. As such they provided models, for European
immigrants unfamiliar with work on the land, of 'true farmers' and of 'people
of the soil'. Given these kind of sentiments, it seems misleading for Liebman
and Don-Yehiya to claim that Arab traditions were never deemed relevant to
the formation of Israel's sacred symbols.

Apart from these linked ideas, of Arabs as being 'like' Patriarchs and 'authentic residents' of the land, there was a view, articulated by Buber and others,
that Palestine should be a bi-national State in which Jews and Arabs could
pursue their different faiths and communal interests side by side. There is even
a glimpse of that possibility in Herzl's *Altneuland*, in which a future Jewish
State is imagined that would provide conditions for mutual economic and
cultural benefit for both communities.

Finally the emphasis placed by the early settlers on 'Hebrew work'—that is,
the idea that Jews should do their own farm work rather than employ Arabs as
farm servants—may well have been primarily about visions of a new Jewish
cultural integrity rather than about how this idea would benefit Arabs, but for
at least for some thinkers the two concerns were closely linked. For Achad
Ha'am (Weinstock 1989: 67) the employment of Arab workers by Jewish immigrants in the first *Aliyah* was not only paternalistic but exploitative, and was
thus to be avoided.

In short, although it is probably true to say that attitudes towards Arabs in
the early days were notable mainly for their absence, there *were* several clearly
recognizable streams of thought amongst both early twentieth-century settlers
and Zionist writers which are relevant to the theme of this paper: that Arabs
looked and behaved like ancient Hebrews and to a certain extent provided
examples for Jewish settlers to follow; that they were different and would
develop their own national feelings alongside Jews; that both they and Jews
would benefit from the establishment of a Jewish State; and that they should
not be exploited as hired labour.

Some of these views persisted into the Independence period. Thus, even
after the 'Arab Revolt' of 1936, which was followed by the 'tower and stockade'
method of establishing Jewish settlements on land farmed by Arabs, and pre-
State military operations, examples of Jews defining themselves within a symbolic arena constructed by both communities may still be found. One
remarkable example of this was the custom amongst soldiers of the *Palmach*,[3]
some of whom also believed in the idea of a bi-national State, to eat pork in
Christian Arab restaurants on Yom Kippur.[4] Here again may be seen an example of Arabs providing conditions for Jews to reject values they associated
with the ghetto. As peasant farmers, Arabs provided an example for Jews to

follow, enabling them to break with the narrowness of diaspora occupations. As pork restaurateurs on Yom Kippur, Arabs provided the possibility of making the symbolic statement that the narrowness of diaspora religious and commensal practices could also be overcome. In both cases Arabs played a key symbolic role.

The purpose of this first section has been to outline some of the ideas which have contributed to the construction of a framework within which a powerful set of attitudes towards, and values about, the landscape have been articulated.

All of this is more or less well-known but it is, none the less, necessary to set it out clearly for the sake of the argument to come. At this point, a cautionary note should be sounded (very loudly, perhaps even with trumpet or sackbut accompaniment). I do not wish to claim that the set of dispositions identified, described, and discussed here is in any sense either exclusive or unchallenged. It may, none the less, be useful to conceive of a more or less 'determining' framework of ideas and values about the landscape and my contention is that the ideas explored here form a part of that framework.

It is now possible to move on to consider some contemporary dispositions towards the landscape. In doing so we may identify the continued presence of many of the ideas outlined above, identify other ideas which are clearly based upon them but are ultimately quite different, and speculate about the reasons for these ideological accretions and transformations. The medium chosen for this explanation is an examination of some of the features of 'nature tourism' as that activity is defined and organized by the SPNI.

2. Landscapes, Nature, and Identity

This section has one overall aim, which is to discuss the role of landscape as key symbol in the construction of Israeli identity. To accomplish this, some aspects of the work of the SPNI, the largest organization in Israel devoted to nature conservation and the promotion of 'nature tours', are considered. This is complemented by a look at two further examples of attitudes to landscape and to 'nature'. The overall argument is that metaphors drawn from landscape constitute part of the moral discourse which is used in the wider distinctions we make between 'us' and 'them', between the 'good us' and the 'bad other'. More precise definition of these metaphors, images and their articulation and con-figuration will emerge shortly.

Nature Tours and Nature Conservation

Elsewhere (Selwyn 1995), I have provided the background to the SPNI. Draw-ing upon the work of Shaul Katz (1985) I described how the SPNI, which was founded in 1953, grew out of several pre-State traditions. These included nineteenth-century touring practices, workers' education movements, the scouting traditions of the *Palmach*, and a way of studying landscape and 'nature' which was based upon both biblical and scientific approaches. Collectively these traditions became known as *Yediat HaAretz*, or 'knowledge of the country'.

With an annual budget of some $15m and a central office in Tel Aviv, the SPNI organizes hundreds of tours for Israelis and a smaller number, with English-speaking guides, for foreigners. Most of the tours take place in the countryside, although there are also regular tours in Jerusalem and other areas of the built environment. Some are for families and these may involve the use of private cars, although all, including these, are based primarily upon walks. Others are for experienced hikers in difficult terrain. Apart from actual walking, tours may involve riding on inflatable tyres down rivers, horseback riding, combinations of walking and swimming, climbing and caving. There are no coach trips at all. Indeed all tours involve a degree of physical exertion.

The most important centres of SPNI activity are its twenty-five field schools which are spread over Israel. These are staffed by trained guides and instructors who are recruited following their army service.[5] The SPNI has approximately 1,000 full-time and part-time staff. The field schools are centres for trips of groups of schoolchildren. Each field school may expect around sixty to seventy such groups per year, each staying for between three and four days. Although part of the cost of each child's visit is met by his or her parents or school, each is also subsidized directly by the Ministry of Education. The significance of this is that between 40 and 60 per cent of the SPNI's budget derives, by way of these subsidies, from central government. This close relationship between government and SPNI is further buttressed by an arrangement with the army to supply a number of serving women soldiers to act as guides.

Tours organized by the SPNI are proclaimed as 'nature tours' and the publicity of the SPNI stresses the primary role of nature in its operations. Furthermore the SPNI guides and participants do spend time studying the flora and fauna of the region. Nevertheless tours are in fact rather more than mere country rambles.[6] The purpose of the tours, particularly those involving children in the field schools, is to experience an area 'holistically', as one guide informant put it. Such 'holism' is arguably the most significant single characteristic of the *Yediat HaAretz* tradition. This involves learning about an area's history, together with aspects of ancient and contemporary social history, local architecture, and so on. As an SPNI administrator put it, this 'weaving together' of all the elements 'results in patriotic feelings' amongst tour members. Such feelings 'start from relating to everything that's in the environment. In this country historical sites and archaeological sites are all part of the scenery. We don't like to say we teach love of country; it just happens by itself; it's fascinating.'

Three Case Studies

A more detailed description of the structure of 'typical' SPNI *tiyulim* (nature tours) appears elsewhere.[7] What is presented in the present chapter consists of three short 'case studies' which provide the ethnographic background to a discussion about how these 'patriotic feelings' are symbolically generated.

The Ashdod Field School: An SPNI Instructor's View   The following account is a description of the Ashdod field centre of the SPNI given to the writer by an informant who is also a member of the SPNI administration:

The field centre is located in the sand dunes near the towns of Ashdod and Ashkelon. Students may learn about the very rich natural life of the area, there being quantities of small sand reptiles (which may be caught in traps at night to be looked at closely in the morning before being released and the tracks of which may be identified and followed) and small desert flowers. Such a profusion of flora and fauna in the middle of the desert may astonish town-dwelling children. The centre is close to the south coast of the Mediterranean and the ancient sea route from Egypt to Mesopotamia. There are the remains of an *effendi*'s house nearby. It is near one of the best-known coastal points where illegal Jewish immigrants landed during the Mandate period, and stories are retold of the nights those immigrants had to pass in the dunes before it was possible to smuggle them into the hinterland. It is also close to the pre-Independence frontier between Egypt and mandated Palestine, and signs of the 1948 war against the Egyptians are readily to hand. Although the centre is in the desert sand dunes, the foothills of the Judean hills are close by and easily visible. Finally there are the two modern port cities of Ashdod and Ashkelon, the latter being built on the site of the biblical town of that name. Children and other visitors to the field school invariably spend much of their time outside during both the day and the night. There are lots of campfire and story-telling sessions for them.

In speaking about his own involvement as a youth leader for the SPNI my informant added:

There are two points about being a group instructor which make me sure that I am part of a good thing. The first is the experience at night: each group of fifteen schoolchildren sits around a fire making food, talking, and singing. It's dark and only the fires are visible. There is no shouting. The second is the experience of the morning. Each group goes its own way with its own guide. Each follows its own individual trail, although they will all meet again in the night camp. All this is more beautiful than all those beautiful Italian people who walk in the Dolomites. They dress well, with attractive boots, socks, and climbing shorts. But all that is only style. Unlike our youngsters they are not a group.

The instructor's descriptions helps us pick out several themes which not only underscore the work of the SPNI at the Ashdod centre, but are also, more generally, characteristic of their mode of tour organization. Before following up his reference to the Dolomites we may pause briefly to suggest what these are. First, considerable effort is made to convey a sense of historical continuity:

students are conducted along a historical trajectory from pre-biblical and biblical times to the present via strategic points of Israeli history, notably the Independence War, illegal immigration, and modern settlements. Clearly this is a 'selective' narrative—with some possible historical aspects (disruption to local Arab populations in the course of recent history, for example) being quite emphatically 'selected out'.

Here it is worth re-emphasizing several characteristics of the SPNI: it enjoys a symbiotic relationship with the Ministry of Education (deriving much of its budget from the Ministry); its guides are recent army graduates; *Yediat HaAretz* courses are an integral part of army training; qualities expected of guides include an ability to be personable and charismatic in their leadership and their encouragement of the sense of historical continuity intentionally engendered by the tours. In the light of all these features, the claim that the 'weaving together' of all the elements surrounding the field school 'just happens' seems open to question. Arguably, it is accomplished with a great deal of help from authorities located at various central departments of State.

Secondly, there are the themes of collectively shared physical, emotional, and intellectual experience in nature. Schoolchildren learn their Israeli history while they are, literally, in direct contact with the sand—as they walk in the dunes, play, sit and sing in them, sleep and eat in them, and scour them for wild animals and plants. In this way natural and social history appear closely and necessarily interlinked. Indeed they appear to be extensions of each other. These features will be picked up and considered again towards the conclusion of this chapter.

Thirdly, there is the theme of the representation of the Arabs. The three 'appearances', or non-appearances, they make are as (*a*) Egyptian soldiers, (*b*) *effendi*s, landlords, and arguably, (*c*) as unremarked presences in the Judean hills. But, in the sense that each of these bears little relation to more 'everyday' figures, such as carpenters, crane drivers, or bricklayers, all of whom commute daily up and down the Gaza–Tel Aviv motorway which runs near the Ashdod field school, one might say that attention is drawn to the presence and reality of the Arabs in the area paraliptically—by omitting reference to them.

Dolomites, Himalayas, and Cans of Beer   Now we may usefully follow the SPNI administrator's reference to the Dolomites. One of the ways in which SPNI guides habitually define the purpose and character of Israeli nature travel is to contrast it with the style of other nations' modes of travel. One SPNI informant compared the styles of European, American, and Indian mountain walking with that of Israelis as follows. An SPNI party recently went walking in the Dolomites. They were reported to be amazed to see Italians, Germans, and Austrians crossing the mountains *all by themselves*. The Europeans were

For an unforgettable experience, put on your hat and walking shoes and come
see, breathe and touch 625 acres of restored Biblical ecology.

Come touch the Bible at

Neot Kedumim

The only Biblical Landscape Reserve in the world

Easy walking English tours: Monday, Thursday at 1:30 p.m., Friday at 9:30 a.m.
Also see the Tuesday tour in the SPNI "Weekly Tours" section.

Fɪɢ. 5.1. Advertisement from an S.P.N.I. brochure: the landscape of the Book.

said to love walking, quite silently, for kilometres: walking just for walking's
sake. Americans share some of these characteristics and have others too. As my
informant put it:

Americans climb a mountain peak without looking at anything . . . they don't look at a
single plant . . . they don't look at the view . . . they don't want to recognize or identify

anything at all. All they want to do is reach the top, say 'cheers', drink their beer, climb down the mountain, and then write in their notebook, 'I was at the peak of the mountain on such and such date'.

On a trip to the Himalayas, another Israeli group observed what happened to an Indian party of freelance walkers who wished to offer encouragement and moral support to a state-sponsored national team of climbers about to climb a hitherto unconquered mountain peak. Some of the freelance party were suffering from exposure. Despite this they were denied access, by Indian guards, to the base camp of the government climbers.

These vignettes are instructive because they illustrate attitudes to significant 'others' against which 'we' of the SPNI define 'ourselves'. The travellers in the Dolomites come straight out of Barthes's (1972) 'Blue Guide': earnest individualists to a person. The Americans have no culture other than one based on raw enterprise and achievement, and the Indians are hopelessly antisocial. For 'us', however, walking in nature is at once determined by and determines a culture based upon social inclusiveness and collective group experience.

These anecdotes lead into the third case study based upon events at a collective *bar-mitzva* at a politically left-wing kibbutz in the summer of 1986. One purpose of this excursion into a kibbutz is to raise another clearly very significant locus for the production and articulation of ideas and values about the landscape. In any subsequent considerations of the role of the landscape in Israeli nationalist thinking, it might be useful to focus more particularly on the institution of the kibbutz itself, although in my view the SPNI actually provides a richer seam of ideas about the landscape than does the kibbutz.

The Rose and the Androgyne   The part of the celebrations which will be described here is the theatrical performance which took place on the final day of the ceremony. Before describing the performance itself, however, the role of the SPNI needs explaining. All children going through the ceremony worked for the SPNI voluntarily for several weeks before the ceremony. Tasks included trimming hedges, tending road verges, collecting rubbish, and generally clearing up the countryside around the kibbutz. It is a good example of the way in which in addition to the organization of tours and its conservation campaigns the SPNI also appears as an organization which is fully 'integrated', as it were, into the daily lives of people in kibbutzim and other settlements in the country.

Following the ceremony itself a play was performed in the kibbutz theatre. It was written by those who managed the children's house and was performed by the kibbutz children. The set consisted of wood panels on which were painted flowers, plants, fields, and mountains. The plot ran as follows.

The opening scene was 'long ago'. The kibbutz people were shown looking after their farms and milking their cows. A religious figure in black, with white *tsitziyot* (the white stringlike adornments worn by religious Jews), stood, bowing and beaming, on one side of the stage. The scene suggested harmony.

Suddenly and brutally the composure of this rural idyll was broken up. The panels were reversed and were revealed as painted with the garish decorations of a discothèque. Lights flashed and disco music flooded the auditorium. All the child actors changed into latex trousers, florid blouses, and dark glasses. They danced while a portrait of Michael Jackson was hoisted on to centre stage. At one point two 'parents' were shown on one side of the stage and a child dancer approached them saying 'What use are your books to us now? Come and join us.' The parents stayed seated. Then, as others danced, one child after another appeared carrying school books. Each was stopped by the disco dancers and persuaded to give up their books in favour of the dance. The last child, who carried a pink rose in his hand, was not so easily dissuaded, however, and he was placed on an operating table by the dancers, some of whom turned into surgeons. They claimed he was suffering from 'too much heart'. He was said to have 'too many principles'. As they held up the rose before tossing it away they said he had 'too much love of country'.

As the incision was made the stage went dark and to its right a platform raised on scaffolding materialized on which sat a figure who claimed to be the grandfather of the children. Clouds of white smoke swirled around the platform. He spoke of the importance of the old values and of the danger of the new ones symbolized by the disco-dancers. The stage was then transformed back once more into the original one. The dancers changed back into their agricultural clothes and rustic charm was restored. This was the end of the formal play but, once the house-lights had gone up, the real parents of the child actors mounted the stage to embrace their offspring and were applauded by the audience. Each child was then presented with a model sickle and a Bible by the 'mother' of the children's house.

The performance demonstrated the central significance of the landscape as a metaphor, for this is clearly a play about the moral context in which Israeli values are forged in a contemporary world dominated by European and American popular culture. It also illustrates the way a break with the essentially secular Zionist tradition of this kibbutz found symbolic expression in the form of the religious figure who appears at the start of the play. Furthermore the central role of parental authority suggests another break. This time it is with the egalitarianism of early Zionism which, as we have seen, stressed the emancipation of youth. Finally, we may perhaps suggest that the appearance of Michael Jackson, rather than, say, Bono, may reflect a preoccupation with boundaries, a preoccupation which is becoming more, rather than less, pronounced. From such a cultural perspective the very last role model needed is an androgyne.

Black Goats, Unholy Land, and Bad Others

So far in this part of the chapter several ways have been described in which landscape metaphors have been used to generate feelings of national solidarity. A sharper edge to these accounts may be fashioned by concentrating on what we might term the 'bad other'. It is against this 'other' that we locate ourselves.

What follows, then, comprises two expressions of this 'bad other' inhabiting his, or its, 'unholy land'. The first comes from the writings of an influential Christian (yet 'Zionist') agronomist, the second from the controversial activities of the so-called 'Green Patrols'.

By the end of the Second World War there was intense superpower rivalry for influence in Palestine. Amongst the first nations to recognize the new Israeli State in 1948 was the Soviet Union. The British Mandate was coming to an end and Israeli independence was on the horizon. In 1944 Lowdermilk's *Palestine: Land of Promise* appeared. Its author was a Christian American soil conservationist, who, largely as a result of his radio broadcasts, had built up a reputation for his views on the use of land and water resources in the area. In the *Encyclopedia of Zionism and Israel* Lowdermilk takes his place alongside other Zionist notables. The *Encyclopedia* records that his most enduring claim to fame was his work in promoting the idea of a Jordan River Authority which would, Lowdermilk argued, provide substantial irrigation opportunities for a new Israeli State. Lowdermilk (1944: 53) started from the premiss that:

During the past 1,200 years the lands of the Near East have been gradually wasting away; its cities and works have fallen into neglect and ruin; its peoples also slipped backwards into a state of utter decline,

and that

The people of Palestine have been plunged into degrading poverty by wars, exploitation and soil erosion. Nowhere has the interrelation between the deterioration of a land and the degradation of its people been so clear as in Palestine.

The two agencies most responsible for this state of affairs, in Lowdermilk's view, are the Bedouin and the Turks. The solution lies categorically with Jewish agriculture. As far as the Bedouin are concerned he compares

groups of black and brown goat-hair tents belonging to semi-nomads, near a patch cultivation of grain that could not have yielded more than five bushels to the acre. This was the most primitive sort of life . . .

with

a modern Jewish dwelling, just over the road, surrounded by a well-tilled orange orchard, its waxy deep-green leaves dotted with white fragrant blossoms and illuminated with ripening fruit. (ibid. 62)

Lowdermilk asserts that the very 'darkest time' in Near Eastern history was the period of the Turkish Empire between 1517–1918. Actively in league with corrupt local tax-collecting *effendis* as well as with powerful Bedouin chiefs, the Turks effectively presided over a population who were 'barbarous, inactive and despondent and in constant fear that the fruits of their labour would suddenly be reaped by any of the oppressing or marauding chiefs who have the strongest hand at the moment' (ibid. 61). This language is remarkably similar to that used by local agents of another imperial power in another place and one cannot help wondering whether Walter Lowdermilk's bedtime reading consisted of the early nineteenth-century history of the East India Company.

All of this fitted a more general world picture in which the 'Nazi-Fascist-Japanese group were fighting to make the individual serve the state . . . forcing conquered peoples into vast sweat shops to work for their masters' (ibid. 21). And so on. Near the beginning of the book, Lowdermilk (p. 24) quotes from Deuteronomy 8: 7–9:

Behold the Lord thy God giveth thee a good land, a land of water brooks and fountains that spring out of the valleys and depths, a land of wheat and barley, of vines, figs and pomegranates, of olive oil and honey, a land in which . . . thou shalt lack nothing . . .

Following which Lowdermilk composed his own 'Eleventh Commandment':

Thou shalt inherit the holy earth as a faithful steward, conserving its resources and productivity . . . thou shalt safeguard thy fields from soil erosion, thy living waters from drying up, thy forests from deforestation, and protect thy hills from overgrazing by the herds. If any shall fail in this stewardship . . . they shall live in poverty . . . or perish from off the face of the earth.

This Eleventh Commandment was first broadcast on Jerusalem Radio in June 1939.

Having described the benefit to land and people of the work of Jewish settlement since the outset of the century, Lowdermilk (p. 26) concluded that 'Arab rule in Palestine would . . . put an abrupt end to the reclamation work now being carried on so splendidly. Erosion would begin to have its way again . . . and goats would make short work of the young forests'.

The three remarkable aspects of all this are as follows. First, there is the uncompromising nature of the language. Bedouin, Arabs, and Turks are energetically cast into utter darkness. Secondly, there is the enthusiastic conjoining of one religious tradition with morally and practically beneficial agricultural practices while another religious tradition is linked to positively malevolent agricultural practices. Thirdly, there is the apparent certainty about the natural partnership between Hebrew agriculture and American strategic interests. In this connection, it may be remembered that, with or without military advisors, the Soviet Union was ferrying arms to Tel Aviv via Czechoslovakia from 1945, that the Jewish Agency was allowed to open an office in Moscow, and that

Gromyko had spoken of the legitimate rights of Jews to their own State (Weinstock 1989: 264).

Lowdermilk's fulminations were to find echoes much later in the activities of the 'Green Patrols'. These were set up in the early 1970s by the Agriculture Minister, Ariel Sharon, as a branch of the Nature Reserves Authority, a government department which (following intense lobbying by the SPNI) had been set up in 1965 and given the task of organizing and protecting nature reserves. The particular function of the patrols was to protect kibbutzim, moshavim, and other settlements from the grazing of the black goat.

In 1975 the Black Goat Law was passed. Bedouin were allowed to graze goats only in particular areas and the patrols were given powers to prosecute goat-owners who allowed their herds to stray into protected areas. To give some idea of the way the patrols went about their work, it may be sufficient merely to quote from an informant working as a guide for a kibbutz-based nature tour organization: 'The official purpose of the drive by the government to settle the Bedouin is to give them better facilities. I consider this a gross lie. The main purpose is that we have to confiscate as much land as possible and the Bedouin sense this. The 'Green Patrols' are there to carry out this policy.' According to another informant from the SPNI, the effect upon Israeli public opinion of the Black Goat Law, of the army takeover of much of the Negev desert, and of the publicity associated with the work of the patrols who have been involved in a stream of evictions of Bedouin from their desert grazing land, was to propagate the notion that the Bedouin constitute a positive danger to Israeli agriculture and its landscape. A well-known aerial photograph from NASA of the landscape either side of the Egyptian–Israeli frontier in Sinai is enthusiastically displayed in nature conservation circles. This is said to 'prove' that the desert on the Egyptian side, where black goats and Bedouin roam fairly freely, is barren, while the desert on the Israeli side is green.

It is time to sum up this second section. I have tried to show how the landscape is used in various ways to provide a metaphorical setting for defining not only 'us' and 'our' values but also the 'bad other'. The argument began from the claim that one influential strand of opinion about landscape, land, and nature in contemporary Israel stems from the ideas and values associated with Labour Zionism which were described in the first section. These were developed during the course of the Independence movement—in the traditions of the *Palmach* in particular—and find expression today in, for example, the touring practices of organizations such as the SPNI and in the *bar-mitzva* play at the kibbutz.

At the core of the set of dispositions I have described lies an association between activity on, and attitudes towards, the land (as manifested in agricultural practices and the social organization associated with these) and the landscape (as manifested in touring practices, and so forth) and the construction of national identity. I have tried to describe an ideological framework in which the symbols of the former two find their way into the latter—and back again. For example, the activities of young people exploring the natural life around an SPNI field school, or tidying up the countryside around their kibbutz as part of their *bar-mitzva* celebrations, are also symbols which help define a moral order in the centre of which lies a vision of a relationship between people and nature which is at once scientific, physically experienced, and orderly. But the images and metaphors grounded in activities on, and representations of, land and landscape help define not only the 'good us' but also the 'bad other'. The evidence presented here suggests that this latter is an amalgam of the following: individualism (associated with the European walkers), materialism (linked to the American climbers), secularism (of Western youth), the agriculturally irresponsible and unproductive (associated with Arabs in general and Bedouin in particular), and the undemocratic and exploitative (again linked to Arabs and Turks). In short, if 'they' are individualistic, materialistic, undemocratic, exploitative, irresponsible, secular (or alternatively too religious), unproductive, and so on, 'we' appear as co-operative, modest, as respecters of parents and tradition—including agricultural and religious traditions—as organized and productive, and as responsible guardians of land and landscape.

3. In Defence of Nature and the State: Landscape as Political Myth

In this final section the aim is to work towards a propositional conclusion which will incorporate the argument of the chapter as a whole. We may conveniently start with the name of the SPNI itself: *Chevra LeHaganat HaTeva* (*hagana* means defence). Recalling that the pre-Independence precursor of the Israeli Defence Forces (IDF) was known as the *Hagana*, the question arises as to whether we can say anything about the relation between the defence of nature—including landscape—and defence of the State. We may begin with a simpler question: why does Israeli 'nature' and landscape need defending? And what does it need defending from?

The first sort of answer is a biological and scientific one. According to one of the founders of the SPNI, Asaria Alon,[8] few regions in the world have a richer natural history than Israel: the region witnessed the origin of scores of cultigens, including wheat, barley, radishes, carrots, and so on and it is presently home to at least 2,500 species of plants, at least 150 of which are not found anywhere else. The first reason for the existence of the SPNI thus lies in the scientific, especially the pharmaceutical, importance of these and similar facts.

In Alon's view the threats to all this 'natural richness' come from several quarters. To start with there are modern farming methods dependent as these are on heavy machinery. Such methods are associated with the modern (Jewish) agriculture which came to replace Arab agriculture in the early days of the State. This was one of the reasons the SPNI came into existence in the first place. Then there are those people, ordinary enough and found in every country, who simply do not look after the countryside; those who go on picnics and leave rubbish or pick wild flowers, for example. Finally there are the Bedouin and their black goats. The problems are thus both modern and traditional (and, according to Alon, it would be quite mistaken to assume that modern Arab agriculture is necessarily always more environmentally friendly than modern Jewish agriculture).

Beyond these sorts of concerns, however, Alon has another set of a different kind. According to him the importance of defending the land and the landscape derives from the fact that the very existence of Hebrew culture, language, and literature, especially the Bible, simply cannot be understood without reference to the landscape in which it is set. 'You can't understand the culture or language if you don't connect them with the nature of this country . . . keeping the landscape, animals and plants . . . means also keeping the Hebrew culture.'

This is a line of thought which is espoused enthusiastically by Rehevam Ze'evi, the Curator of the Museum of Israel, founder of the *Moledet* (Homeland) Party and, for a period of time, Minister Without Portfolio in the Israeli Cabinet. One of Ze'evi's best known achievements during the 1980s was to translate into Hebrew, edit (adding period engravings), and publish in popular form a series of nineteenth-century accounts of journeys to the Holy Land by European Christian travellers and pilgrims. An example is the Italian traveller Pierotti's *Customs and Traditions of Palestine: Illustrating the Manners of the Ancient Hebrews*. According to Ze'evi what Pierotti wanted to show was that 'everything in the villages is based on the Bible'. Ze'evi starts from the proposition that 'What the Arabs do is to demonstrate exactly our forefathers' way of life and traditions.'

For Ze'evi, nineteenth-century accounts, many from the Palestine Exploration Fund (PEF), are valuable because they were written by people who were at the same time romantic, Bible-loving, and empire-building. They (especially the British) were able to imagine themselves in a biblical landscape while paying considerable attention to finding out place-names and making maps. But Ze'evi also has what is probably an accurate image of nineteenth-century British travellers 'coming with their hats, standing under their umbrellas, asking the Arabs about names of places'. They were, consequently, in some respects, gullible, and many of the names they recorded in their accounts were clearly wrong. Some names were the result of Arab jokes. Ze'evi cites the numerous examples of places marked on British maps with the name *Mush Aref*, Arabic for 'I don't know'. Other names were 'wrong' in a different sense. Examples of these include Rumana, Rechebe, and Abde; all Arabized versions of the biblical settlements of Ramon, Rehovot, and Ovdat. In short, apart from removing the jokes, Ze'evi's editions 'correct' the place-names by using the Arabic names to 'get back' to the 'real' biblical names.

Here the landscape appears as a sort of stage-set enabling the biblical landscape to be experienced by contemporary Israeli travellers, whether clients of the SPNI or readers of Ze'evi's recycled travelogues. The political function of all this is well expressed by two senior administrators of the SPNI. For the first, nature touring serves the fundamental function of uniting a potentially divided society. He sees Israel as being split between orthodox and non-orthodox Jews, between Ashkenazim and Sephardim, between the political left and right, and so forth. The *only* common factor they have is a properly organized landscape. This is the only arena in which Jews from all these divisions, as well as others from abroad, can be guaranteed to express their common nationality. The second informant expresses essentially the same view more precisely. He refers back to the time in the early 1970s when the Ministry of Education acknowledged the importance of the SPNI's touring activities for Israeli schoolchildren. A senior SPNI administrator recalls the context—the shelling of northern settlements by the PLO, actual incursions by PLO fighters into Israel, the Black Panther movement of disenchanted Sephardi Jews in the early 1970s, the subsequent desertion of these from the Labour Party, a growing awareness of the relative poverty and the social problems in the 'development towns', populated in the main by Eastern Jews. According to my informant the role of the SPNI towards the population of the 'development towns' was to make them feel part of the mainstream of Israeli culture. He puts it thus: 'The Ministry of Education realized they had to invest in these people; otherwise they would run away. There was a terrible sense of insecurity and a strong feeling that something had to be done.' These views go some way towards understanding why the Israeli landscape is felt to need defending. A line of thought of one of the SPNI informants cited above brings us closer to answering the question about what it has to be defended from:

The nation symbolized by the landscape must be defended because without it people would leave themselves open to cultural and religious *contamination*. If that happens nothing but imminent destruction can follow. The contamination may derive both from the influences of an Arab population which will outnumber the Jewish one in a matter of years and from the increasing stocks of glitzy American consumer goods in Tel-Aviv department stores [emphasis mine].

Conservation of the landscape, and intimate contact with it, thus appears as the surest way of protecting the nation as a whole, both from internal schisms and external influences and threats. In that sense the Israeli government is right to recognize the part played by the SPNI—and the Israeli landscape it defends—in the war effort. To a significant degree, defending nature is an inseparable part of defending the State: a case of defending a metaphor with an army.

We have clearly worked our way back to a point which resonates with the words of two of our forefathers (Fortes and Evans-Pritchard 1970):

Members of an African Society feel their unity and perceive their common interests in symbols, and it is their attachment to these symbols which more than anything else gives their society cohesion and persistence. In the form of myths, fictions, dogmas, ritual, sacred places . . . these symbols represent the unity and exclusiveness of the groups which respect them. They are regarded, however, not as mere symbols, but as final values in themselves.

The social system is, as it were, removed to a mystical plane, where it figures as a system of sacred values beyond criticism or revision.

Conclusion

Using evidence of various kinds—from the writings of early settlers to the writings and broadcasts of Walter Lowdermilk, from the activities of the SPNI to the recycled accounts of the 'Holy Land' by members of the PEF[9]—the argument of this chapter has been that key cultural and political dispositions, and the changes that these have undergone throughout this century, show up clearly in the way that Israelis have read their landscape.

In the early days of Jewish settlement in Palestine the landscape served as a strategic metaphor in a political process in which the renaissance of Jewish culture and nationhood was understood to be not merely inseparable from but actually defined by, first, the establishment of a socialist movement, and, secondly, by the rejection of traditional religious and other values associated with European ghetto life. All this was symbolized by co-operative work on the land and knowledge of the landscape through extensive travel. Arab agriculturalists, when thought about at all, may have been perceived romantically as being in some way like ancient Hebrew farmers, but they were also regarded pragmatically with some admiration as 'sons of the soil'. To this extent they were models of the very type of knowledgeable farmer which the immigrants themselves aspired to be. Perhaps the principal theme of the life of the new immigrants, as this was reflected in their relationship to the land and landscape, was their attempt to lead lives which were definitively secular—in which, as Liebman and Don Yehiya put it—'the ultimate authority . . . was transferred . . . from God to society' (1983: 5).

Ironic therefore that at the end of the twentieth century the landscape seems to have become one of the means of re-establishing that link with God which was severed at the beginning of the century. Although the work of the SPNI and other agencies and institutions involved with nature conservation and 'nature tourism' still retain features which derive from their socialist origins, the landscape has now become a strategic metaphor in the reconstitution of the very values from which the early settlers attempted to liberate themselves.

The conceptual and perceptual shifts needed to advance any peace process in the region would seem inevitably to entail wide-ranging reflection by all concerned on the way that the landscape is used metaphorically there. (The events in Hebron of February/March 1994 may be thought to underline this point). As far as Israel itself is concerned such reflection will, also necessarily, take place within a context circumscribed by the fact that its landscape continues to be used (with increasing passion by some) to construct myths in which 'we' appear as its defenders against several different kinds of people and forces who would seem to threaten it and, by so doing, threaten us too.

Notes

The ideas for this chapter derived in the first place from field experience, gained while I was a member of the Department of Sociology and Anthropology at the University of Tel Aviv, 1982–5, and in subsequent visits to Israel, participating in some thirty tours organized by the SPNI, with Hebrew and English-speaking guides. In addition to this, I held extensive interviews with other tourists on these tours as well as with SPNI tour guides and administrators. Some of the interviews with these have been recorded on tape (some forty hours or so) and some as handwritten accounts. I owe debts of gratitude to many SPNI personnel and would like, in particular, to thank Asaria Alon, Amir Eidelman, Gadi Sternbach, Avner Goren, Danny Rabinowitz, Joseph Shadur, Amnon Nir, and Nissim Kedem.

1. Joseph Shadur, former editor of the English-language edition of the SPNI newsletter; personal communication.
2. Incidentally, and ironically, the historian Nathan Weinstock fields a considerable amount of evidence to suggest that Palestinian Arabs of today are, to a greater or lesser extent, the descendants of intermarriages between the ethnically diverse population of the region and Jews left over as peasants in Palestine at the end of the Byzantine era in the sixth century.
3. The élite commando unit of the pre-Independence Israeli armed forces.
4. Tuvia Gelblum: personal communication.
5. Since advertisements for SPNI positions always specify that applicants should have done army service, this effectively means that the majority of Arabs are barred from holding positions in the SPNI.
6. This is not to say that organizations such as the English Ramblers' Association are in the business of organizing *mere* rambles in nature. One only needs to consult recent editions of the Ramblers' monthly journal to be aware that such walks are part of a long tradition of English radicalism closely associated with ideas about rights of public access to land and the privatization of water, for example.
7. Selwyn 1995.
8. Personal communication.

9. One of the ironies of the use by Rehevam Ze'evi of PEF writings (especially if seen as being coupled with the influence of Lowdermilk) is that Christian visions of what might constitute a 'Holy Land' can be seen to be playing a substantial role in the reconstitution of biblical political rhetoric in contemporary Israel.

References

BARTHES, R. (1972). *Mythologies*. London: Jonathan Cape.

Encyclopedia of Zionism and Israel (EZI) (1971). New York: Herzl Press/McGraw-Hill.

FORTES, M., and EVANS-PRITCHARD, E. E. (1970). *African Political Systems*. Oxford: Oxford University Press.

FRIEDMAN, M. (1982). *Martin Buber's Life and Work*. London: Search Press.

KATZ, S. (1985). 'The Israeli Teacher-Guide', *Annals of Tourism Research*, 12: 14–17.

KATZNELSON-SHAZAR, R. (ed.) (1975 [1932]). *The Plough Women*. New York: Herzl Press.

LACQUER, W. (1972). *A History of Zionism*. New York: Schocken.

LIEBMAN, C. S., and DON-YEHIYA, E. (1983). *Civil Religion in Israel*. Berkeley, Calif.: University of California Press.

——(1984). *Religion and Politics in Israel*. Bloomington, Ind.: Indiana University Press.

LOWDERMILK, W. C. (1944). *Palestine: Land of Promise*. London: Gollancz.

MENDES-FLOHR, P. R. (1983). *A Land of Two Peoples: Martin Buber on Jews and Arabs*. New York: Oxford University Press.

RUBENSTEIN, A. (1984). *The Zionist Dream Revisited*. New York: Schocken.

SELWYN, T. (1995). 'Atmospheric Notes from the Fields', in his *The Tourist Image: Myths and Myth-Making in Tourism*. London: John Wiley.

WEINSTOCK, N. (1989). *Zionism: False Messiah*. London: Pluto.

6

Chiefly and Shamanist Landscapes in Mongolia

=====

CAROLINE HUMPHREY

The Western idea of 'the landscape' arises from objectification and is closely related to practices such as painting, map-making, song, and poetry. The secular, appreciative gaze is certainly not unknown among the Mongols. But it was historically intermittent and was inspired by non-Mongol kinds of representation, such as Manchu maps, Chinese and Russian landscape painting, or the 'genre' scenes in Tibetan religious paintings. In Mongolian culture itself landscapes are more in the nature of practices designed to have results: it is not contemplation of the land (*gazar*) that is important but interaction with it, as something with energies far greater than the human. The Mongols do not take over any terrain in the vicinity and transform it into something that is their own. Instead, they move within a space and environment where some kind of pastoral life is possible and 'in-habit' it. That is to say, they let it pervade them and their herds, influencing where they settle, when they move, and what kinds of animals they keep. However, this is not a pre-reflective or spontaneous existence, but one recognizing human choice and agencies, which are conceived as interrelated with and subordinate to the agencies attributed to entities in the land. Thus the Mongols choose to avoid forests and narrow ravines, preferring wide-open steppes, where the land is before them in a limitless expanse. But the most featureless plain has its gentle curves, or bushes, or marshy patches, and even such entities are credited with powers of some kind. I shall use the word 'landscape' to designate the ways in which these energies are envisaged, or, to put this another way, to describe the concepts by which social agencies constitute the physical world.

There are at least two ways of being in the landscape, which are simultaneous possibilities for any Mongol group. Each combines its own sense of place with spatial awareness.[1] The extent to which either of these emerged in history is a function of complex political, economic, and religious interrelationships, and this chapter, which aims to provide an overview of a vast region (see map) in both time and space, will be able to provide only schematic explanations of the processes involved.

The two landscapes engage different notions of energies-in-nature and the social agencies by which such powers may be harnessed to human benefit. One is that of the chief or ruler, and the other is that of the shaman. Both chiefs and

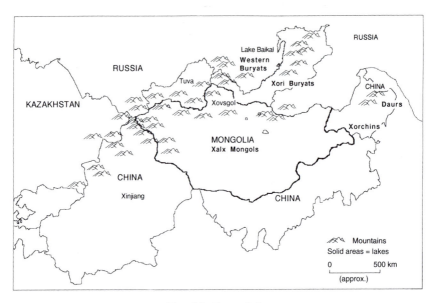

FIG. 6.1. Inner Asia.

shamans 'have power', but such powers should not be seen as if they were metaphorical substances somehow 'gained' or acquired by a pre-existing subject. Rather, they emerge by the exercise of different forms of agency which are socially constituted in basically asymmetrical ways. Very briefly, chiefly agency derives from patrilines of males which constantly reconstitute themselves as 'the same' through generations, and they are successful in so far as they can prevail upon the powers in the land, which are often anthropomorphized as kings and warriors, to produce fertility, health, and prosperity among people and livestock. Shamanist agency, on the other hand, acknowledges and celebrates difference. Shamanic legitimation derives directly from the ability to manifest in inspirational performances the energies perceived in 'nature' (*baigal*, 'what is', an idea of nature which is not separate from but includes human beings). The energies in the land are not envisaged as ranks of similar male spirits but as the myriad abilities of beings in the world: the ability of a fish to live under water, of an evergreen tree to flourish through the winter, or of a falcon to swoop on a virtually invisible prey. Shamans also use ideas of anthropomorphic spirits which are the 'souls' of the deceased, but these tend to dissolve with time into the nameless energies of particular beings or sites, a process which will be described later in this chapter. The more various the abilities (*chadal*) which can be cumulated magically in the shaman the better.

Common to both views is the idea that entities in nature have their own 'majesty' (*sur*) or effectiveness (*chadal*) which does not derive from human spirits but is simply there. This idea is often the first to be expressed when Mongols talk about the land and is perhaps a more fundamental Mongolian attitude than the idea of spirits. Power relationships between natural entities are used as explanations of the visible features of the land. In northern Mongolia the play of fierce sun and shade has resulted in a relief of bare south-facing slopes and forested north-facing ones, a dappled pattern stretching as far as the eye can see. The flat, sandy Gobi region, on the other hand, is dotted here and there with tamarisk bushes.

According to Arash there was once a war between the tamarisk or *jagha* and a tree called *khara modo*. The name means black-wood, but it turns yellow in winter. Perhaps it is a juniper. Arash did not know what was the cause of the war, but the tamarisk won and remained in possession of the sands. The black-wood ran away, and to this day is found only on the northern sides of mountains in Outer Mongolia. A single tree may stand on the crest, or several may look over the ridge, but they never come further. (Lattimore 1942: 207)

It seems that the black-wood, when it burns, crackles and throws off sparks. But Arash told Lattimore that this crackling and spitting stops if you put some of the 'victorious' tamarisk on a black-wood fire; the black-wood will be frightened and keep quiet (ibid.).

The human relation to natural entities is analogous: their unpredictable energies and beneficial powers can be tamed by ritualized actions. People have their own relationships with particular mountains, cliffs, or trees[2] which they feel to be especially influential in their lives. A Mongolian friend told me that when he was travelling and unable to make offerings to 'his' mountain, he nevertheless called upon it in case it should be angered by his neglect: 'My mountain (*minii uul*), please help me! I haven't forgotten you, my mountain, I have just had to go away for a necessary reason.' Such an individual relation with a mountain is documented from as long ago as the thirteenth century,[3] but this chapter will be concerned with the social aspect of this attitude. Some physical objects are worshipped[4] only by a few people, some by whole communities, and a few by virtually all Mongols (Abayeva 1992). It will be suggested here that even a family ritual of worship partakes of a 'view' with regard to the natural object. The 'family' may constitute itself as a subsection of a patrilineage or as the group defended by a shaman, and in these cases two alternative landscapes present worlds in which there are different objects of worship. Both chiefs and shamans engage with the land on behalf of social groups. Characteristically the chiefly social group does not include women, whereas the shamanic one does.

Chiefs and Shamans: Background to a Latent Conflict

The points of view, which create their own landscapes, are just that. It is important to note that they are not in principle identified with 'societies'. Thus it would be incorrect to say of some Mongol group that they 'are shamanists' as though that is all that needs to be said. All groups have both chiefs and shamans, as well as a number of other socio-cultural categories of people with 'supernatural'[5] abilities and their own views on the world (midwives, smiths, bone-setters, diviners, hunters, astrologers, and others). This chapter singles out the landscapes of chiefs and shamans because the views of these two categories are engaged in large-scale rituals which involve all members of the local group, whereas midwives, bonesetters, etc. have a more restricted realm of practice. But as regards any given person the chiefly and shamanist views are not exclusive. To take the early twentieth-century Buryat Mongols as an example: a shaman as a lay person (not a shaman) would attend a ritual directed by a chief, just as a chief would often find occasion to be present as a patient or client at a shaman's ritual. Today the ritual calendar of Buryat collective farmers comprises a series of both kinds of ritual, and lay people attend both (Abayeva 1992).

It is because chiefly and shamanic rituals present different views on the world, and people in general can find one or the other more compelling, that there is a latent tension between them. There is an important asymmetry here, in that chiefs have historically aspired to global power in society, whereas shamans do not have such aims and in any case are limited by the face-to-face and oral nature of their constituencies. Chiefs in the process of military expansion repressed shamans in an attempt to obliterate alternative kinds of agency (see Humphrey 1994). On the other hand, when native political organization came under threat and was generally seen as weak and unsuccessful, the people might turn their allegiance to shamans. This happened, for example, when Russian peasant settlers backed by aggressive Cossacks encroached on Western Buryat lands in the nineteenth century, causing widespread poverty, brigandage, and a sense of humiliation. With the collapse of the Soviet Union, and the consequent weakness of the Mongolian government, there has also been a resurgence of shamanism in north and western Mongolia.

Having recourse to a shaman often had direct influence on use of the land. From 1865 to 1870 a series of droughts convinced the elders of the Gushid Buryats that they should abandon their village and move to a different region. To confirm this decision they invited a famous shaman. He, however, said that they should on no account move. The problem was that they had been cutting wood at Upxyr nearby, 'angering' the forest. The Gushid obeyed his command to stop cutting down the trees of Upxyr, and in a few years a thick young wood had regrown, a dried-up spring gave water again, and this enabled the people to irrigate their pastures. In thanks to the shaman and the spirit of the spring the Gushid instituted an annual sacrifice (Mikhailov 1987: 118). Such was the prestige of shamans among the colonized and downtrodden Western Buryats in the nineteenth century that chiefs in many places declared themselves also to be shamans and practised as such. In other parts of West Buryatia shamans took over the customarily chiefly task of sacrifice to ancestral spirits domiciled in the land (Mikhailov 1987: 115). In such rituals the shamans acted in the chiefly idiom on behalf of patrilineal groups. The chiefly ritual repertoire consists mainly of prayers, sacrifices, and offerings, and the 'beckoning' of spirits down to accept them. This contrasts with the shamanic experience of spirit presence through trance. The fact that shamans could operate in the chiefly way did not prevent them from performing in the shamanic idiom on other occasions (curing, exorcising, conducting consecrations of vessels for spirits, contacting spirits to divine future events, etc.), all of which were done by means of trance. This dual role of shamans in circumstances when chiefly efficacy was in doubt is discussed in Humphrey (1994).

The asymmetry between chief and shaman derives from the fact that although the category of 'chief' could vary in practice from a dominant elder of a sub-lineage to an emperor, the idea always was that this was a social role, usually legitimated by patrilineal descent. Being a 'shaman', on the other hand, was not in essence a social role or a profession but was seen as an ability, something which could descend on anyone, women as well as men, by choice of the spirits. However, in the end, a chief too was successful not just by descent but by something like ability, his destiny (*zayaga*). Chiefly destiny was seen as an absolute, manifest in the power, militancy, and achievements of the leader, and brooking no interference or dilution. This is why successful chiefs could not tolerate the myriad and unpredictable powers of shamans, for whom 'destiny' was but one among a host of forces about in the world.

Thus the imperial patriline of Chinggis Khaan,[6] known as the Borjigid, which has provided leaders throughout most of Mongolia since the thirteenth century, was thought by the Xorchin Mongols to be incompatible with shamanism. On the other hand, the Borjigid were said to include and to accord high respect to another category of inspirational practitioners, bone-setters.[7] This may be connected with the symbolism of bones, which not only metaphorically stand for male descent in general but are also used (by counting the joints in the limbs) to reckon generations in genealogies.

Given social groups in different historical circumstances have emphasized one or other of the two views. Explanations for this are bound to be complex and multilayered. A change, say from a predominantly shamanic to a more chiefly ritual process, can be explained by analysis of the economic, political, and religious circumstances in which the shamanic field of agency was contested. However, it is also observable that over the longer term (since the thirteenth century) some peripheral regions of Mongolia have never developed strong chieftainship and are renowned for their shamanism, whereas other areas have repeatedly seen the rise of empires, princedoms, and other forms of centralized polity, which was accompanied each time by repression of shamanism. When the State collapsed shamanism reappeared. The centralized polities emerged in the vast region of the central treeless steppes. The more shamanically inclined groups are found on the western, northern, and eastern peripheries, where grassland is interspersed with forests, mountains, great rivers, and lakes. These observations are not, however, meant to imply that I see 'chiefly' and 'shamanist' viewpoints as timeless, changeless structures within Mongolian 'culture', somehow separate from particular human agencies. On the contrary, I would see Mongolians through history as constantly changing and re-viewing the images by which the world was seen. Nevertheless, it would be an act of wilful historical blindness not to recognize that they often came up with new views which were in many ways 'the same' as those from an earlier time or a different place and using the same vocabulary, though it is beyond the scope of this chapter to attempt a full explanation of this. Chiefly and shamanist landscapes may be seen as reiterative in this sense.

The missions of the Lamaist Buddhists were crucial in the to-some-extent historically recurrent landscapes of the Mongols. There were three phases of advance succeeded by retreat, following in each case the emergence of centralized states: in the fourteenth century under Khubilai Khaan, at the turn of the sixteenth and the seventeenth centuries with the short-lived States of Xalx, and in the eighteenth and nineteenth centuries with the consolidation of the Manchu Empire in Mongolia. This last mission was a successful expansion into virtually the whole of the steppe region. Buddhism allied itself with the chiefly sacred geography, and lamas became in effect priests for political leaders. But Buddhism also introduced a moral shift. Spirits were pronounced to be 'good' and 'bad', and furthermore the whole practice of worship of entities of the land was denigrated in comparison with the religious goal of individual salvation. Thus Buddhist lamas took an extremely active part in mountain worship, but they said it was 'not religion'. Indeed, high-ranking Buddhist lamas could adopt a definitely chiefly idiom for the occasion. A prominent lama active in Inner Mongolia in the 1920s wrote:

When I, as a high-ranking *gegeen* [incarnation], went to the *oboo* [mountain-cult site] to participate in the ceremonies, I was always accompanied by various high-ranking lamas and lay disciples. Inasmuch as this was not a Buddhist ceremony, I did not dress in a customary Buddhist gown, but rather in the costume of a lay leader, with a flint and knife in my belt. The dress is formal, with the knives on the right side and the flint and other ornaments on the left. The worshipful bowings at the *oboo* were not performed in the traditional Buddhist custom [. . .] but rather were a kowtow in the old tradition. (Hyer and Jagchid 1983: 89)

It was comparatively easy for lamas to take over ritual operations at sacred sites hitherto managed only by elders or chiefs. But they ran into opposition, as we shall see, where shamans had added a priestly function at lineage sites to their own inspirational practices elsewhere. Sometimes shamans retreated from these sites and accepted a subordinate status; elsewhere they fled rather than submit. At yet other places an uneasy syncretism evolved, an example of which will be described at the end of this chapter.

A Common Substratum of Landscape Concepts

The energies in nature should exist and reproduce themselves in harmony. Lying below, as it were, any of the ritual practices referred to above, there is what Lattimore called 'a "code of the laws of nature and the harmony of man with nature" which grows in a spontaneous way out of the practice of being a nomad but is also partly a kind of mystical idealization of the practice' (1942: 211). The 'mystical idealization' Lattimore refers to has effect in a series of injunctions (*yos*), which differ greatly from place to place, but are always precise and always express the idea that the features of the landscape have their own being and nature which should not be disturbed by the activities of man. Now since human beings also have their way of being, which is the pastoral nomadic way of life, this is as valid a part of nature as any other. The *yos* essentially state that any unnecessary disturbance of nature must be avoided, and this includes inanimate entities. So it is wrong to move stones pointlessly from one place to another, or scuff the ground and make marks on it. Such marks must be wiped out with the foot before leaving a place. The circle left on the ground by a kettle should be erased. Burying things in the ground is done only with special rituals. It is wrong to interfere with the reproduction of nature: one must not take eggs, catch nestlings, or hunt young or pregnant animals. Grass should not be torn out by the roots—only withered grass should be collected (Tatar 1984: 321–2).

Injunctions of this kind indicate that the landscape is conceptually divided up into constituent entities credited with their own ongoing form of being. This can be seen, for example, from the rules about where it is forbidden to urinate: in rivers, the ground of the yurt, the livestock pound, on roads, or on places which are the domains of other creatures, e.g. in burrows or in hollows which animals have made to rest in. It is wrong to pollute a river by washing in it, but it is quite allowable to take water out of the river and then wash in it. In other words, it is not water as a substance which is pollutable, but the river as an entity.

A Mongolian landscape seethes with entities which are attributed with anything from a hazy idea of energy to clearly visualized and named spirits. Each planet, mountain, river, lake, lone tree, cliff, marsh, spring, and so forth, has some such 'supernatural' quality, as do animals, birds, fish, insects, humans, and even artefacts, such as tools, or guns, or man-made hay meadows. It is not possible to discern a coherent cosmology in all this. A question about how the spirit of a tree relates to the spirit of the *nutag* (homeland) within which it is found is often unanswerable. However, I shall suggest below that certain limited practices of conceptually 'putting together' landscapes exist and have rather different properties in chiefly and shamanic contexts.

The Chiefly Landscape

The assumption that humans are nomadic beings is one point where we may start. I shall suggest that it implies, in the chiefly landscape, an ego-centred universe, and thereby the idea that 'the centre' moves. If we understand the landscape, as the Mongols do, as everything around us, then the landscape includes the sky and its phenomena, such as blueness, clouds, rain, lightning, stars, and rays of light. The sky (*tnggri*) is the power above all powers. Not only does it give the light, warmth, and rain which make the earth fertile and allow humans and animals to live, but it also expresses this by means of its will (*zayaga*) which sets out the destinies of all living beings. With this in mind, the idea of 'the centre' is not so much a point in a horizontal disc on the earth, as a notion of verticality, for which position on the earth does not matter. The aim is reaching upwards, the making of a link between earth and sky, as with the column of smoke from a fire. 'The centre' is established anew when people make a halt. It is, in other words, not a place but an action.

It is this notion of power which I suggest was emphasized in the chiefly, hierarchical and statist periods of Mongol history (though it was also present in the practice of the patriarchal family or lineage even in times of political disintegration). The use of space by the steppe Mongols for subsistence, for reasons perhaps largely ecological, in effect 'spirals' on a time axis, as people move through the annual cycle of pastures and repeat such cycles from year to year. Yet although the helical trajectory of Mongol subsistence-space use through time enables their very existence, the ruler-centred politico-religious orientation provides a kind of centripetal force which collapses the spatial dimension around the time axis (Fig. 6.2).

The Polish ethnographer Szynkiewicz (1986: 19) showed that the journey between camps is felt to be an event outside the ordinary run of life; people set out at an astrologically determined time, they put on special clothes and use festive harness for their horses.

On the way, young men compete with one another, showing off their horsemanship and prowess. The moment such a caravan is spotted from yurts along the way, all haste is made to prepare tea and carry it out as a testimony of welcome. Those on the move become the guests of all who live on the steppe. At the same time, this ritual comprises a negation of the fundamental principle of nomadic life, namely change. The ritual emphasizes . . . continuity, particularly the idealized permanence of the place occupied in space.

The ritualized journey is thus a spatial liminality, into and out of the otherness of 'travelling that is not travelling'—paradoxically an otherness which serves to

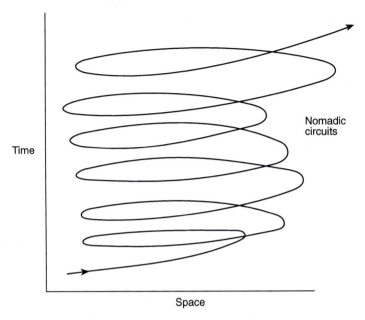

Fɪɢ. 6.2. An idealized representation of nomadic circuits in time and space.

reassert the nomadic way of life—thereby negating movement in the everyday world. The time axis, which is universal, and thus locates each household at the centre of the cosmos, is the *axis mundi*. This is an idea which the Mongols do not usually express as a generality, but often come out with in specific instances: the hearth of the tent, with its vertical column of smoke, the worshipped mountain, and the pole which supports the roof-ring are all symbolically the centre of the world. The deified sky alone of all phenomena is given the epithet 'eternal' (*mönke*) by the Mongols of the central steppes. In this landscape, with the collapse of subsistence-space into some kind of 'co-ordinate singularity',[8] we find in its place a social space constructed around the time axis. Time here is ideologically constructed as invariant repetition. Each category of person occupies a certain social space, which is conceived as unambiguous and invariant, repeated at each stopping-place, in a trajectory through time.

The tent itself has an invariant organization of social space, as seniors, juniors, males, females, guests, and animals are accommodated in specific places in relation to the central hearth and the orientation of the door to the south. Males sit to the west and females to the east, seniors to the north and juniors (including servants) to the south. Animals are kept by the door (Humphrey 1974). The concept of 'seniors' (*axmad*) varies in content according to the predominant principle of male-focused social organization; at one time genealogical, in recent times it is more likely to be reckoned by standing in local administration or simply by age.⁹ A similar setting-out of social space is constructed at the site of mountain-worship (see below).

How does such a view construct a landscape? One way of denying movement is not to recognize that places are unique, or intrinsically different from one another. I shall take as characteristic of the chiefly landscape the conceptualization of the central Mongolian plains, an area dominated for the past three centuries by the Manchu state and the Buddhist hierarchy. Here place-names are virtually all descriptive types. So the same rather limited number of names are repeated all the thousands of miles from the Altai to the Hsinggan Mountains. There are numberless examples of *Ulaan Uul* (Red Mountain), *Xar Bulag* (Black Spring), *Elest* (Sandy), *Xujirt* (Place with Soda), or *Bayan-gol* (Rich Valley). It might be thought that such terms are not really names in the sense of designating something specific. But this would be incorrect because there are regions within which, as with the colours of a map, the names are not repeated. Kazakevich (1934: 6) suggests that north-central-Mongolian extensive pastoralism in the pre-collectivized period required a radius of no less than 25 km. from any given camp (the distance a horse-herd could venture in a day). The length of annual routes was between 25 and 40 km., and occasional droughts, searches for lost animals, and so forth, would increase the area herdsmen needed to know intimately to a radius of about 150 km. It is such an area which the Mongols call their 'homeland' (*nutag*) and in which, I suggest, descriptive terms are in effect names.¹⁰

To turn now from toponymy to the descriptive terminology for the chiefly landscape we see that it is largely metaphorical, and consists of a mapping of the parts of the body on to the land (at least it is reasonable to suppose, as suggested by Lakoff and Johnson (1980), that the metaphors are extended from the body to the land, and not vice versa). The ways the terms are used suggest that land-entities are seen as 'wholes', or 'bodies', centred on mountains (*uul*; literary Mongolian: *agula*). The system is ego-centred, as though ego were the mountain, and it is orientated, in that the front is always to the south. Mountains have backs and fronts. The northern (or back) side of mountains is given the following epithets: *uulyn shil* (nape), *nuruu* (spine), *seer* (vertebra); the eastern and western sides are: *uulyn zuun/baruun xatsar* (east and west cheeks), *mör* (shoulders), *shanaa* (temple, cheek bone), *xavirga* (ribs), *suga* (armpit), *tashu* (side); and the southern or front side has: *magnai* (forehead), *xomsog* (brows), *övdög* (thigh) and *eleg* (liver) (Zhukovskaya 1988: 27, quoting Mongol sources). A hill standing on its own, or a high summit in a mountain range, is called *tolgoi* (head). A mountain cape, or elevated prong, is its *xoshuu* (nose, beak, snout). A valley opening from a mountain is *am* (mouth). This certainly suggests the mountain as some kind of gestalt, viewed from its summit or centre, as Ego views his or her own body.

It can be seen that mountain terminology in this central region is dominated by skeletal or bone metaphors. This is Lévi-Straussian *Elementary Structures* country. The Mongols, like other peoples of North Asia, associate the bone with patriliny and descent through the father (the word for patrilineage in some dialects is 'bone', *yasun*); descent through the mother is linked with flesh/ blood. Rivers or river valleys are called *gol*, which means centre and also aorta, the blood-vessel of life (it is by tearing the aorta that Mongols kill animals). Rivers are seen as descending from, or depending on, mountains. Terms for lake, pond, stream, spring, bog, etc. are mostly non-metaphorical and uncon- nected with one another. Essentially, these are appendages of mountains. The engendering of the landscape in this way is much more marked in central Mongolia than in the periphery. In the Altai, the shamanist Buryat areas, and even in the far east among the shamanist Daur, bone metaphors for mountains are much less prevalent, and the spirits of mountains may even be 'grandmothers', or 'girls', or they may consist of a man and wife.[11] In the central steppes, on the other hand, mountains are virtually all called *khan* (chief, prince).

Spirits in the chiefly landscape in general are termed 'rulers' or 'masters' (*ezen*, or *ejen* pl. *ezed*). The term is used for human rulers as well as the spirits and it occurs at all social levels, from the 'master of the tent' to the emperor, who was called the Ezen Khaan. These days the Mongolians are privatizing their economy and beginning to think about the possibility of allowing owner- ship of land. The expression coined for this is 'land master' (*gazarin ezen*). But this term has been used for centuries with quite another meaning, the *genius loci*. The original Mongolian 'landlord' from whom permission had to be obtained to use the land was not a human but a supernatural being.[12] The *ezen* of a locality provides generalized well-being, good weather, and fertility, or, if 'angered', drought and pestilence. In the chiefly idiom the major *ezed* are the masters of 'mountains'. In flat areas these may be no more than mounds, hardly visible except in the slanting rays of the setting sun. But nevertheless any particular mountain is the site at which to call upon the spirits of the whole landscape relevant to the agent (the social group or individual). Characteristic- ally such invocations involve lists of mountains and culminate in appeals to 'skies' which are spoken of as spirits of clear, stormy, etc. skies.

Careless pronunciation of the names of worshipped mountains is held to be dangerous anywhere in their vicinity, just as junior people must not speak aloud the names of senior male relatives in their hearing for fear of offending them. It is difficult to convey the variety of occasions on which, even today, mountains are behaved towards as if they are real presences. Just as 'they' may be annoyed by someone blurting out their names, 'they' take offence if bold young Com- munist officials defy them and dig up wild onions from their slopes. Many stories are told of disasters which were caused in this way. In their presence mountains are called *xairxan* (dear one), and they are offered animals for their herds—not sacrifices, but live animals, which the former owners care for as though they belonged to a powerful human patron.

In the Manchu period 'land masters' were actively used in the political process. For example, the Kanjurwa Khutagt, a prominent Mongolian Lamaist reincarnation, wrote in his memoirs that during the visit of his second incarnation to the court in Peking a supernatural event occurred:

The emperor, it is reported, seemed to see a person standing behind him and inquired who it was. Turning to see for himself, the incarnation replied that the *ejen*, the spirit of the Serku region in Kokonor, was standing there. This pleased the emperor who then conferred upon the *ejen* a yellow jacket and a red button, the headdress symbol of special rank, denoting the second rank in the hierarchy of the imperial bureaucracy. Such bestowals from an emperor were rare and greatly prized.

This tradition was [the Chinese Emperors'] means of demonstrating that they regarded themselves as supreme not only over local rulers but even over regional gods. The bestowal of recognition was not limited to a particular spirit but was also upon the place where the deity was customarily believed to reside. Because of this incident, my previous incarnations over the centuries were always searched for and found in this Serku area. (Hyer and Jagchid 1983: 28).

If this was the emperor's way of pinning down the powerful Ganjurwa reincarnation to a certain territory, it is not surprising that Mongolians recognized that a political process was involved and themselves sometimes dared to treat a mountain as a resource. Bawden (1968: 103) mentions a story about an eighteenth-century governor of Urga (now Ulaan-Baatar) who went out to celebrate the spring worship of Bogdo Uul Mountain and was caught in a heavy storm. He reproved the mountain: 'I came here to worship you as a duty, not because I wanted to. What do you think you are up to?' Then he condemned the mountain to a whipping and to wear fetters, which were deposited on the cairn normally used for rituals of worship. Later in the year, still not satisfied with the weather, he came back and fined the mountain all its horses, confiscated them, and drove them away.

The main site of worship in the chiefly mode is a mountain-top altar, which is called *oboo*[13] (see Fig. 6.3). All worshipped mountains have *oboo*s on their summits. Physically, the *oboo* is a cairn of stones, to which each participant must add a stone or a bundle of branches contributed by those present and bound together. Modern *oboo*s in Buddhist areas are often concreted in and painted white, becoming neat cylinders or shaped like an inverted bowl. *Oboo*s should be built around a central vertical pole or have one in their vicinity. The term *oboo* is polyfunctional and refers to the cairn, to the spirit-master, and to the mountain or other entity worshipped (Abayeva 1992: 74). The rituals are seasonal, and the *oboo* is 'renewed' by adding new stones to it, inserting new branches, or tying on ribbons, horse-hairs, and flags. *Oboo*s are occupation-marks, in the sense of 'We are here', and they are also orientation-marks for travellers. Smaller and more ephemeral *oboo*s are also placed on roads at mountain passes. During the year nomads move between lands, each land with a governing and protecting *oboo*; a new one can be erected if a place has none. In

FIG. 6.3. A modern Mongolian painting showing circumambulation of the mountain cairn (*oboo*) by a nomadic group prior to making offerings. The skulls of favourite horses are placed on the *oboo* as a sign of respect for these animals.

my view, the *oboo* not only enacts the idea of the social group (a heaping-up of like things, stones, or branches), but is also the physical mark of the denial of horizontal space, a vertical statement. Just as the 'mountain' embodies the idea of height and hence of closeness to the sky, the *oboo* represents its peak. The ritual (*dallaga*) always involves circular movement, circumambulation of the site and the 'circular beckoning' of blessings from on high into sacrificial meat which is then shared and eaten.

The *dallaga* is not only performed at the *oboo*. It is one of the commonest rituals of the household head today in Mongolia. In regions with a strong shamanic tradition it was also performed by a shaman, acting on behalf of the patrilineal group. Among the late nineteenth-century Xori Buryats the shaman, having 'beckoned' down the blessings, would take a bucket full of the *dallaga* meat to the master of the group and say, 'This is the unbreakable blessing of the princes, the origin of the patriline *(ug garbal)*, the endless happiness of the wish-granting jewel (*chandamani*), the great *dallaga*, from which one becomes rich and populous!' The *dallaga* meat was never given to any outsider, even the smallest piece, and generally for three days after the ritual people took care not to give anything to people outside the group (Poppe 1940: 68, quoting the Buryat chronicler Yumsunov).

The *oboo* rituals enact a kind of closing-up and binding-in. Many of the *oboo*s made of branches were in the form of a conical tepee, with the offerings laid inside, as if in a small room (Carruthers 1910: 246). Stone ones often have a small opening in one side, or a hollow in the top. This creates an enclosure, a sheltered space, which in Mongolian is closely connected etymologically with secrecy and with sacredness (*xori-*, *xorigul*). It is an aspect of the denial of real spaces that the idea of the enclosure takes the place of the territory with a boundary. There is a linguistic link between the word *oboo* and *obooxoi*, a refuge or shelter. In the Mongolian landscape a shelter is principally a hideout from the wind, which is the agent of movement, unpredictable, bringing discomfort and change, coming from no one knows where. The *oboo/obooxoi*, like the Mongol tent, can thus be seen as an escape from the real landscape by recreating its conceptual structure in miniature, protected space.

Chiefs and elders created their own landscapes with anthropomorphic spirits of mountains and other dominant objects, but the effect of the centralized Buddhist system was to reduce imaginative variety and standardize the mountain rituals. In 1893, for example, the chief lama 'discovered' a text for an *oboo* ritual, composed as it were by one of his previous incarnations, and issued it to all the hereditary princes of central Mongolia to be performed to avert plague, famine, and cattle-sickness at all worshipped mountains (Bawden 1958: 57–61). The text consisted of fixed formulas, within which local princes executing the order were invited to insert lists of all the local mountains, springs, rivers, etc. they wished to invoke. The Buddhist hierarchy also attempted to standardize the sensibility attributed to mountain-spirits: blood sacrifices were forbidden and it was even decreed that executions of criminals must not take place within sight of major mountain-rulers, in case they be offended at the sin of killing (Pozdneyev 1971: 50).

Princes and high lamas loved to be patrons of the great *oboo*s, to arrive with the most impressive suite, to donate most livestock, to have their wrestlers and their horses win the games in the festivities which followed the rituals. The athletic games were to restore male virility and strength. If the *oboo* was the axis of time, it was a kind of timeless time, a perpetual harmony, a setting out of the ideologically permanently recurrent structure of society—for which the archetype was the Imperial lineage, recurrently primed in its vigilance and valour. Participants in the ritual sat in an order regulated by social status.[14] Women and foreigners were excluded from the *oboo* ritual itself, quite simply because they were not members of the patriarchal group (though they could take part in the festivities held afterwards).[15] Shamans were also excluded in many places; though members of the lineage, they were destabilizing pretenders to a different and more direct access to the spirits. In all of this the detailed knowledge of genealogies was not important. This is because the idea of the patriarchal group slid easily between the notions of lineage, clan, residential group, political division, and military unit. What was being enacted was the 'beckoning' of the energies of nature to the advantage of the male group, a kind of recharging of the batteries of virility, in which gender mattered more than any other principle of group organization.

The Shamanic Landscape

The picture so far is of a simplified 'punctual' landscape dominated by mountains and bone terminology, with water and lowland as inconsiderable appendages. Shamanic practice has the effect of opening up the vision of the cosmos. Here the earth as a whole, with its complexities and its subterranean depths, is seen in relation to the sky, with its ethereal layers. The earth (*gazar*) is now explicitly female, the Mother Etugen, while the sky (heaven) is male and a father. These associations recur through the sources, right back to the period of the Mongol Empire. The earth, old Mother Etugen, was given little attention in the State-dominated religion of nineteenth-century central Mongolia. But in regions on the shamanic fringe she was celebrated, incorporating both fertility and nurturance, and a kind of animal complexity. The following is from a late nineteenth-century Buryat invocation to Xangai (*xangai* means forested hilly region):

> Eternal silk-faced Sky!
> Eternal butter-faced Mother Etugen!
> Eternal Sky with speckled eyes!
> Mother Etugen with golden ears!
> I accomplish the great fumigation-ritual [to you].
> Mountain, called Ishi [root, origin] Khan,
> River-mother, called Queen . . .
> Your bending spinal-range,
> Your filled up udders,
> Your squeezed crevices,
> Your sticking-out shoulder-blades,
> Your huge armpit . . .
> You have an unencompassable body . . .
> Queenly earth-water,
> I make an offering [to you]! (Galdanova 1987: 26).

No one will be surprised to learn that the Mongols have cults of caves as well as mountains and these are often called *umai* or *eke umai* (womb, mother's womb). The ordinary word for 'cave' or 'grotto' is *agui*, which has no bodily reference, and this is used for those caves occupied by a Buddhist ascetic in contemplative retreat. But here and there along the northern borders of Mongolia, in Buryatia and in the Xorchin region of Inner Mongolia there are special caves, the ones called 'wombs', and here there are shrines for female fertility cults. The rituals at these cults must be performed by shamans, not lamas. They involve women penetrating through the narrow crevice of the cave. In the Dayan Derke cave of the Xövsgöl region of north-west Mongolia there were a series of chambers. The shaman said to the person clambering through: 'Look up, what do you see there?' The shaman would interpret what the person saw in the gloom. It was good if a ray of light seemed to suggest a child or an animal (Galdanova *et al.* 1984: 6).

As has been pointed out, Buddhism and shamanic spirit-cults were not in some harmonious 'structural' relationship here, as depicted by Tambiah (1970) for north Thailand. They were bitter competitors in the construction of rival ideologies concerning the reproduction of society. The lamas of the peripheral regions therefore took action against the cave-spirits. Unlike their attitude to patriarchal cults, they did not attempt to make use of the female power but tried to destroy or negate it. Indeed, the idea of real this-worldly physical birth was anathema to the reiterative male ideology outlined above, in which celibate lamas were the priests for patriarchal groups. The reified representation of the female ability to give birth in the cave cults was frightening as well as abhorrent to the lamas. Since the idea was that the power in the caves derived from the untamed sexual drives of the female spirits within, one of the lamas' feebler tactics consisted of setting up male sexual organs, carved out of wood, facing the caves. This was no more than a containing device, which acknowledged the spirits' power. In central Mongolia, where Buddhist State-oriented society had long since triumphed, lamas were able to dismiss such spirits as unimportant (indeed I do not know of any significant cave cult in this region). In the shamanic peripheries there were women-only cults of rivers[16] some distance from the settlement (attendance on such cults was known among the Daurs as *daud gara*—to go out on the *daud*, which was the distance a pheasant[17] could fly before having to come down for a rest). There were also prominent female spirits of the land in these regions.

If the 'punctual' landscape focuses on centrality, the shamanic landscape involves an idea of laterality and crucially, it acknowledges movement. To give an example: the contemporary Selenga Buryats worship a female spirit who is envisaged, at least by some people, as wearing dark-blue clothing and mounted on a black stallion. The story goes that this is the spirit of a woman who was travelling in the direction of the Xori Buryats to the north. Stopping on the southern slope of Bayan-Tugud hill she tied her horse to a single tree and then she died of disease. The local people buried the woman there, untied her horse and let it wander off. The horse was caught by people of the Selenga Tubsheten clan, who killed it and used it as food. They began to die of a terrible disease. Only after sacrifices were made to the spirit (woman and horse) did the disease disappear. Although the sacrifices are now (1980s) made at the tree, the spirit is considered to be the *ezen* of a lateral section of land which extends between the Bayan-Tugud hill and another called Olzeitei-Ondor and this area is known as *güideltei gazar* (literally, 'running-track land', a *güidel* being a track or a run of a spirit or animal) (Abayeva 1992: 78). The idea of the 'track' is homologous, in many other stories, with the movement of women between male social groups, a movement which often fails in one way or another (through ill-treatment, divorce, and flight of the wife with nowhere to go). This creates a hiatus of abandonment, from which asocial place the female spirit wreaks her revenge.

We may begin to explain this by observing that the distinction between the chiefly/Buddhist and the shamanic world-views rests on radically different theories of empowerment. Both chiefs and Buddhist lamas derive their legitimacy from social processes: from genealogical descent, from political or military structures, from teacher–pupil lines in the Buddhist system, and so forth. Shamans, on the other hand, think of themselves as acquiring their abilities not so much from social training as directly from the energies of the world, conceived as spirits which decide who is to be a shaman.[18] This distinction means that chiefs need only acknowledge external power as some abstract energy, driving and revivifying the social group (for example, 'destiny', or the 'land-masters' which are everywhere more or less the same). Shamans on the other hand must acknowledge the variety of the world, the infinite multiplicity of beings which people feel to have power. This view does not exclude human society, but constructs it as relying on interaction, waxing and waning with its exchanges, conflicts, enticements, depredations, and restitutions *vis-à-vis* other powers. Shamans act relationally, usually as intermediaries between entities conceived as different from one another, whereas the patriarchal group is constructed ideologically as if it were self-perpetuating.[19]

Though shamans tend to specialize in the introduction of this or that spirit, and are also said to 'inherit' spirits, if one looks closer it turns out that a shamanic predecessor is in fact not an ancestor as ordinarily conceived but 'naturalized' (cast into the world) in the very process of becoming a spirit. Buryats, for example, say that deceased shamans 'become cliffs' (*xada bolxo*, the term *xada* meaning both 'cliff' or 'rocky hill' and the spirit of such a place (Galdanova 1987: 32)). A *xada* is also said to be the son or daughter of a sky (*tengeri*). How a spirit can be both a deceased shaman and the child of a sky is not explained—as I noted earlier, landscapes are not coherent and invariant 'structures' applicable on all occasions, but ways of thinking and speaking in particular contexts. Although the term *ezen* (master) is a common way of talking about such spirits in shamanic discourse there also exists a variety of other terms for them.[20] Furthermore, for ordinary people a spirit is usually considered a single being, but in shamans' songs it may comprise numerous energies which are its metamorphoses, its helpers, instruments, and parts (this will be explained further below). The shaman thus cumulates varied external powers, while the chief, in his ritual role, and the lama unify, regulate, and rank them.

The shaman puts on a gown which, among some Mongolian groups, is itself a 'landscape' representation. The Daur shaman, for example, appears as a fortified city, an extravaganza of symbolic openings and closures to the world.

Seventy-two small bronze mirrors sewn horizontally in bands round the costume are the strong city walls; eight large bronze mirrors sewn down the front are the gatehouses through which the shaman's soul can pass; sixty bells are the guards on the city wall; a female bird and a male bird on the shoulders are messengers to the spirits; twelve embroidered cloth strips down the back represent different birds and animals together with the various trees where they perch or dwell; another twelve strips symbolize both the months of the year and twelve passages or paths by which spirits come and go; 365 cowrie shells studding the gown are the days of the year and also a kind of armour against penetration by vengeful spirits (Batubayin 1990).

Of course, the self-representation of shamans by their costumes varied greatly, but the above example hints at one extremely important shamanic concept, the way or path. To explain this idea let me first take a detour by contrasting the shamanic with Buddhist ideas of the underworld or the world of the dead. Getting at an understanding of this contrast is difficult, since all of the Mongolian culture area has been subject to Buddhist influences at some period or other, and some Buddhist-type representations have remained even in areas where shamans are recently the only ritual practitioners. The 'underworld' is one of these. It was moralized by Buddhism, becoming a series of hells or prisons for sinners. It was reached through a cave, or a well, after crossing a bridge or a river, after passing guards, a gatehouse, walls and sentries, and it had a huge palace, many storeys high, with glass windows, with armed officials, and scribes writing in their books, and crucially it contained many prisons and torture chambers. It was ruled by a king, Erlig Khan, who informed dead souls of their sentences and punishments before they could be reborn on earth, all of which was written in his secretaries' records. In other words, this was a representation of the State, the dark vision of the real government institutions.[21]

Now it is true that there are accounts (e.g. the Manchu and Daur tales of Nisan Shaman) of shamans visiting exactly just such an underworld to rescue a soul and bring it back to earth. But there are other accounts, which seem more purely shamanic, where the world of the dead is not a 'State', but is simply 'somewhere else', across some void separating life from death, but not even definitely down below. Sometimes this other world is just nearby, across the mountains, or round some bends in a river, or inside a cliff, but it is just that ordinary people have lost the knack of finding it. In yet other ways of talking about this, the other world is this world, here, only we cannot see it. But sometimes it can be felt, or heard, or smelt. In other words, it is apprehended through the prism of faculties. But ordinary human organs of perception are not enough. This explanation is used to account for why shamans must acquire the abilities of their ancestor-spirit and animal helpers, which can see better, track down better, fly, or swim underwater. The exercise of such abilities constructs the 'ways' or 'paths' of shamans and spirits.

A vision of this kind in effect transforms the landscape. The souls of the dead are no longer trapped underground in a king's dungeon, but are somewhere in this world. The real land is inhabited by remembered ancestors, giving a sense of place. Now what is significant is not only big obvious things like mountains but the capacity of nature to conceal, contain, and host even insignificant beings, because disguised among them may be a spirit of vital importance to one's well-being. This is accompanied by mythological 'maps' superimposed on real space. For example, the Buryats say that the spirit of Lake Baikal has nine sons and one daughter, i.e. the nine rivers which empty into the lake and the Angara River which runs out of it, the former bringing him benefit and the latter only loss (Khangalov 1958: 318).

It is the shamanic accounts which can explain the presence of spirits in the world. The chiefly model simply deals with them as given. But in shamanism it is the souls of the remarkable dead people, or people who died in a strange way, who *become* the spirit-rulers of the land. In particular, shamans themselves, after their funerals, are given a second burial after a period of time during which their souls are transformed into spirits, and they are then acknowledged and invoked as *ezed*. This is clearly explained in a seventeenth-century Mongolian account of the death of one powerful shamaness, who became, three years after her first burial, *ezen* of a mountain in East Mongolia (with her husband as a kind of side-kick spirit) (Heissig 1953). This account is unusual, in that it is a written text, composed by a lama who was attempting to convert this spirit to Buddhism, but it accords with numerous ethnographical descriptions, by Mongolians and Europeans from all over the culture area. Shamans used to prepare their own coffins and chose the sites for their interment and metamorphosis. They then became spirits of those regions, in some cases an extensive domain and in others reduced merely to the site itself. The shamans who are their descendants inherit their power and are also able to go to these places to call them 'into reality', to explain what they want, or what people should do to obtain their magical benefactions.

This means that, in contrast with the chiefly model, it is absolutely vital to remember shamanic genealogies, and it also means that particular places, where shamans really were buried in the past, do matter. Where a social group remained in one place, its shaman ancestors were stacked up, as it were, and joined previous spirits, becoming collective 'masters' of the place. But in cases where the group moved this is apparent from the ritual sites of spirit rulership. So the Hungarian ethnographer Dioszegi (1963) was able to draw a nine-generation genealogy of shamans, and show how the shamans dying in each generation were the spirit-rulers of a series of different places. This chart showed the particular group to have migrated some hundreds of miles over this period. These sites are not only remembered in the shamans' songs, but people travel back to them to make offerings many generations later.

We may compare this with the death-ritual of elders and chiefs. Here, burial sites are avoided, may often be unknown, and even be secret and deliberately erased. This matter is historically complicated. The Buddhist practice was the exposure of corpses on the surface of the ground, such that they should be rapidly eaten by wild animals and birds. For all ordinary people it is considered ideal if no trace remains, if the land appears absolutely untouched as soon as possible. But with the Manchu Dynasty and the influence of Chinese ancestor-cults, the bodies of prominent aristocrats were embalmed and placed in huts at graveyards. They were allotted families of hereditary attendants, but the main role of these people was to keep people and animals out, to prevent the sites being despoiled. The main point is that these graves never coincided with places of worship (*oboos*), and the dead souls of chiefs did not become spirit-rulers of the land. The paradigm of the Imperial ancestor is Chinggis Khaan; his burial site, said to be at the legendary mountain of Burxan Xaldun, was ridden over by horses to erase any traces. His grave has never been found, though generations of foreign archaeologists have searched for it (many Mongols object to this). Although Chinggis is still worshipped and rumours still circulate about his reincarnation, as is the case with several other famous Mongolian warriors in history, a connection with any particular place was deliberately obscured, and indeed one can see why a political hierarchy composed of highly mobile sub-units would operate in this way.[22]

The shaman's first 'burial' site was avoided, since the soul was considered dangerous until transformed into a spirit. Among Western Buryats it consisted of a platform between trees, so as to be open for the soul's journey to the 'other world'. The shaman's accoutrements were hung up at the site, and since many of them were made of bronze or iron they last for a considerable time. Physically such a dual structure (see Fig. 6.4) contrasts with the circular 'punctual' construction of the *oboo*.[23] At the second burial, frequently the shaman's bones were merged with a natural object by placing them inside a hole made in a growing tree. Such a burial place, the site of subsequent worship, could be beside a lake, cliff, grove, spring, cave, or river. The ontology of such a 'naturalized' spirit is entirely unclear: is it an anthropomorphic being, or the very tree, cliff, spring, or so on, of burial, or is it the animal 'incarnations' which seem to live around that place? All we can say is that shamanic invocations speak as though the spirit has its 'seat' at this particular place and often moves around and changes shape. It may 'become' a bird or animal. These journeys and metamorphoses are significant since they indicate the geographic and zoological range of shamans' pretensions to power. The two are linked in that according to the specific animal or bird metamorphosis, e.g. as a black mouse, or a crow, or a kind of beetle, or a wolf, the 'tracks' and 'running courses' vary too. The shaman's speech is poetic but the imagery stays with the likeness of real places.[24] For example, the Tarsai spirit-rulers, an important shamanic line among the Western Buryats, said via the shaman (Khangalov 1958: 117):

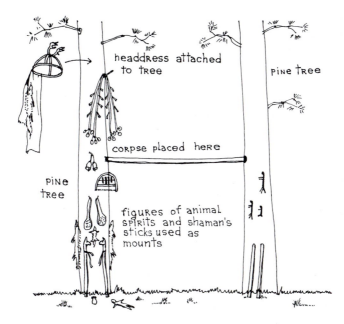

FIG. 6.4. A shaman's burial site of the Western Buryats, based on a sketch by M. N. Khangalov. The shaman's corpse is laid on a wooden platform between two trees. The shaman's implements (metal crown, bells, wild animal skins, sticks representing magical horses, models of helper-spirits, etc.) are attached to the trees.

> Our trail is that of the grey hare,
> The dark wolf is our servant,
> The honking crow is our incarnation,
> The Hoto eagle is our envoy.
> On the summit of Bortoi mountain,
> Having turned into dark wolves,
> Curving our backs, we ran.
> Whose son did you see there?
> On the summit of Tarsai mountain,
> Having become five geese,
> Crying out, we came in to land.
> Whose son did you see there?

There are other places in the shamanic landscape which commemorate the mythical adventures of particular shamanic ancestors when they were alive: the place where an enemy was defeated, or a wife was turned to stone, or simply where the ancestor urinated and a big cedar tree grew up. These become place-names. It is not that there are no recurrent toponyms of the 'black cliff' variety found in the steppes, but this shamanic landscape adds to them personalized and historic names, which are a constant reminder of links between known individuals and places.

The shamanic second burial site is not conceived as spatially central, but as a resting-point on a journey. It situates the end of one life and also the beginning of a spirit existence which is at the same time the start of the shamanic life of the next recipient of these abilities. Receiving the *udxa*, becoming a shaman, involves symbolic death and a rebirth which ritually acknowledges the complex (male, female, animal) components of shamanic power. We see here a concept of time, made up of lifetimes, which is different from the seamless reproduction described for the patriarchal vision. One Mongol of my acquaintance, brought up as a shamanist, claims that the notion of eternity and changelessness (*möngke*) is foreign to shamanism, which emphasizes metamorphosis.

In shamanic regions the site of chiefly worship and the shaman's second burial site occasionally coincide, but usually they do not. The reason for this is that the principle of shamanic transmission is not patrilineal descent, but 'choice of the spirits'. In practice this only sometimes resulted in transmission inside the clan and more often in a zigzag line through male and female relatives of the deceased shaman. So although shamans were often thought of as 'belonging' to given clans, in practice most of them had ancestral powers from a variety of places. This derived initially from the first spirit in the line (very commonly a girl or married woman who had suffered and died at the hands of the patrilineage and was thereafter bent on revenge) but it also gathered powers from the wayward track of the *udxa*, which could move through affines, wandering migrants absorbed into the group, illicit lovers, or even magical animals whose power was transmitted to a shaman by some strange event. All this added to a shaman's power. The great shaman 'lines' among the Buryats were worshipped separately by several different groups, each having some mythology of its own about their relationship with the spirit. The resulting situation was extremely complex, and it is impossible to do justice to it here. I can only summarize by saying that weak chiefs could try to make use of the power of shamanic lines by incorporating them into the cycle of sacrifices and treating them as patrilineal 'ancestors', while, conversely, as mentioned at the beginning of the chapter, powerful shamans sometimes took on the main role at the chiefly communal sacrifices, acting as chiefs or priests for them. Each community reached its own accommodation in this matter. To give an example: the Buret settlement of Idinsk Western Buryats at the end of the nineteenth century held eleven communal sacrifices each year. Eight of them were in honour of spirits of patrilineal ancestors, stones, cliffs, waters, hayfields, etc.; three were sacrifices in honour of deceased shamans. The Buret people also travelled annually to Baitag Mountain in the Kudinsk district for a great sacrifice at which all groups of the Exirit clan in the region were represented, some 2,000–3,000 people (Mikhailov 1987: 68).

Buryat and Xorchin history suggests that whatever accommodation a given group reached between chiefly and shamanic power could be rapidly altered by some social or economic disaster, such as an epidemic or loss of lands to foreign colonists. In such a case the prevailing power was felt to have failed (to be ineffective with the spirits) and people turned to the alternative. The massive wealth and crusading zeal of the Buddhist missionary advance during the nineteenth century lent additional weight to chiefly pretensions. Lamas saw shamanic 'ruler-spirit' sites as power points, to be controlled, obliterated, or converted. Latent opposition, which was really perhaps just difference, between the shaman and the elders in the acephalous, clan milieu then became real conflict. In many documented cases, as recently as the beginning of the twentieth century, there were battles, when shamans were killed, or forced to renounce their calling, their sacred equipment burnt on the order of lamas backed by ruling princes. Conversion meant the turning of chiefly and shamanic cult sites into *oboos*, the introduction of a new ritual, usually in Tibetan, and the imposition of the 'punctual' view of the landscape.

But we also know that in many regions of the non-centralized fringe these missionary ventures were only partly successful. If local political and economic organization was not in fact sufficiently successful to support monasteries of non-productive lamas, and if in general the people were not apparently benefiting from the new Buddhist petitioners for the blessings of the land, then the lamas had a hard time of it. Shamans hated and cursed the lamas. They said the Buddhist books and paintings were not real, just paper and paint.[25] In the isolated and forested Darxad region of Xövsgöl, north-west Mongolia, the monastery was forced to move three times during the nineteenth century when epidemics among the lamas were attributed to the activity of a female shamanic spirit (Dioszegi 1961: 202). Sometimes shamans and lamas both maintained competitive cults at a single site, an example being the Dayan Derke cave in the Kubsugul region mentioned above.

The Dayan Derke cave was a place where women went to become fertile and shamans travelled to acquire spiritual abilities. Shamanists saw Dayan Derke as a powerful and cruel spirit (*xatuu onggon*) who caused as much suffering as joy. He was a shaman or warrior who stole the wife or daughter of Chinggis Khaan. Fleeing from the vengeful emperor he avoided a death blow by turning himself into stone. Now petrified, Dayan Derke became the 'black master' of the Xövsgöl region. Until the end of the 1920s, when it was carted away by zealous communists, a man-sized vertical stone stood outside the cave, and the cleft at its summit was said to have been caused by Chinggis's sword. Some people say that the stone once lay flat and raised itself to a vertical position. The stolen woman is said to have hidden herself in the crevices of the cave, her breasts giving out spouts of health-giving water. Lamas give the spirit a different biography, according to which the shaman Dayan Derke was defeated by the

Dalai Lama and converted to Buddhism. The shaman ran away from Tibet to Xövsgöl, stealing a wife on the way, and was turned to stone. To 'calm down' the angry Dayan Derke spirit, lamas built a monastery and conducted rituals at the stone, wrapping it in cloth and laying offerings before it. At the main Lamaist annual ritual the stone was said to become wet and to give off the smell of human sweat. On the same day shamans held seances for Dayan Derke, but inside the cave. Rather than 'calming down' the spirit as the lamas tried to do, they celebrated its power and transferred it to neophyte shamans from all over North Mongolia and southern Buryatia. The subsequent history of this cult deserves further research. The monastery was destroyed in the 1930s. However, a complex syncretistic cult continues, perhaps largely for reasons of secrecy, inside the cave where, at this time (1980s), there are Buddhist paintings, a statue of Dayan Derke as a warrior, and a long text painted on a cloth. This text is in what I have called the chiefly idiom, mentioning success for the Soviet space programme, the uprising by a warrior-hero called Ayush, the undertakings of Soviet and Mongolian political leaders, and a eulogy in honour of the 1980 Moscow Olympics (Galdanova *et al.* 1984: 3–6).

We can observe that shamanism remained more powerful, and the chiefly/ Buddhist mode more defensive, in forested mountainous regions broken up by large rivers and with relatively small amounts of open pasture. This suggests that the chiefly mode can only gear itself up to a totalizing vision of the world in wide steppeland, which not only corresponds in some way to the reiterative sameness of the conceptual landscape but also provides the ecological conditions for the reproduction of nomadic patri-focused groups. We may perhaps also conclude that the shamanic vision is not simply a mapping of human differences and adventures on to the land but is also a response to the actual diversity, of species and habitats, touching on people's lives and which they feel to be important. The contrast between the central Mongolians' ritual denial of travelling, which for them is a boring, laborious necessity, and shamanic enacted celebration of 'tracks' and 'ways' through difficult obstacles, seems to fit with actual environments. But however tempting such ecological observations may be they are insufficient, since they do not account for the dynamics of the concepts involved: headmen and chiefs died and entered the ranks of unmarked and identical male ancestors, but shamans (and suffering women), by dying, went on giving birth to spirits. Each vision implies the other, though they might not acknowledge it. As a result the two landscapes are always superimposed on one another, even if, at a given time and place, one or other is in the ascendent.

I hope I have shown that there is a connection between topographies, descriptive terminologies for landscapes and political structures, and that these 'place' different kinds of *ego* in the world. In the case I have described, the two kinds of 'person' are ideally male members of replicating hierarchical lineages on the one hand, and mediating, birth-giving, persons-in-transit on the other (perhaps ideologically 'females'). But actual people, whether men or women, can take either or both of these stances.

Notes

I am grateful to Mark Lake, whose essay on Mongolian pastoralism helped formulate my ideas about the dynamism of pastoral circuits.

In transliteration from Mongolian languages I have used standard modern Khalkh as a basis (though without differentiation between the front and back g). The exception is the term *khan* as opposed to *xan* (chief, king) which is generally known in English by the former spelling.

1. By this I refer to the ways the Mongols see themselves as *in* the landscape (a sense of place) and the ways in which it is conceptualized as *out there* (a sense of space).
2. A friend from the Xorchin region of Inner Mongolia said: 'When our family moved to a new village, my father told me he saw a beautiful tree growing nearby. It was all on its own, with thick bushy leaves, and this was an area with no trees, just sand and some bushes. "That tree must be something," he thought. "A village should have a tree to worship." He took big rocks the size of a human head and put them at the foot of the tree, and he made that tree the *shanzh mod* (sacred tree) of the village.'
3. For example, in the 13th-c. chronicle, *The Secret History of the Mongols*, it was a mountain, Burxan-Xaldun, which saved the life of Chinggis Khaan, when he was fleeing from his enemies, the Merkid. Chinggis then vowed that he and his descendants would worship the mountain ever after (Mostaert 1953: 319–20).
4. This term is used for want of a better one, since what is involved is not just worship in the usual sense of the term but also bargaining, pressurizing, and exchange with the entity.
5. I use the word 'supernatural' to indicate that the abilities would be so considered in Western academic discourse. The Mongols, however, do not have the idea of the supernatural. Certain people, they say, simply have greater abilities in understanding and manipulating *baigal* (the way things are) than others.
6. *Khaan* (lit. Mongolian *khagan*) is the term for Emperor; *khan* is the term for a lesser prince or chief.
7. 'Taij kün böö baixgüi, Xarts kün böö baina.' (An aristocrat of the Borjigid cannot be a shaman. Common people are shamans.) A. Hurelbaatar, personal communication.
8. A co-ordinate singularity is a point which is not intrinsically special but appears singular when a co-ordinate system has been chosen in a specific way, e.g. if latitude and longitude have been chosen then the North and South Poles are co-ordinate singularities.
9. The tents at a camp are also ranked by seniority, from west to east.
10. No one has done the work, but it would be interesting to investigate the relation between repetitions of naming systems, the extent of nomadic journeys, and the notions of local community or 'homelands' in different parts of Mongolia. An indication that some relation would be found can be seen from the fact that along the border of Mongolia with Siberia from Lake Xovsgol to the Xangai Range, a

distance of some 1,000 km., there are six mountains named Burin Khan, giving an average of 166 km. in each section.

11. The names and visualization of mountain spirits is complicated by the fact that Buddhist lamas 'transformed' earlier native spirits, renaming them as a category (*sabdag, luus*) and conflating them with various minor deities or demons in the Lamaist pantheon. This process did not succeed in eliminating the earlier ideas of the spirits in many regions. However, the Lamaist deities are very various in form, including anthropomorphic, animal-headed, and other images. Today hardly any Mongols know these partly assimilated spirits, and they continue to worship the mountains with a blank space bracketed off for the spirit ('the spirit of the mountain, if only I knew what it looks like or what it is called').

12. I am indebted to John Gaunt for this point.

13. The term *oboo* derives from the verb 'to pile up', 'to heap'. This term is used in the Lamaist cult and also in some shamanist areas, e.g. among the Daurs, but elsewhere the chiefly cult in the shamanist idiom used other terms for the stone altar.

14. At Buryat non-Buddhist *oboo*s this was generally by lineage membership and age, elsewhere by rank (e.g. clerics above laymen, aristocrats above common folk, elders above juniors).

15. Widows of aristocratic men, who were the residual heirs of their husbands, did act as patrons at the mountain cults, but they would find an excuse—feeling tired, etc.—not to climb to the summit.

16. In regions with a more prominent chiefly ritual practice than among the Daurs, river cults were not the exclusive domain of women.

17. Women were often likened by Daurs to pheasants, with their bright feathers and plump shape.

18. I am indebted for this important point to an unpublished paper by Sherry Ortner concerning the decline of shamanism among the Sherpas of Nepal.

19. The question of the recognition by shamans of the female role in social reproduction is complex and cannot be dealt with adequately in a chapter on landscapes. (I have mentioned that shamans acknowledge and even prioritize 'female' kinds of powers in the landscape.) The matter is complicated in that all north Asian societies have several different kinds of inspirational practitioners (whom I have lumped together as 'shamans', though they have different names in native languages). Some of these practitioners specialize in rituals to do with women's fertility. They are always women shamans. However, there are certain great shamans, who may be either male or female, who have pretensions to mastery of the entire range of shamanic activities. This creates a zone of potential rivalry between them and the specialist practitioners.

20. For example, among the Buryats: *kugshen*, 'old women'; *ubugun*; 'old man'; *baabai*, 'father'; *eji*, 'mother'; *xada*, 'cliff'; *onggon*, 'spirit'; *shudker*, 'demon'.

21. By contrast, the inhabitants of the sky are pictured without all this constructed, built apparatus. They seem to float about separately, riding horses or other animals, but somehow perched on clouds.

22. There is a Chinggis Khaan mausoleum at Ordos in Inner Mongolia where elaborate rituals of worship take place. It is not considered to be his burial site but is a shrine to his battle-standards and other relics. The mausoleum has been moved several times this century.

23. Ritual structures involving two or more trees, with ropes strung between them representing the 'ways' of spirits, were very common throughout north Asia (Poppe 1940: 60–1; Batubayin 1990).

24. The poetic forms used are parallelism, metre, and control of vowel harmony.

25. Sunchig, a young female shaman aged 25, had a son who was put into the Darxad monastery at age 5. In grief the mother hanged herself, after having cursed her child as follows:

> I want you to lose your all!
> I want you to lose everything you have in this world!
> Have no place on earth!
> Let them tear up the collar of your cloak
> Let them cut your bald head in two! [. . .]
> Let the ravens tear out your tongue, you cur!
> 'Buddha, buddha', you keep saying.
> Though it's but paint and canvas! [. . .]
> 'Lama, lama', you keep saying,
> Though they are but shorn-headed wranglers.
> 'Sacred book, sacred book', you keep saying,
> Though it's but ink and paper!
> 'Religion, religion', you keep saying,
> Though it's but clay and oil paint! (Dioszegi 1961: 202)

Unfortunately, the ethnographer gives no date nor any other information about this incident.

References

ABAYEVA, L. L. (1992). *Kul't gor i buddizm v buryatii*. Moscow: Nauka.

BATUBAYIN (1990). *Customs and Folklore of the Daur People* (in Chinese). Beijing: Press of the Central University of the Nationalities.

BAWDEN, C. R. (1958). 'Two Mongolian Texts Concerning Obo-worship', *Oriens Extremus*, 5/1: 23–41.

——(1968). 'Mongol Notes', *Central Asiatic Journal*, 12/2: 101–43.

CARRUTHERS, DOUGLAS (1910). *Unknown Mongolia*, i and ii. London: Hutchinson.

DIOSZEGI, V. (1961). 'Problems of Mongolian Shamanism', *Acta Etnographica*, 10/1–2.

——(1963). 'Ethnogenic Aspects of Darkhat Shamanism', *Acta Orientalia*, 16: 55–81.

GALDANOVA, G. R. (1987). *Dolamaistskie Verovaniya Buryat*. Novosibirsk: Nauka.

——*et al.* (eds.) (1984). *Lamaizm v Buryatii: XVIII v.–nachala XX v*. Novosibirsk: Nauka.

HEISSIG, W. (1953). 'A Mongolian Source to the Lamaist Suppression of Shamanism in the Seventeenth Century', *Anthropos*, 48: 1–29 and 493–536.

HUMPHREY, CAROLINE (1974). 'Inside a Mongol Tent', *New Society*, Oct., London.

——(1994). 'Shamanic Practices and the State in Northern Asia: Views from the Centre and Periphery', in N. Thomas and C. Humphrey (eds.), *Shamanism, History and the State*, 191–228. Ann Arbor, Mich.: Michigan University Press.

HYER, P., and JAGCHID, S. (1983). *A Mongolian Living Buddha: Biography of the Kanjurwa Khutughtu*. Albany, NY: State University of New York Press.

KAZAKEVICH, V. A. (1934). *Sovremennaya Mongol'skaya Toponimika*. Leningrad: Akademiya Nauk SSSR.

KHANGALOV, M. N. (1958). *Sobraniye Sochinenii*, i. Ulan-Ude: Buryatskoye Knizhnoye Izdetal'stvo.

LAKOFF, G., and JOHNSON, M. (1980). *Metaphors We Live By*. Chicago: Chicago University Press.

LATTIMORE, OWEN (1942). *Mongol Journeys*. London: Travel Book Club.

MIKHAILOV, T. M. (1987). *Buryatskii Shamanizm: Istoriya, Struktura i Sotsial'nyye Funktsii*. Novosibirsk: Nauka.

MOSTAERT, A. (1953). *Sur quelques passages de l'histoire secrète des Mongoles*. Cambridge, Mass.: Harvard-Yenching Institute.

POPPE, N. (ed. and trans.) (1940). *Letopisi Xorinskikh Buryat: Khroniki Tuguldur Tobyeva i Vandana Yumsunova*. Trudy Instituta Vostokovedeniya XXXIII. Moscow: Akademiya Nauk SSSR.

POZDNEYEV, A. M. [1896] (1971). *Mongolia and the Mongols*, i, ed. J. KREUGER, Indiana University Uralic and Altaic Series, 61. Bloomington, Ind.: Indiana University Press.

SZYNKIEWICZ, SLAVOJ (1986). 'Settlement and Community among the Mongolian Nomads: Remarks on the Applicability of Terms', *East Asian Civilisations*, 1: 10–44.

TAMBIAH, STANLEY J. (1970). *Buddhism and the Spirit-Cults in North-East Thailand*. Cambridge: Cambridge University Press.

TATAR, MAGDALENA (1984). 'Nature-Protecting Taboos of the Mongols', in E. Ligeti (ed.), *Tibetan and Buddhist Studies Commemorating the 200th Anniversary of the Birth of Alexander Csoma de Koros*, ii. Budapest: Akademia Kiado.

ZHUKOVSKAYA, N. L. (1988). *Kategorii i Simvolika Traditsionnoi Kul'tury Mongolov*. Moscow: Nauka.

7

Seeing the Ancestral Sites: Transformations in Fijian Notions of the Land

CHRISTINA TOREN

Remarking Places and Events

Where I lived in Fiji, in the chiefly village of Sawaieke on the island of Gau, people routinely remark on the most ordinary events.[1] So, when the truck that twice a day makes a circuit of the villages is sighted in the distance or its horn heard someone is bound to say, *Lori*! Or it might be the doctor's van, or the drum for church, or women returning from fishing, and all of us present can see or hear whatever it is, but even so someone always remarks 'Doctor!' or, 'There beats the drum!' or, 'Here come the women from fishing!' And any walk with others elicits similar remarks as the group passes a landmark: '*Ia*, the old village!' or '*Ia*, Crabshit Pool!' or '*Ia*, the school!'

One might indeed wish to go to meet the truck or attend the church service, or stop at the place named, but this is rarely the point of the utterance. Rather it seems to be the very fact that the happening is expected or the place known that renders remark on it proper and even satisfying.

What is implicitly remarked on is the passing of time, often in terms of places and landmarks that function as reference points for the succession of events. Historical time too can be marked by the succession of places; the Lands Commission of 1916 recorded histories of the social divisions on Gau and their claims to land: these name various apical ancestors, but more important is the recital of the succession of places where they had made villages.[2] This made it clear that the social division called the *yavusa* was constituted as much by the land to which people belonged as by the people to whom that land belonged. The remarking of places and routine events by contemporary villagers likewise has implicit in it their sense of belonging to those places and that round of events. In this sense of belonging, space and time are experientially dimensions of one another: the self is always placed in time, whether 'here now' or 'here then'.[3]

This awareness of 'time emplaced' informs the process through which Fijian villagers constitute their identities, their sense of themselves, as rooted in their natal land. This chapter addresses their conceptions of the land in so far as these can be gathered from historical records, from accounts of the ancestors, and from what people say and do in everyday life in the *vanua* (country, land, or place) of Sawaieke.[4] The focus is on the land as it is experienced or lived in terms of people's active engagement with it. For Fijian villagers, the idea of the person as rooted in his or her natal place is powerfully real; one is virtually a material manifestation of that place. The corollary of this is that the passing of time, and personal experience of the changes time brings, are made manifest in the land itself.

Moreover, the transformational potential inherent in the awareness of 'time emplaced' renders the ancestral past not as a frozen, timeless, mythical domain, but as historical and dynamic. And even as this dynamic past continues to inform the dynamic present, the changes wrought in the present are made integral to the land, and the present comes to overlap, becomes as it were continuous with, that ancestral past.

Vanua may refer to a part of the world, to a part of Fiji, to a confederation of villages (*vanua ko Sawaieke*, the eight villages of Sawaieke country), to the people who occupy it, to a subset of those people who are classified as landspeople, to a certain spot, or to a place on one's body. Fijian villagers are holders and users (*i taukei*, lit. 'owners') of land, but because this birthright is grounded in an idea of people as materially belonging to the land, being an owner does not allow one to alienate it. The people are *lewe ni vanua*—*lewe* being given in Capell's (1941) dictionary as 'the flesh or inner part of a person or thing'; in other words, people are the land's very substance.

The phenomenological world of villagers is one where the power immanent in land and sea, and manifest in exchange relations and ritual, materially informs their identity as particular Fijian persons. Their ideas rest in part on verbal representations of the land, but are as much visceral as intellectual; in their daily lives, villagers emphasize embodied sensuous experience: that which seems experientially to be unmediated, directly derived from seeing, hearing, touching, and smelling the land and consuming its products.[5]

Historically more recent ideas about Christianity, 'development', and commoditization of the economy, also inform villagers' conceptions of the power immanent in the land; so they inform too their conceptions of themselves as persons and their relations with one another. That these conceptions remain peculiarly Fijian is a function of the inherently transformative nature of cognitive processes: in taking on ideas introduced over the past 150 years, Fijians have transformed not only their indigenous ideas and practice, but also those introduced by missionaries and colonizers.[6]

Given their centrality for identity, Fijian conceptions of the land have profound politico-economic implications. In ritual, balanced reciprocity in exchange across groups is transformed into tribute to chiefs, and in day-to-day life villagers routinely appeal to traditions of chiefship. Chiefly ritual appears able to contain equally salient practices of equality, so villagers come to conceive of hierarchy as a given dimension of social relations. But what the analyst finds is a struggle to make hierarchy contain relations of equality, and a recognition that the very continuity of this hierarchy depends on the dynamic of those equal relations, which cannot ultimately be contained by ritual, but only by raw power—by superior physical force. So, in daily village life, hierarchy and equality are set one against the other and each is made at once to reference and to subvert the other.[7]

This historical (and continuing) tension between tribute and balanced reciprocity, between hierarchy and equality, is inscribed in the very features of the land and is evident in people's conceptions of it. But as I show below, the 'meaning' of these features has been and continues to be transformed.

Ancestral Places

The term *yavusa* is derived from *yavu*—the earth foundation of a house in which, in pre-colonial days, the bodies of the dead were buried.[8] The names of house foundations are conceived of as eternal so they were given to new *yavu* when people deserted old villages and established new ones; people were (and still are) understood to belong to the *yavusa*, or group of related houses, that was founded by their ancestors.[9]

The existence of old gardens can be inferred from levelled land and the nature of secondary growth, old village sites from the remains of the deserted *yavu*. The height of the *yavu* varied with the status of its owners: a chief's house might be 1.5 metres or more above ground level. So the higher the *yavu* the more powerful its owner, and tributary relations were inscribed in the topography of the land. But equality was implicit here too for houses were built 'facing each other' (*veiqaravi*) with the 'land' side of one house facing the 'sea' side of the next; this referenced balanced reciprocity in exchange relations across households.

The term for kin (*weka*) may be extended to include all ethnic Fijians and kin terms are routinely used in reference and address. With only one exception, all kin relations are hierarchical and require varying degrees of respect and avoidance. The exception is for kin who are possible spouses or siblings-in-law, i.e. cross-cousins.[10] Cross-cousins are equals, but across sex they are equals only outside marriage; any husband is axiomatically above his wife so 'every man is a chief in his own house'. Even so, equal and hierarchical relations are predicated on one another, because marriage depends on relations of equality between cross-cousins across exogamous clans (*mataqali*), both across and within sex.

So, in any village, the varying height of the *yavu* and the disposition of houses evinces an antithesis between hierarchy and equality, between non-marriageable kin (where the paradigmatic reference is to the hierarchical household and clan) and marriageable kin (who as cross-cousins are equals across households, clans, and *yavusa*).

Yavu tabu or 'forbidden *yavu*' are distinguished from old village sites and from the *yavu* of the present village; they are usually situated on garden land belonging to a *yavusa* or to a clan, whose honorific titles are derived from the names of their forbidden *yavu*. Adults say one should not tread on such a place, but one young man told me that children today do not care—if they see a coconut fallen there they go and take it; when he was a child one did not do so. If one wants a thing from a *yavu tabu* one should ask its owners to fetch it.

Only the owner of the *yavu* can be bold enough to fetch something from the top of his *yavu*. . . . If you tread or lay a hand on the top of a *yavu tabu* or one of those dangerous places—places where the ancestors had their gardens—then you will fall ill. If you tread on it, your feet will swell . . . until you can't walk at all.

Old village sites belong to their long-dead owners, as do the abandoned gardens inland and the ruins of the fortified hilltop villages; one visits such places only with good reason and in company, for who knows what one might find there? So too, if one is coming home from or visiting another village at night, one goes in a group and talks and laughs loudly to scare away any devils that might be lurking in the bush that borders the road. But some men walk alone at night between villages, and two told me they do not believe in *tevoro* (lit. 'devils', the ancestors, *kalou vu*, in their malign aspect).

A *vu* or ancestor is one who died before the coming of the Christian church, and most adults maintain that while they continue to exist, they are no longer so effective (*mana*) as once they were. This is because the *mana* (lit. 'efficacy') of an ancestor, like that of a chief, of the old gods, and of the Christian God is said to be augmented, if not brought into being, by the attendance of people upon them.[11]

Methodist missionary success in Fiji was assured when Cakobau, the most powerful of high chiefs, converted in 1854. Today virtually all ethnic Fijians are Christians, the vast majority still being Methodists and assiduous church-goers.[12] Services take the form laid down in the prayer book, but they differ from those held in Methodist churches elsewhere: the layout and use of church seating evinces hierarchy in the relations between *yavusa* chiefs and the congregation, whose own seating is differentiated in terms of an interaction between rank and seniority (see Toren 1990: 119–37).

People attend on (*qarava*, lit. 'face') the Christian God, who is above all. The old gods and ancestors still exist but their power has waned for they are no longer the object of the people's sacrifices; so the Christian God is invoked not as 'the only god' but as 'the only god who is served'. But the ancestors resent any meddling with their own places. When the Gau secondary school was built in the late 1970s, a full *yaqona* (kava) ceremony was performed on the site with libations of the drink being poured to placate the ancestral owner. But later he took revenge by attacking at night some teenage boarders at the school who woke to find this devil on their chests trying to choke the life out of them. More ceremonies had to be performed. Older people with orthodox Christian views may deny these occurrences, but most people I know give credit to them.

Villagers in Sawaieke country attend up to four or so church services a week; they also assert ideas of immanent ancestral power and the continued existence of old gods such as Degei (the snake creator god) and Daucina (see below). In their benign aspect under the sway of the Christian God, the ancestors bless their descendants, while misfortune may be their punishment for wrongdoing. But they may be empowered too by those who, ignoring the true God, offer them sacrifices and so unleash their malign powers—a matter I return to below. So the ancestors have still to be feared and their dwelling-places treated with circumspection, for their intentions towards the living seem always to be equivocal.

Besides the obvious *yavu* one may also see great mounds of earth or stones like Naivinivini ('Heaped-up'). Its present owner, a member of the former priestly clan, told me it was the house foundation of a founding ancestor and the biggest in Fiji. The (edited) story of this *yavu* is given below in the words of an elderly man of chiefly birth (not the owner):

Once there was a founding ancestor [*vu*] in this country of Sawaieke ['There's-water-here'] called Ravuravu ['Killer-with-a-club']. His *yavu* is over there at Nagaga ['Drinking-hole'] a beach on the way to Somosomo village ['Mangrove-mud']. The people used to go there to serve him. But for firewood this chief required trees like the *dawa*, mango and chestnut—tall and heavy trees; it took who knows how many people to drag a tree-trunk all the way there.

One day a war happened between Sawaieke and Nukuloa ['Black-sand']. Nukuloa was weakening so they searched Fiji for a powerful person to help them. The message went to Dama in Bua ['Frangipani-tree'], to a chief called Radikedike ['Fire-fly']. You can see his *yavu* at one side of this village; this [was the beginning of this] *yavu*.

The Nukuloa chief and Radikedike agreed to become allies. Radikedike was told to come through the reef at Nagali ['the Solitary One'] opposite Nukuloa. But he came through at Sawaieke. The Nukuloa chief had said 'You will see a *tavola* tree on the hilltop; it marks where I live.' But at Ravuravu's place there also stood a big *tavola*. Radikedike saw it and came ashore at Vatoaleka ['Short-blessing']. If you go there you will see his footprint on top of a stone. This is proof that he came to Gau.

But when he arrived, no one took any notice of him and he realized his coming here was a mistake. He was carrying a hundred huge chestnuts that hung from his arm—so what about the size of this victorious chief? He wanted to roast his chestnuts, so he climbed up to Ravuravu's house. 'What do you want?' 'I want firewood to roast some chestnuts for me to eat.' Ravuravu said, 'The only firewood is that beside you. If you can carry it, fine'. Radikedike took one of these firewoods, stripped off its leaves, and went outside. Ravuravu was astonished. What a strong man! It took fifty Sawaieke people to drag such a tree so far as here , but this was only one man. 'I am getting old, I shall hand the country over to him and let him lead it.' So these two changed over at that time . . .

Now Radikedike always wanted women. The ladies then used to go net-fishing at Muana ['Its-tip']—just as you do. On their way back they used to sing until they reached Naivinivini. He built his mound [his *yavu*] there where the women ceased to sing. Near Denimana ['Crabshit Pool'] you will see the [deserted *yavu* of the] old village, which was situated there when Radikedike took over.

That this story is taken to be a valid account of the past was evident in the teller's insistent linking of its details to the present; moreover, it was prefaced by observations on the ritual duties of *yavusa*, on the remarkable physical size and powers of the chiefs of former times, and a comparison between their strategies in war and the teller's experience of war in Malaya. But for both the teller and his audience (myself and half a dozen children), the continuing power of such a story lies in its references to known landmarks, whose salience is presumed to be of the same order for the hearers as for their forebears. The past referred to is distant and radically different from the present, but the story emphasizes material and manifest continuity between the present and that past.

It explains that Naivinivini is the house foundation of an ancestor god and, given that the height of chiefly *yavu* inscribes hierarchy in the land itself, suggests that its size reflects glory on Sawaieke people whose ancestor was so great as to merit it. The storyline is a common one: a founding ancestor arrives as a stranger, shows himself to be *mana*, and is given power by an aging but still powerful local god. That this warlike chief has to be warmed by fires made of the trunks of fruit-bearing trees denotes his waning powers, that those powers are still great is given by the size of the trees thus consumed. Ravuravu must be overcome if the rebellious tributary village of Nukuloa is to triumph over Sawaieke. His name denotes war, so the heat [*katakata*] he absorbs will make him *yalo katakata*, hot-spirited or angry. A tall *tavola* tree marks the dwelling of Ravuravu; its wood is used for making the great slit drums on which, in pre- and early colonial times, one group challenged another to war and beat out the rhythms of its success in killing and eating the enemy (Seeman 1862: 363; Clunie 1977: 25, 27). Given that a boy's umbilical cord is buried and a tree planted on top of it, tree and man are identified; the war-drums and Ravuravu manifest the land's immanent power converted into material form via consumption of its sacrificed products. Ravuravu's power derives from the burning of fruit-bearing trees, a form of consumption here analagous to explicit sacrifice: to killing and eating subject people and to drinking *yaqona*.

In telling how Sawaieke village emerged victorious and how peace came to Sawaieke country, the story explains and justifies Sawaieke's precedence as the chiefly village and the paramount position of its *yavusa* chiefs. The very presumption of Nukuloa, in seeking to escape from its tributary relation to Sawaieke, makes Radikedike mistake his entry through the reef. He leaves his footprint on a stone as he comes ashore and climbs the hill where he takes firewood, not to spend its fruitfulness in generating in himself a warlike heat, but to roast chestnuts to eat. The huge chestnuts denote his own fruitfulness and strength, and his eating of them gives him another form of the heat that is proper to men, the heat that makes a man desire women. The leadership of Radikedike and the attendance of the Sawaieke people upon him is implicit in their allowing him to build his great *yavu* at the spot where the women returning from fishing ceased to sing; it also implies that he had many wives and fathered many children.

Radikedike may be identified with gods of other areas, e.g. Daucina, the Lamp-Bearer, famous all over Fiji (Hocart 1929: 191). In the form of a handsome stranger or a desirable cross-cousin, Daucina haunts coastlines and streams and seduces any woman foolish enough to bathe alone at night. In Gau, Radikedike is not identified with Daucina; the latter is a *tevoro* (devil) whereas Radikedike by contrast is considered a local ancestor—one whereby Gau people have the same founder god, *veitauvu*, as people from Vanua Levu, the island from which Radikedike originated. Those who are *veitauvu* are 'owners' in each other's country: this joking relationship references the equality between cross-cousins, and I return to it below.

Today the *yavu* of Radikedike stands in a grove of trees at one side of Sawaieke village; and, like the deserted *yavu* of the old village and the forbidden *yavu* in the bush, is respectfully avoided. Young people seem not to know that the dead were once buried in the *yavu* of houses, but children do not play in such places, nor does anyone walk there. The villages of Sawaieke country, including Nukuloa, continue annually to make formal tribute to Sawaieke chiefs; though as the Lands Commission records show, Nukuloa chiefs were attempting to assert their independence as late as 1916. The *tauvu* relation between Gau and Vanua Levu is still observed and their joking is unremitting; a visitor from Vanua Levu is an honoured guest for whom no attention is too much and to whom nothing can be refused. Likewise, young women continue to be vulnerable to the attentions of Daucina. Eating and *yaqona*-drinking are also, at least implicitly, still forms of sacrifice: a prayer is said before every meal (even morning or afternoon tea), every *yaqona*-drinking helps constitute the position of chiefs *i cake*—above—and the drinking of the installation *yaqona* makes the paramount chief one who has 'all the ancestors in Gau at his back'. Older wooden houses in Sawaieke are built on *yavu* of varying height, but many of the new houses of concrete breeze-blocks are not; their layout within any village is still that of *veiqaravi* (lit. facing each other). And at three different times on Sunday and three or four times during the week a great drum made of the wood of the *tavola* tree calls people to church, which stands at the centre of the village on one side of the *rara*, village green.

Ancestral Powers in Land and Sea

In prayers and sermons in church one is regularly told that the Christian God made the world and everything in it. But many of the stories told to children in school or that one hears when people are gathered to drink *yaqona* or to work together stretching pandanus for making mats, suggest that it was the original ancestors who formed the land in distinctive ways. The water of Waiboteigau, 'Water-broken-from-the-middle', the stream that rises in Gau's inland hills, was stolen from two powerful ancestresses whom the Sawaieke chiefs claim as theirs.[13] The water was carried away by the first of ten brothers in a leaf of a plant called *salasalaqato*—so fine-textured, said the teller, one would not believe water could be carried in it. When the first brother—Radua—arrived at the top of a hill he saw that his nine brothers had set sail without him; in anger he threw the leaf full of water to the ground and the course taken by the water that flowed from it retraced that marked by the water which had dripped from the leaf as he had made his way from the ancestresses' house to the top of the hill. Radua slipped and fell on the hillside and there he left his handprint in a stone near the source of the stream.

Besides these features—the *yavu* of the old villages, the deserted gardens, the occasional mound or cairn of stones, the foot- and handprints of the ancestors—there are the graves of forebears. Villagers in general hold that the material substance of the dead should become one with the land from which, in life, they obtained their food by virtue of the fertile powers of its first owners— their founding ancestors. So the bodies of those who die elsewhere are sent home to their native village to be buried in the land of the clan or the *yavusa* to which they belong.[14] And once a year young men are ordered to make 'clean' (*savasava*), that is, to weed, all graves in preparation for the holiday and ritual season that is Christmas and New Year. Thus all the dead, including the pre-Christian ancestors, continue to be respected.[15]

In the days when the *tabu* (prohibition) still had force, a chief might forbid any taking of fruit or fishing of streams. The place would be marked with a pattern of crossed sticks or somesuch and one who offended against the *tabu* would fall sick and even die. These kinds of *tabu* were called *vakatalele* (lit. 'something hung up'). The powers that inhabit the land still protect themselves and their products—their efficacy being manifest through the imposition of a *tabu* by one who has the ancestral right to impose it and who does so under proper circumstances.[16] During my first fieldwork a married man in his 40s told me that even today 'the *tabu* according to the land is still effective'. He had tested this himself. Some years before, on the death of a person of high chiefly rank, he had laid a *tabu* on the salt water from Sawaieke to Navukailagi; fishing could take place only right out near the reef. One night he and his wife were coming back from such a trip and were close to Sawaieke when they saw a large crab and he speared it. His wife was angry with him for breaking the *tabu* he himself had instituted but he told her it did not matter. 'I wanted to know, Christina, I wanted to see for myself if the *tabu* according to the land was still *mana*.' When the hundred nights were over and the *tabu* was formally lifted and everyone went net-fishing, he was there, swimming along to join the others, when suddenly a fish with a sharp snout came leaping towards him, in and out of the water, making straight for him very fast and it struck his face with a glancing blow to the cheek, cutting it there. 'And then, mother of Manuel, I realized the *mana* of the *tabu* according to the land. I saw it. I had proved thereby the *mana* of that *tabu*.'[17]

All parts of the country are owned and inhabited—even if one does not always know by whom. Indeed many references to old gods and ancestors are oblique; so I was often told by young people in their late teens that 'something' (*e dua na ka*) was there, or likely to be there, in spots we passed on those occasions when I went to the gardens—in a large and beautiful bamboo grove, in a stand of *ivi* trees on a hillside and, always, in any spot where the remains of old *yavu* were to be seen. The knowledge of all these places and landmarks as formed, held, owned, guarded, used, inhabited, by human or ancestral beings, enters into villagers' conceptions of what the land is and who they are themselves.

The Land and Personal Identity

Implicit in much Fijian cultural practice is the idea that land and sea literally empower those who belong to them (at once their 'substance' and their 'owners') by providing for their material needs—the hardwoods and softwoods, the bamboos and vines for housebuilding; the paper mulberry for barkcloth; pandanus for mats; the coconut for food, oil, string, baskets, bowls, and other things; and the many tubers, fruit trees, fish, shellfish, seaweeds, and so on that form the basis of the subsistence economy. People need money for clothes, kerosene, certain foods, and consumer goods, for secondary-school fees for their children, for weekly donations to church funds and, intermittently, to community projects such as new school buildings; but land and sea still provide the necessities when money fails—a common occurrence in a mixed subsistence and cash-cropping economy.

This potency of land and sea is transformed into equal relations between people via the balanced exchange of goods and services across households and *yavusa*, and into hierarchy in tributary prestations of *yaqona* roots (*Piper methysticum* or kava) to chiefs, under whose aegis it is transformed into drink and redistributed to the people. Chiefs reciprocate tribute with *tabua* (whales' teeth).[18]

Throughout central Fiji, with respect to ethnically Fijian people, everyone is either 'land' or 'sea' in relation to others. Within Sawaieke village, members of *yavusa* Sawaieke are 'land', members of the chiefly *yavusa* Nadawa are 'sea'; in relation to the island of Batiki, Sawaieke country (all eight villages) is 'land' and Batiki is 'sea'; so even though one is born into a given classification, one may be 'sea' *vis-à-vis* certain people even while one is 'land' *vis-à-vis* others.

Chiefly *yavusa* are 'sea', but this does not mean that 'sea' is above 'land', for the exchange relation between them is one of strictly balanced reciprocity. So, when eating in each other's company, people classified as 'sea' do not eat fish and those who are 'land' do not eat pork; each makes available to the other the products of their labour.[19] That one is by birth either 'land' or 'sea' can explain personal behaviour or dispositions, for example, one is no good at fishing or gets seasick because one is 'land', or skilled at fishing because one is 'sea'.

Men as gardeners who provide 'true food' (*kakana dina*, root vegetables essential to any proper meal) are associated with land, and women, who provide fish, with sea.[20] A baby girl's umbilical cord is placed under a stone in a stream or on the reef so she may become skilled at fishing; a boy's is buried at the base of new-planted tree so he may become a good gardener. A tree may prompt the remark, 'I planted this for so-and-so' or 'That is my tree'; and if such a tree does not flourish a boy's elders may express worries about his health.

These formalizations of the way land and sea enter into identity are aspects of the material but still implicit senses through which one knows oneself to be attached to a place and a very product of it—knowledge that is rendered explicit in the responsibilities one bears in relation to others.

In Sawaieke, people do not make much of what were once important associations between certain fish, trees, birds, and each *yavusa*. They talk more of the privileges they have in other 'countries' (*vanua*) as a function of ancestral links to them, or describe the forms which their own *sevusevu* (tributary offering—usually of *yaqona*) takes in these different places, or how the style of their *yaqona*-drinking ritual is distinguished from others. These identifying distinctions are linked to land and sea and to conceptions of oneself as a product of one's native place—but they are made between countries, as much as within them. Links between countries rest in the relation between their ancestors; those who are *veitauvu* (lit. 'of the same root') have the same ancestor god or *vu* while those who are *veitabani* (lit. 'mutually branching') have ancestors who were cross-cousins to one another. These joking relationships denote balanced reciprocity between people of two countries.

Households, *yavusa*, villages, and countries are linked by *sala ni veiwekani*, 'paths of kinship' created by marriage; so relations between *veitauvu* and *veitabani* denote chiefly kinship and reference ancestral marriages. These paths are affirmed and in part constituted in the many life-cycle rituals and in everyday *yaqona*-drinking; they are the route too for the connections between village churches within a country. Marriage takes place between groups whose relative status differs, but it does not itself create hierarchy because the exchange relations are reciprocal and balanced over time. The hierarchical relation created by marriage is that between husband and wife; it is the basis of hierarchical kinship within the household.

In all journeyings about their country, people traverse the paths of kinship created through marriage, and the equality of cross-cousins (and of those who are *veitauvu* and *veitabani* across countries) makes these paths ideally level. But the paths connect households within which hierarchy is axiomatic. Chiefly ritual projects on to the community at large an image of the hierarchical household and references the height of chiefly *yavu*. So inside any given house, village hall, or church, hierarchy appears to become dominant because one has inevitably to find one's appropriate place on the above/below axis that describes the internal space of all buildings. In certain villages one may be above others and the object of their deference and respect; in others one may be below and have oneself to defer. However, in all villages one may find too one's cross-cousins, with whom one may sit as an equal.

Women are embodied paths of kinship because they 'carry the blood of posterity' (*kauta na dra ni kawa*); a woman goes to a man as his equal, his cross-cousin, but as a wife in her husband's house she is never an owner (*i taukei*); on his death she is likely to return to her own village where her brothers are bound to provide her with the staple vegetables. Married women eat 'true food' from land belonging to their husbands' ancestors; once married, even the fish a woman catches are implicitly provided by the same ancestral source, for if she is pregnant and does not yet know it, she ruins the fishing for all the women present. Because one of their number has yet to recognize that she will bear a child who will belong to her husband's house, his ancestors withhold from her, and from all the other wives present, that which their own labours must provide.[21] Thus a lack of success in fishing implicitly reminds the women that they are not owners in their husbands' houses. Women's low status as wives, by contrast to their status as sisters, is historically dependent on their material relation to land, which rendered them unable to attend on and be empowered by their own ancestors; this low status is being transformed by Christian practice whereby a woman can approach God directly without the mediation of a man (see Toren 1988).

The ancestors' benign power from the Christian God makes the land fertile and enables a man to fulfil his obligations to produce 'true food' for consumption and exchange and *yaqona* for tribute to chiefs. But invocations of the ancestors are usually only implicit, for example in the names of the forbidden *yavu* that form the honorific titles of *yavusa* and clan. Even so, in accepting an offering of *yaqona*, one highly respected man of chiefly birth called not only on the Christian God, but on 'the ancestors of the land [*na vu ni vanua*, lit. 'the roots of the land'] that they might also bless our living in the manner of kinship'. Explicit references to fertile power tend more often to invoke the Christian God; so one young man told me that he began each day's work in his garden with a prayer that his work would be fruitful.

God and Commodity Exchange as Sources of Material Power

In prayer and other formal expressions of belief, villagers assert the Christian idea that humans are 'the highest' of God's creation. Thus in a prayer offered at a meeting of the island-wide council, the Sawaieke preacher prayed extempore: 'To Heaven, to the holy dwelling place. You the true God, you the God whom alone is served . . . you created the heavens and you created the earth too that we people might inhabit it. We the people know that we are the most excellent of the creation in your hands . . .

The Christian God and his holy dwelling place come first in any recital of names and places,[22] and Christian practice continues to transform the land; so the landmarks of power today include those wrought by 'development' (*veivakatorocaketaki*, lit. 'moving upwards together'). In 1981 some unused *yavu* in Sawaieke were levelled in the cause of development, making one old man weep and rail impotently at the bulldozer, 'now our *yavu* are lost, those that belonged to our ancestors'. Some old people sympathized, but most people I spoke to did not; 'it is good that the village be made clean', they said.

That villagers associate development and Christianity is clear in a sermon I heard in 1983 in which the preacher—a Sawaieke villager aged about 43—talked about the kingdom of heaven and urged us all to change our ways so that we might be worthy of it. He made development (e.g. the opening up of new roads), and by implication the congregation's involvement in development projects, identical with the progress of Christianity and personal enlightenment. The church and our sincere membership of it are, he told us, the very foundation (*yavu*) of all that is good about life in Fiji.

In another sermon, primarily directed towards children, a man in his 50s, an occasional preacher, said: 'The most important thing for you is your gardening land (*qele*, lit. "earth, soil"). We can't obtain what Indian people can. No. Therefore we must look after the soil that is ours. The soil is ours, it does not belong to the Indians. The soil is ours, it is yours.' He prefaced this statement with the story of an industrious man who every day worked hard on his land and who, when about to die, told his two sons, 'Look, you have your soil, in that soil is hidden a pot of gold; one day it will become visible to you.' Then he died. The sons looked hard for the gold, turning over every patch of earth and incidentally planting crops. These they sold, and because they never ceased to work their land they prospered, and at last the meaning of what their father had said became clear. 'This was their pot of gold; they already had it, it was just their own soil.'

Here is a version of the Protestant ethic, for this tale is not about producing crops for consumption, exchange, and tribute so as to fulfil one's duty to kin and chiefs; it is about producing commodities for sale. The preacher emphasized that land is the material source of well-being for Fijians and does not belong to (and so cannot empower) Fiji Indians who, in other contexts, are often said to have 'no kinship' and to be fully conversant with 'the path of money', which itself implies that commodity exchange might be antithetical to kinship. However, the telling of this tale in church suggests that the diligent production of commodities is desired and blessed by the Christian God and thus implies that it is not antithetical to 'the way according to the land', which is itself held to be at once Fijian and essentially Christian (see Toren 1988). But kinship is in part constituted in gift exchange, so at least some of the profits from the sale of produce must be fed back into exchanges between kin.

One cannot alienate land, but one can alienate its products and thus one might get rich (*vutuniyau*, have plenty of valuables) and gain lots of money. The term for money, *ilavo*, was derived from that for the fruit of the *walai*, a vine that is used for lashing together the parts of temporary houses which, by implication, have no proper *yavu*, foundation. Today, by contrast, money derived from producing commodities is made an explicit foundation for prosperity. So the story suggests that to get rich by selling the land's products is entirely legitimate; but during my 1981–3 fieldwork, no adults ever suggested that one could actually get rich through hard work, though clearly one might use the idea to encourage good practices in the young. Then I was told that a villager could become rich only by attending on the ancestors in their devilish guise, i.e. by witchcraft. One could 'drink *yaqona* on one's own', pour libations to an ancestor and name one of one's close kin—who was thus offered as sacrifice—and so empower the ancestor *and* oneself, so that riches simply came to one. Here personal riches resulted from a selfish, evil act that was antithetical both to kinship and chiefly authority.[23]

However, by 1990, *yaqona* had become a lucrative cash crop and one could indeed become relatively rich by dint of hard work. So on my second field trip I heard people respond to the sight of a garden well filled with mature *yaqona* plants with estimates of how many thousands of Fijian dollars the crop would raise. Money gained by cash-cropping *yaqona* had conspicuously enriched those families with many sons who had remained in the village and had raised their status too, for it enabled them not only to build new houses of concrete blocks, to buy videos and boats, but also to contribute substantially to village projects; in one case where riches had not, at least in part, been redistributed, people suggested that they were ill-gotten gains, obtained by embezzling certain public funds.

So commodity transactions have not precipitated a sharp break with tradition, for money and commodities are not allowed to escape the kinship nexus.[24] Illegitimate riches—by definition those one keeps to oneself—are associated with tradition in the form of an appeal to the ancestors in their malign guise and with 'the path of money' in respect of immoral behaviour. Legitimate riches are those one is prepared to give away and in so doing at once demonstrate and constitute kinship; they are associated with tradition in so far as they are obtained through exploitation of the land, whose ultimate owners are one's own ancestral gods, and with development and Christian practice in so far as the latter are seen to augment the power of chiefs and increase the well-being of the community at large. So villagers' ideas of a transformed and transforming tradition—*cakacaka vakavanua* (lit. 'working, acting, doing in the manner of the land')—allow for a notion of themselves as truly products of a land that has assimilated market exchanges and Christianity (in the case of Gau people a thorough-going Methodism) to itself.

Transforming the Emplaced Past in the Present

Fijian villagers emphasize direct embodied experience of the land: seeing, touching, hearing, and smelling. In old *meke* songs that accompany narrative dances and songs that are more lately authored and sung to guitar music, they regularly celebrate their villages and countries by name, the song of the birds that live there and the smell of flowering trees and plants that grow there. The smell of a place can be a mark of certain ancestors: this is true of the vanilla-like scent of the sand at a beach near Sawaieke, while an inexplicable bad smell in the house alerts one to the potentially malign presence of 'the two ladies' (*Ko i rau na marama*). Smell is a feature of personal attractiveness, so the flowers that women wear to community celebrations (and later usually present to male guests) are selected as much for their scent as for their appearance, and when a man comments on a garland he is likely to suggest that its smell is seductive: 'The scent of your garland is wafting my way' (*E boi vinaka mai na nomu isalusalu*). Here the act of smelling is implicitly a form of consumption and may be allied to the idiom for sexual intercourse, whereby the man 'eats' and the woman is consumed.

Consumption by smell is powerfully evoked in mortuary ceremonies or *reguregu* (lit. sniff-kissing). The corpse is laid out on the floor of a house in the honoured place above, and just before the coffin is closed and removed for burial, the close kin of the dead come one by one, press their noses against the cheek or forehead of the corpse and sniff deeply, taking into themselves its sweet, rotting smell. This ceremony implies that, in the past, death as a radical conversion of substance was pivotal to the cycles of consumption and exchange between the people and the land. The intangible substance of the dead was consumed by their living kin and their tangible substance became part of the foundation of houses to constitute immanent ancestral efficacy (*mana*).

This immanent *mana* was made material in the fertility of land and people and, crucially, in the person of the paramount chief. The people were the land's substance; they gardened and fished, consumed the products of their labour, and exchanged them in terms of a balanced reciprocity between land and sea. At the same time they rendered certain relations hierarchical through the transformation in ritual of balanced reciprocal exchange into tribute and thus constituted husbands as heads of houses and certain heads of houses as chiefs.[25] The sacrifice of death broke the cycle of exchange and tribute between people, and between people and the land, for the dead were removed from those exchanges between kin to become objects of consumption. But just as consumption of the food products of the land fuelled the living and created the heat of sexual desire that produced children, so the land's eventual consumption of the material substance of the dead constituted the ancestral *mana* that drove the entire process. His installation made a chief at once the object of sacrifice and the sacrifice itself; in drinking the installation *yaqona* he died as a man to be reborn as a living god (Sahlins 1983). His sacrifice rendered the *yaqona* root he received as tribute a medium for the conversion of immanent and dangerous ancestral *mana* into a material form whose effects could be known by the lesser chiefs (i.e. married men) who drank after him.

A paramount chief also received tribute in the form of people taken captive in war; they were sacrificed on such occasions as the building of his house where they were buried upright at the base of its corner posts, or their bodies might form the rollers over which his outrigger canoe was launched. Such prisoners were also regularly eaten; thus 'the flesh of the land'—but of land that was not one's own, for one did not eat close kin—was directly consumed by the high chief, to at once express and constitute his *mana*, which was dispensed to other men who ate after him. In his own person he converted immanent ancestral power into a manifest efficacy in war and into fertility and so came to embody his country's prosperity, while his talking chief or herald was literally its face or eye (*matanivanua*).[26]

Today death can be a sacrifice only to the Christian God and villagers are likely to deny that any other ideas are implicit in mortuary and installation rites and in day-to-day *yaqona*-drinking. But the transformations of earlier ideas evinced in what is said and done by contemporary villagers continue to bind their identities to the land itself. And even as the land has been and continues to be transformed by human action, so villagers transform their conceptions of the land and the past in which it was formed.

Historically these conceptual transformations were rendered more radical by the move from war villages in the hills to more peaceful confederations of villages on the coast—villages that nevertheless were sometimes at war; then with the 'coming of the light' (*ni lako mai na rarama*) and mass conversions to Christianity in the wake of conversion by powerful chiefs, the coastal villages became settled once and for all. Under British rule the land claims of all were written and mapped; graphic and written representations of the land began to enter into people's consciousness of themselves in relation to land and tied their ideas more closely to genealogy than is likely to have been the case in the past. Today one cannot be deprived of one's land rights because one does not use them, but neither can one formally give land to others; that land rights were written (even though these records are open only to chiefs) rendered the giving of land and the gaining of it by force of use, largely impossible.

The ancestors inhabit the land they formed and through the cycles of production, consumption, exchange, tribute, and sacrifice of which the land is an integral part, they continue to impress historically constituted relations on their descendants. So the tension between competitive equality and hierarchy, between balanced reciprocity and tribute, that is evident in the topography of the land still informs tussles for higher status and chiefly rivalry, both of which are today manifest in a competition to contribute larger sums of money to community projects than others can do. But the actions of the ancestors are not immutable, because the land itself has been and continues to be transformed— the *yavu* levelled, roads built, buildings erected. And in any village, beside the green and adjacent to one another, stand the church and the village hall, where community-wide meetings are held and committees formed to oversee day-to-day village affairs. So relations between people may be 'in the way of the church' (*vakalotu*) and 'the way of central government' (*vakamatanitu*) even while they continue to be 'in the way of kinship' (*vakaveiwekani*), 'the way of chiefs' (*vakaturaga*), and 'the way of the land' (*vakavanua*).

This chapter rests on adult conceptions, but in writing it I have had in mind contemporary village children who, in constituting their own personal identities as Fijians, are inevitably coming to understand the material world (and thus their relations to one another) differently from their elders. So when, for example, adults remark on banal occurrences and the places one has reached on one's way, these utterances and the uttering of them willy-nilly become part of what it is to be a Fijian agent in language. In this sense the kind of thing that is said by adults today was said by their parents and their parents' parents before them, and will be said again by future adults, but what has changed and will continue to change is the significance of the utterance—i.e. that to which it refers in a material sense external to the person and that to which it refers conceptually in terms of the manifold associations that any given utterance may carry in its train.

Thus a future ethnographer will collect data that may at once seem very similar to my own and significantly different—not only because each person's experience is always unique, but also because the tenor of village life is changing even while it remains the same. During my 1981–3 fieldwork young children engaged in commodity transactions only on behalf of their elders, but in 1990 they were doing so on their own behalf—for example, selling their labour and the products of their labour to get the money for admission to a house where the owner of a video shows tapes of films and sporting events. These children are also engaged in relations which, in impressing upon them the obligations of kinship and chieftainship as constituted in giving and tribute, render purely market transactions as potentially threatening to 'the way according to the land'. In the course of all their complex relations with others, to household and kin, to land and sea, to the Christian God and the ancestors, they are cognitively constituting their identity as particular persons who are at once products and producers of a specifically Fijian history.

Like their forebears, these children are experientially placed in time, in a continuing and transforming present in which the transformed and transforming past continues to inhere. They themselves experience how this past continues into the present through the sights, sounds and smells of the land and through fishing and gardening; but like their elders before them, their conceptions of that past are mediated by their relations with their own contemporaries as well as with adults and so must inevitably differ from the conceptions held by adults. This process of cognitive construction in particular persons, mediated by their relations with others, underpins the continuity of culturally specific concepts even while it transforms them, and allows for the appearance of fixedness in a situation of radical change. In this specific, Fijian, case it makes the ancestral past continue into the present even while, for any given person, it effects transformations in the meanings of that past and thus in the meanings that 'the land' can have for present and future generations.

Notes

1. Fieldwork in Fiji was carried out during twenty months from June 1981 to March 1983—supported by grants from the Social Science Research Council and the Horniman Trust, and for five months (May–September) in 1990—supported by a Brief Award from Brunel University. I am grateful to fellow participants in the conference on 'The Anthropology of Landscape' for their comments, and especially to the editors of this volume. The paper was substantially revised for publication in 1992 during my tenure as Macquarie University Research Fellow in the Politics of Tradition in the Pacific.

2. For example: 'Our founding ancestor is Ro[ko]taloko, this ancestor I heard came from Nakauvadra [Pandanus tree], then went to Vanualevu [Great Land] and to Dama in Bua [Frangipani tree] then came here to this island of Gau [Middle] and made a village here, Nukubolo [Sand strewn with coconut leaves] near to Navukailagi [Flew to the sky]. After that they went up higher to live in Qilai [Branches pulled down with a forked stick]—an empty spot . . .' Note that these place names tend to refer to features of the land or to events that occurred there.

3. I am indebted for this insight to Professor Nancy Munn, who made this point in a seminar discussion during the 1992 Conference of the Australian Anthropological Association. See Nancy Munn (1986) for an extended analysis of how spatio-temporal concepts inform cultural praxis on Gawa, in Papua New Guinea.

4. In 1981–3 the population of Sawaieke country was about 1,400 and of the village, 260; by 1990 the population of the country had risen to 1,700–1,800 and the population of the village to about 290. About half Fiji's population (approximately 750,000 people) are of Indian descent, living mainly in towns. There is no Indian community in Gau.

5. This distinction is implicit in villagers' insistence on the validity of direct personal experience as opposed to second-hand knowledge derived from what other people have told one. However, from an analytical point of view no experience can ever be unmediated, as indeed is clear from the ethnography that follows.

6. Ideas are not received 'ready-made' but have always to be cognitively constructed over time by particular persons—this process being inevitably mediated by their relations with one another. Here structure and process are aspects of one another, rather than theoretically separable entities; thus cognitive processes are autonomous and inherently dynamic systems whose products are *always* emergent rather than fixed. Cf. Sahlins (1985) who tries to resolve the Saussurean split between structure and process, but for whom structure remains an ahistorical model of possibilities: 'the system of relations between categories, without a given subject'. *Contra* Sahlins, I would argue that human cognition is itself a historical process because it constitutes—and in constituting transforms—the ideas and practices of which it appears to be the product. In other words, human cognition renders intentionality as inevitably historical (see Toren 1993).

7. Toren (1994), analyses the antithesis between hierarchy and equality in the history of Fijian chiefship.

8. Regarding burial of the dead in the *yavu*, see e.g. Williams (1982: 191), Capell (1973: 186), Waterhouse (1978: 43), Hocart (1912: 448; 1929: 182), Thompson (1940: 222).

9. In previous publications I have translated *yavusa* as clan and represented it, as Fijians often do, as a patrilineal descent group. However, see Toren (1994) for an analysis of Fijian social organization in terms of the relations between houses along the lines suggested by Lévi-Strauss (1983: 163–87). Cf. Sayes (1984: 87) who argues that 'the idiom of descent is used to disguise a power relationship. The true formation process would appear to be one in which the different co-residential groups have been drawn together by intermarriage and . . . the dominance of one of the component groups.'

10. Fijian kinship is classificatory and thus allows for the extension of kinship terms. So, for example, anyone my mother addresses as sister, I call mother; anyone she addresses as brother, I call father-in-law. Similarly anyone my father calls brother, I call father; and anyone he addresses as sister, I call mother-in-law. Thus the children of anyone I call mother or father are my siblings, and the children of anyone I call mother-in-law or father-in-law are my cross-cousins. I cannot marry anyone I call sibling, but marriage is possible with a man whom I call cross-cousin. Spouses are cross-cousins by virtue of marriage, even if their relation to one another before marriage is unknown. Kinship terminology is Dravidian; kinship and marriage practices in Sawaieke largely accord with those described by Nayacakalou (1955) for Tokatoka, Sahlins (1962: 147 ff.) for Moala, and Hocart (1929: 33–42) for Lau.

11. So Thomas Williams describes attempts to effect success in war by attendance on particular ancestors who had not, previous to the threat of war, been the object of any particular attention (Williams 1931, ii. 282, 516). Similarly, a paramount chief becomes *mana* (effective) through the attendance of the people upon him in the installation ceremony, where he is 'made to drink' the installation *yaqona* (kava) by the installing chief, who is also chief of 'landspeople'.

12. For accounts of missionary activity in Fiji, see e.g. Calvert (1858) and Clammer (1976); the latter attributes the success of missionaries to their policy of establishing a widespread literacy whose objects were religious texts. In Sawaieke country there is virtually 100 per cent adult literacy, but reading matter is largely confined to the

Methodist Prayer and Hymn Book, the Bible and, sometimes, religious tracts. Villagers read newspapers and books relatively rarely. See Toren 1988 for an analysis of the way that Fijian villagers constitute 'tradition' as the site of continuity and change in respect of their conversion to Christianity.

13. These two ancestors are probably those goddesses who are known elsewhere as *ko i rau na marama*, 'the two ladies'. What I was told about these two by a 30-year-old woman (not by the man who told me the story of the stream) implied that my informant took them to be ancestresses of her own *yavusa*, but I may be mistaken here.

14. The colonial administration tried to make people bury their dead in designated graveyards (apparently for reasons of hygiene)—but as far as I can tell, the practice was not followed for people of high status and today seems to have been completely discontinued.

15. The graves in the graveyard are unmarked and the identity of those buried on gardening land may be known only to people who witnessed the burial.

16. Dening (1980: 53) argues for traditional Marquesan society that 'to know the *tapu* was to know a social map of Te Henua [the landscape]'. Bradd Shore (1989: 143), in his fascinating paper on *mana* and *tapu* in Polynesia, remarks that Dening's reading of *tapu* distinguishes the noble from the common. Certainly one could say for old Fiji that to know the *tabu* was to know a social map of the *vanua*—land or country, but the *tabu*, while it may have been the prerogative of chiefs, was not confined to those who came from chiefly *yavusa*; I was told that any *tabu* imposed on the use of lands, streams, sea, etc. was the prerogative of the chief of those *yavusa* classified as 'land' (i.e. commoners). The *tabu* on the salt water that I refer to in the text was imposed by a man who was, at the time, 'acting land chief'.

17. My informant distinguished this kind of *tabu* from one announced by persons who do not want others to take fruit or watercress etc. from their land; these are dependent for their effect on goodwill and people may not take much notice of them; they are not *mana*—effective, as is the *tabu* that is announced, under the proper circumstances, by one with traditional authority.

18. For an extended account of the significance and uses of *tabua*, see Hooper 1982.

19. In *yaqona*-drinking in Sawaieke, 'sea' is above 'land' when the high chief (sea) drinks before the chief of the *yavusa* whose prerogative it is to install him (land); but 'land' is above 'sea' when the chief of the landspeople *yavusa* drinks before the chief of the sea-people *yavusa*.

20. This does not mean that in general men are 'land' and women are 'sea'; rather both are 'land' and 'sea' in different ways. So women as makers of mats and barkcloth are associated with the land, and men as fishers for turtle and for big fish (such as the *saqa*, whose eating is the prerogative of chiefs) with sea. Sahlins (1976: 26–42) explores these associations in some detail; however, where I take the relation between sea and land to denote balanced reciprocity in exchange relations, he takes sea to be above land and nests it within an opposition between nobles (*turaga*) and land (*vanua*, i.e. the people).

21. Note that *bukete*, meaning 'pregnant', is derived from *bukebuke*, meaning a mound of earth on which yams are planted or, possibly, from *bu*, green coconut, and *kete*, belly—both yams and coconuts being male products.

22. From one point of view Fijian Christianity has taken on the appearance of an

encompassing value, but here too it is possible to show that an ethic of equality is equally dominant and that Methodism (which contains its own inherent tension between equality and hierarchy) is in the process of taking on a distinctively Fijian form (Toren, forthcoming).

23. Chiefs are empowered by *yaqona*-drinking, but today this legitimate, collective, drinking is under the auspices of the Christian God.

24. Villagers have incorporated them both into ceremonial exchange such that 'the way according to the land' emerges intact from the confrontation with 'the way according to money'; see Toren (1989) for an analysis of the way that money and commodities derived from the market economy are 'laundered' in ceremonial exchange. Thomas (1991: 35–82) discusses the applicability of the gift/commodity distinction to exchange systems in the Pacific; for Fiji, he argues that while the objects of gift exchange were themselves alienable, ceremonial exchanges 'create a lien, and in that sense have "inalienable" ramifications' (p. 67).

25. For a detailed description of these processes in contemporary village life, see Toren 1990: 50–64, 90–118, 238–44.

26. In the course of accepting a *tabua* (whale's tooth) the speaker sniff-kisses it (*reguca*) several times and continues to hold and gaze at it as he speaks. Given that *tabua* are chiefly products given in exchange against tributary products of the land, this behaviour suggests that the speaker is implicitly consuming an intangible chiefly substance that inheres in the tooth.

References

CALVERT, J. (1982; orig. 1858). *Fiji and the Fijians*, ii. *Mission History*. Suva: Fiji Museum.

CAPELL, A. (1973; orig. 1941). *A New Fijian Dictionary*. Suva: Government Printer.

CLAMMER, J. R. (1976). *Literacy and Social Change*. Leiden: E. J. Brill.

CLUNIE, FERGUS (1977). Fijian Weapons and Warfare, *Bulletin of the Fiji Museum*, Suva.

DENING, GREG (1980). *Islands and Beaches: Discourse on a Silent Land, Marquesas 1774–1880*. Honolulu: University of Hawaii Press.

HOCART, A. M. (1912). 'On the Meaning of *Kalou*', *Journal of the Royal Anthropological Society*, 42: 437–49.

——(1929). 'Lau Islands, Fiji', *Bulletin of the Bernice P. Bishop Museum*, 62, Honolulu.

HOOPER, STEPHEN PHELPS (1982). 'A Study of Valuables in the Chiefdom of Lau, Fiji', Ph.D. Thesis, University of Cambridge.

LÉVI-STRAUSS, CLAUDE (1983; orig. 1979) *The Way of the Masks*. London: Jonathan Cape.

MUNN, NANCY (1986). *The Fame of Gawa*. London: Cambridge University Press.

NAYACAKALOU, R. R. (1955). 'The Fijian System of Kinship and Marriage', *Journal of the Polynesian Society*, 64: 44–56.

SAHLINS, MARSHALL (1962). *Moala: Culture and Nature on a Fijian Island*. Ann Arbor, Mich.: University of Michigan Press.

——(1976). *Culture and Practical Reason*. Chicago: Chicago University Press.

—— (1983). 'Raw Women, Cooked Men and Other "Great Things" of the Fiji Islands', in P. Brown and D. Tuzin (eds.), *The Ethnography of Cannibalism*. Washington, DC:

Society for Psychological Anthropology.

——(1985). *Islands of History*. London: Tavistock Publications.

SAYES, SHELLEY ANN (1984). 'Cakaudrove: Ideology and Reality in a Fijian Confederation', Ph.D. Thesis, Canberra, Australian National University.

SEEMAN, BERTHOLD (1862). *Viti: An Account of a Government Mission to the Vitian or Fijian Islands*. Cambridge: Macmillan & Co.

SHORE, BRADD (1989). '*Mana* and *Tapu*', in Alan Howard and Robert Borofsky (eds.), *Developments in Polynesian Ethnology*. Honolulu: University of Hawaii Press.

THOMAS, NICHOLAS (1991). *Entangled Objects: Exchange, Material Culture and Colonialism in the Pacific*. Cambridge, Mass.: Harvard University Press.

THOMPSON, L. M. (1940). 'Southern Lau, Fiji: An Ethnography', *Bulletin of the Bernice P. Bishop Museum*, 162, Honolulu.

TOREN, CHRISTINA (1988). 'Making the Present, Revealing the Past: The Mutability and Continuity of Tradition as Process', *Man*, NS 23: 696–717.

—— (1989). 'Drinking Cash: The Purification of Money Through Ceremonial Exchange in Fiji', in J. Parry and M. Bloch (eds.), *Money and the Morality of Exchange*. Cambridge: Cambridge University Press.

——(1990). *Making Sense of Hierarchy: Cognition as Social Process in Fiji*. London: Athlone Press.

——(1993). 'Making History: The Significance of Childhood Cognition for a Comparative Anthropology of Mind', *Man*, NS 28: 461–78.

——(1994). ' "All Things Go in Pairs or the Sharks Will Bite": The Antithetical Nature of Fijian Chiefship', *Oceania*, 64/3: 197–216.

——(forthcoming). 'Cosmogonic Aspects of Desire and Compassion in Fiji', in Daniel de Coppet and André Iteanu (eds.), *Society and Cosmos*. London: Berg.

WATERHOUSE, J. (1978; orig. 1866). *The King and the People of Fiji*. New York: AMS. Reprint of the 1866 edn. published by the Wesleyan Conference Office.

WILLIAMS, THOMAS (1982; orig. 1858). *Fiji and the Fijians*, ed. G. S. Rowe. Suva: Fiji Museum. A reprint of the 1858 London edn.

——(1931). *The Journal of Thomas Williams, Missionary in Fiji, 1840–1853*, ed. G. C. Henderson. Sydney: Angus & Robertson.

8

Landscape and the Reproduction of the Ancestral Past

=====

HOWARD MORPHY

The Dreamtime was a ground of consummation. The doctrine of the Dreaming is a sort of eschatology, a doctrine of final things which were also first things. (Stanner 1984: 170)

I was walking along a narrow river valley in the Snowy Mountains on the border between New South Wales and Victoria, with open temperate woodland on either side. I was accompanied by Narritjin Maymuru, a Yolngu, an Aboriginal person from north-east Arnhem Land, a continent away to the north. We came to a place where the river opened out to form a shallow, oval lake, tapered at one end, with sharp pebbles strewn on either side (Fig. 8.1). We sat down beside the lake and Narritjin began to interpret its mythology for me. It was, he said, land of the Dhuwa moiety connected with the Marrakulu and related clans of the Trial Bay area of the Gulf of Carpentaria. It was land connected with Ganydjalala, an ancestral woman who, with others, hunted kangaroos through the forests with stone spears. Ganydjalala is associated with the origin of stone spears as well as with one of the great regional ceremonies of Arnhem Land, the Djungguwan. The ancestral women cut down trees in the inland forests as they looked for honey. In different places, where the trees fell, they created water courses and lakes, or ceremonial grounds, or stone-spear quarries.

I asked Narritjin how he knew it was Dhuwa moiety country since neither of us had ever been there before. Moreover, little was known of the mythology of the people who had once lived in the area, before their lives had been so rudely interrupted by European colonization in the middle of the last century. Narritjin pointed to the sharp pebbles that lay beside the stream that were Ganydjalala's stone spears, and he pointed out the trees that were similar to those in the forests through which Ganydjalala hunted, and finally he reminded me of how the lake she created was represented in paintings on the *djuwany* posts made for the Djungguwan ceremony by his brother Bokarra, and how its shape resembled the shape of the lake by which we were sitting (see H. Morphy 1991: 121). Yes, we were in Dhuwa moiety country.

Many people who have travelled through the southern states of Australia with Aboriginal people from the north have had similar experiences. In the

FIG. 8.1. Narritjin Maymuru walking through a valley in the Snowy Mountains near Nimitabel in 1976. The open stretch of water in the river course and the sharp stones on the river bed and along the bank reminded him of places in Arnhem Land that had been made by the ancestral woman Ganydjalala, the creator of stone spearheads, as she hunted for honey through the forests (see Morphy 1991: Fig. 9.4).

nineteenth century the colonial frontier moved rapidly across Australia from south to north. Eventually climate, Aboriginal resistance, and the changed historical context of colonialism slowed its movement. Many Aboriginal people in northern Australia remained distant from the most destructive processes of European colonialism until the middle of the twentieth century, by which time it had become increasingly difficult (though not impossible) to appropriate Aboriginal land and deny Aboriginal people their rights to have a say in their own future. With the passing of the Aboriginal Land Rights (Northern Territory) Act in 1976 many Aborigines in the Northern Territory regained secure title to their land almost before realizing they were threatened with its loss (see e.g. Hiatt 1984). In the 1960s Yolngu people had been at the forefront of the Aboriginal struggle for land rights and most of their land was transferred to Aboriginal ownership without them even having to go through the process of making a claim. However, Yolngu are fully aware of the catastrophic process of colonialism that the Aboriginal population of the south was subjected to, of the decimation of population, the forced removal of people from land, and the separation of children from their parents. They are aware that the land had a history before European colonialism, they recognize the existence of ancestral forces in the land, and they feel the spirits of generations of the dead in the surrounding land. It is important to them to be able to interpret the land so that the permission that would have been sought, were the people still alive, can at least be thought, and so that the possibility of avoiding spiritually powerful or dangerous places can be recovered, thereby enabling them to act properly, if with an uncomfortable uncertainty (see Williams 1986a). When I travelled with Narritjin in isolated places, where the masking presence of Europeans was less heavy, he would be continually trying to place himself in the landscape, interpreting signs in the land that could link it with the mythological past, which to him remained very much part of its present.

One of the significant things about what I would term Narritjin's 'reinterpretation' of the Snowy Mountains landscape is that for him it was not a reinterpretation but a process of discovery or revelation. The ancestral presence was there and immutable. And in parts of Australia where Aboriginal people have remained in a continuing and active relationship with their land I have argued that there are mechanisms which act to maintain the stability of the cosmic framework (H. Morphy 1988, 1990). Each place is part of a network that connects places together in a chain, and the links on either side depend for their connection on the one in the middle. The condition of moving into a place to take over from other people is that links of the same type continue to remain in place. People do not move in and take over a country by imposing new myths: rather they move in and act as if *they* are taken over by the new country. This makes the political struggle for land no less intense, but it preserves the illusion of continuity between people, place, and ancestral past. If the transmission of knowledge about place does break down or if people are moving into previously unoccupied land, then, as Narritjin's story shows, there are mechanisms for creating or recreating the linkages.

I have argued elsewhere that the resilience of the network of linkages between ancestral beings and places is a reflection of the fact that the attachment of people to place through the mediating process of the ancestral past is part of the core structure of Aboriginal society (H. Morphy 1990). The relationship between landscape and Aboriginal conceptions of the world has been a central theme of Australian Aboriginal anthropology at least since the works of Spencer and Gillen and Karl Strehlow. The centrality of the 'totemic landscape' (to use Ted Strehlow's (1970) phrase), to Aboriginal concepts of creation, spiritual power, and world order has been well brought out in the works of Stanner (1966) and Munn (1970, 1973a). It is not simply that landscape is a sign system for mythological events, as is now well understood. Rather, the landscape is the referent for much of the symbolism. Too often landscape has been seen as an intervening sign system that serves the purpose of passing on information about the ancestral past. I would like to argue that landscape is integral to the message. I will be concentrating on the landscape of eastern Arnhem Land, the area inhabited by the Yolngu-speaking peoples. In other parts of Australia there are major differences in the way in which totemic geography articulates with social organization. None the less, much of my analysis relates directly to discussions of other areas of the continent.

Time, Space, and Landscape

I am concerned here with three processes: the ancestral mapping of the landscape, the sedimenting of history and sentiment in the landscape, and the way in which the individual acquires a conception of landscape. To elucidate these processes I examine the triadic relationship between the individual, the ancestral past, and the world in which he or she lives. The question of the relationship between structure and action in terms both of social theory and of Aboriginal metaphysic, is also central to my analysis. My argument, in its simplest form, is that interaction with the landscape is part of the process whereby the Dreaming as a component of the cultural structure of Aboriginal society is reproduced. I do not give the Dreaming *per se* the role of some kind of privileged determining structure, but neither do I allocate that determining status to the level of reality represented by action in the context of historically based social relations, as contemporary social theorists such as Bourdieu (1977) and Giddens (1979) tend to do. I adopt a position in which culture and society are best conceptualized as relatively autonomous but mutually interdependent components of reality, the former being a co-determinant of the socio-cultural trajectory, the latter being a necessary component of its reproduction. The concept socio-cultural is not a fudge: I use it deliberately to emphasize the interdependence of these two dimensions of reality. Both are abstracted from the ongoing and continually transforming process of human life. The Dreaming is not 'culture' but it is an excellent example of something that makes a concept of culture necessary to anthropological analysis: it is a level of reality that is a co-determining component of the process of socio-cultural reproduction. The Dreaming represents a structure, rather than a set of rules—a structure which has in part been lived and has, as a consequence, connotations. It had its origins in the past, in its separation from the flow of Dreamtime events. It has gained its connotations through its incorporation in subsequent history, through being reproduced in a form which enabled it to accommodate to the exigencies of historical events.

As elsewhere in Australia, the physical form of the earth is believed to have come into being through the actions of ancestral beings who travelled the earth from place to place, leaving evidence of their actions in the form of topographical features. Where they cut down trees, river courses or ceremonial grounds were formed by the impression made in the ground; where they bled, ochre deposits were formed or waters of a particular colour were left behind. However, the relationship between ancestral beings and the land is a much more generalized one. The land, taken as a whole, was the land over which ancestral beings hunted and gathered, and every aspect of the landscape can be thought to have connotations of the ancestral beings—the scents and sounds and flavours of the land today are the scents and sounds and flavours that they too experienced.

In that respect the ancestral beings are not so different from previous generations of human beings who lived in the land, who are the immediate emotional referents for much that can be more distally associated with the ancestral beings. The landscape is redolent with memories of other human beings. The ancestral beings, fixed in the land, become a timeless reference point outside the politics of daily life to which the emotions of the living can be attached. To become this reference point the ancestral journeying had in effect to be frozen for ever at a particular point in the action, so that part of the action became timeless. Place has precedence over time in Yolngu ontogeny. Time was created through the transformation of ancestral beings into place, the place being for ever the mnemonic of the event. They 'sat down' and, however briefly they stayed, they became part of the place for ever. In Yolngu terms they *turned into* the place. Whatever events happened at the place, whatever sequence they occurred in, whatever intervals existed between them, all becomes subordinate to their representation in space. Sequences in time are represented only if they were spatially segregated and occurred at separate places in association with separate features, and even then synchronicity or perhaps timelessness is built into the way they are presented. What remains is the distance between places rather than the temporal distance between events. The time it took ancestral beings to complete their journey, the interval between events, is never part of the re-counting of myths, there is no 'and many years later on' in Yolngu myth telling, though there are certain identifiable strata of time or bands of synchronicity. Transformed into features of the landscape, mythological events are represented simultaneously even if they could be said to have occurred at different points in time.

This subordination of time to space is reflected in Yolngu languages, where distance in time is expressed by the same terms as distance in space and there is clear evidence that the spatial vocabulary is primary. The inflectional system of Yolngu verbs is primarily aspectual and modal rather than tense-based. Aspectually, the languages distinguish between the end points of actions and events rather than situating them in their totality in relation to the present. Perfective aspect marks events or actions whose end point has occurred before the time of speaking, in contrast to prospective aspect, which marks events and actions whose end point has not been reached at the time of speaking; ancestral events are always perfective and thus by implication situated in the past, in the sense that they are actions that have been completed. The modal distinction in the perfective aspect is between discrete, unique events which actually took place (indicative) and all other categories of events or actions (non-indicative). Perfective non-indicative alone, with no accompanying particles, marks events or actions which are now completed, but which cannot be described as bounded in space or time—they were habitual or oft-repeated events and activities. Ancestral events are almost invariably described in the perfective non-indicative. Thus ancestral events are not described as unique events which can be firmly anchored in time in relation to one another. Moreover, this way of referring to ancestral events as ones which can be repeated over time fits well the Yolngu idea that ancestral events can be re-performed through ritual action and re-presented through sacred objects and paintings. Hence they are not located forever as something that happened at a particular point in time.[1]

The subordination of time to space is reflected pervasively in the syntax, morphology, and semantics of Yolngu languages. For the most part temporal markers are derived from, one might even say are parasitic upon, the languages' devices for describing spatial relations.[2]

The Dreamtime encoding of ancestral events in the features of the landscape for all time represents something of a contradiction in the production of the world—it cuts across the free flow of ancestral events and fixes them in a form that makes them subject to structure. The untrammelled creativity of the ancestral beings is lost precisely because they created the world in a form that could be passed on from generation to generation as 'the' order of the world. The flow of action was fixed for ever by the very fact of its transmission to landscape; it becomes a structure that exists outside the ancestral world. The ancestral beings carried on, regardless of the fact that part of their subjective experience had been transformed into the forms of the landscape; they journeyed on, leaving their frozen experiences behind to be of significance to the lives of others. In some parts of Australia there are particular categories of ancestral beings who provide a meta-commentary on the creative acts of the others, converting them into the form of ancestral law that is passed on for a human purpose. These ancestral beings in effect say such things as, 'and here the crocodile was changed into the shape of a hill, and from now on you must pass this knowledge on to your children' (H. Morphy 1990). Such ancestral beings are the gospel writers of Arnhem Land, the mythic transmitters of myth, who provide the means of connecting the myth to the future world. In the world of the generations of the living the process is carried on in reverse. The ordered, frozen world of the ancestral past becomes part of the subjective experience of the individual, through the acquisition of knowledge of the ancestral past as he or she moves through the world. But this individually acquired knowledge attaches the person in a particular way to a structure of places and the significance of those places which exists outside the human world. This structure is where the human world and the ancestral world meet, but it is a part of neither.

The Ancestral Co-ordinates

North-east Arnhem Land is criss-crossed with ancestral tracks that provide the co-ordinates of the mythological map of Yolngu land. Ancestral beings travelled in groups or as individuals, creating the land-forms that subsequently marked their passage. The intersection of routes and events created particular places and can consequently be used to locate those places. Almost universally in Australia places are named after mythological events and each place has its own unique mythological marker. The origin of the landscape could be said to be quite independent of the origins of the human groups who subsequently occupied it. However, the ancestral beings operated under the same constraints that they subsequently imposed on the human occupants. They created a land divided on the basis of moieties, and when they subsequently created people, or some of them did, those people had to fit into the moiety-structured landscape. The intersections of ancestral tracks created a checker-board-like pattern of alternating opposite moiety units, into which groups of people are fitted. I have shown elsewhere (H. Morphy 1988) how this system accommodates over time to the demographic and political exigencies of Yolngu life, and I can only summarize my argument very briefly here.

Each contemporary Yolngu clan holds a number of areas of land in common. Where there is no dispute over the ownership of the land or over the corporate existence of the clan, the senior members of the clan and of other clans will present the situation as having existed since time immemorial. The clan is said to exist in direct continuity with the founding human ancestors of the clan, who were given their land by ancestral decree. Ownership of the land entails ownership of the sacra associated with the clan lands—the paintings, songs, dances, and sacred objects that are manifestations of the ancestral beings who created the land. Continued occupancy requires that memory of the ancestral beings be kept alive by the use of the sacra in ritual. Over time, clearly, some groups expand and others decline and there are continual adjustments in the relationships between people and land. However, the ancestral grid remains fairly constant, with new groups occupying existing spaces and taking over the sacra and the spiritual responsibilities that were exercised by those who preceded them. In a sense the new group takes on the clothing of the old group so that, from an ancestral perspective, nothing has changed. As Morton (1987: 104), summarizing Munn (1970), has written 'the land and the sacra are always there basically unchanging through the generations which "hold" and "look after" them'. Again, time is subordinated to space. The new group is soon defined in terms of its distance from other groups in space: as it becomes identified with the group it has succeeded over time, time is condensed through its association with place. The emphasis on continuity continually reimposes the structure of a spatial pattern on human events. This structure is separated from the politics of everyday life, though it is continually the subject of political action.

The systematic nature of the association between landscape, ancestral being, and social group is reflected clearly in the artistic systems of the Yolngu. Place, ancestral being, and social group are encoded precisely in the content and the form of paintings and song. Paintings include in their form sets of related geometric designs which are associated with particular ancestral complexes. For example, the wild honey/fire complex is widespread, and is linked with many places belonging to clans of the Yirritja moiety. Each such place has a series of unique mythological events associated with it, though there are overlaps and connections with events that happened at other places. The uniqueness of each place is signified by unique characteristics of its design, which is differentiated from all the other designs in the set (Fig. 8.2). Songs which are associated with particular ancestral tracks are similarly recognizable on the basis of stylistic features. At a more general level, language and naming systems are also closely connected with place. The emic model is that clans speak

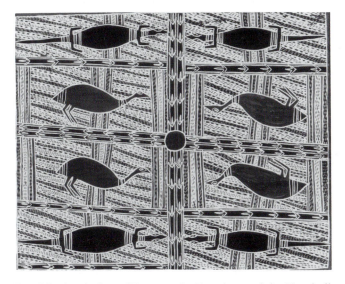

FIG. 8.2. A painting of Darawuy by Larrtjanga of the Ngayimil clan, Yirrkala 1976. The painting shows water goannas and bustards, *walpurrungu*, around a waterhole created by the Djan'kawu, female ancestral beings. The geometric background pattern represents the swampy surrounds covered with *dara* (wild banana) and the footprints of the birds in the mud. Each *Dhuwa* moiety clan associated with the Djan'kawu mythology owns a variant of the design centred on a waterhole or set of waterholes in their country. But in this case the particular configuration of the design, with the birds' feet, combined with the incorporation of the white dotted lines into the pattern, is associated with the Ngayimil clan.

distinctive dialects and that the dialects, like the songs and the paintings, are part of the ancestral inheritance of groups (F. Morphy 1977). From an etic perspective, grammatical and morphological variation and similarity in every-day speech unites or distinguishes groups on a regional basis. Dialect variation is sufficient to identify a set of places with which a speaker could be associated, but does not have the specificity of paintings. On the other hand, at the level of specialized vocabulary, and in the use of certain clan-specific words, place and ancestral being are signified. Naming systems for people, dogs, canoes, and, latterly, cars, are all directly linked to, and from a Yolngu perspective derive from, place. Personal names belong to particular ancestral complexes and are often associated with specific places, and the names for dogs and canoes are clan-specific. The person's name does not necessarily signify clan affiliation since names belonging to a number of different clans may be given to an individual; it does, however, reflect the person's ancestral identity in the broad-est sense.

Thus the Yolngu landscape is divided into segments which reflect the as-sociation of ancestral beings with particular areas of land. Because the ancestral beings not only created the landscape, but placed people in a particular re-lationship to it as perpetuators of the ancestral inheritance, the landscape is viewed simultaneously as a set of spaces for people to occupy. The dual aspect of the landscape—that it is both created by ancestral transformation and divided up between people—is reflected in the set of representations associated with land. Almost everything that is associated with social groups is also in some respects a sign of land. For example the artistic system clothes the landscape in a tartan of clan designs, providing the graphic component of a system for ordering relationships between people, ancestral beings, and land.

Ecology and the Ancestral Nature of Place

Commonalities between places, which exist independently of any political subdivisions of the landscape, are represented in the totemic geography. As one would expect in a hunting and gathering society, Yolngu languages have a rich vocabulary for describing topography and the environment which precisely distinguishes environmental zones and links them in with seasonal resource exploitation (Rudder 1977; Williams 1986b: 66 ff.). Since the mythological system is closely linked to the environment, focusing as it does on the flora and fauna associated with particular places, one might expect there to be a close correspondence between topographical zone and ancestral track, and a logic to the distribution of ancestral beings that accords with the distribution of natural species.

Certainly, representations of totemic landscape and 'natural' landscape ar-ticulate at the level of detailed description. Two kinds of correspondences can be sought. One is the association between the tracks of particular ancestral beings and ancestral complexes, and particular ecological zones. The other is mythical representation of the characteristics of particular kinds of environment. Myths take the form of the journeys of ancestral beings across land; much of the sacred law of particular places consists of commentary on the landscape (see e.g. Berndt 1952 or Clunies-Ross 1978). The ancestral beings sang songs which, for example, describe the animal species that they saw at a waterhole, or which describe minutely a bird as it feeds at a particular time of year. The myths recount how the ancestral beings named particular sets of species, how they thought of them and sometimes how they hunted them and cooked them. These descriptive aspects of myth are almost invariably 'in place', in the sense that the songs reflect the present characteristics of the locality. However, in terms of the event structure of the myths, these flora and fauna are only minor characters, albeit ones which make up the major content of the ancestral 'law' relating to any place. The major figures are the ancestral spirits who created the 'law' for each place at which they stopped on their journey and who named the flora and fauna.

The major ancestral beings are referentially complex entities. They frequently have no set form but transform from animal or inanimate form to human form and back at different stages of the myth. Often it is not so much a matter of transformation from one state to another: different accounts, songs, dances, paintings seem to assume different states of existence. The myths recount not so much that 'Ngulumun changed from human into a king fish' as 'then Ngulumun [who had earlier thrown a spear with his hand] swam as a fish'. Clearly, ancestral beings who are thus unconstrained by nature need not be constrained by ecological zone. And indeed the journeys of these beings often cut across widely differing regions, many of which may be inappropriate to their animal or species transform: salt-water species travel through freshwater country, water species move on land, fire burns under water, and so on. For example, many of the major sites associated with the shark, *maarna*, are inland, though the species itself is associated with the sea. The shark was speared in the waters of Buckingham Bay and in its death agony it tore inland, gouging out riverbeds and sometimes diving under the earth to emerge further on in another country (Fig. 8.3).

Although there is no logical reason why ancestral tracks should have any association with particular ecological zones there is, in many cases, a strong association between the two. Some ancestral tracks, such as that of the salt-water crayfish, link places where the species occurs today. In the Djan'kawu mythology the major sites are associated, on the whole, with a narrow range of coastal environments and inland plains, and in the case of each clan on the track of the Djan'kawu a similar set of songs is associated with similar kinds of places (Keen 1989). Even in cases such as the Yirritja moiety wild honey/fire complex, where the ancestral complex is associated with markedly different

Fɪɢ. 8.3. A painting of the shark *maarna* at Wurlwurlwuy by Maaw' Mununggurr, assisted by his wives, Yirrkala 1974. The background pattern represents the death agony of the shark reflected in the cloudscape.

ecological zones, both inland and on the coast, the inland and the coastal sites form discrete sets, the members of which share a set of overlapping characteristics.

The association between ancestral being and place is so precise that minimal information about an ancestral being in the form of song or painting allows for precise identification of the location. This keying into place gives productivity to Yolngu ancestral representations: all the information associated with the actions of the ancestral being in that place is released as a potential source of interpretants for paintings and other sacra. It is more difficult to move from a type of environment to a particular ancestor because each kind of environment has many different characteristics, only some of which are drawn on as aspects of particular ancestral identities. The two moieties select quite different aspects, since species of flora and fauna are moiety-specific. None the less, in interpreting landscape, people often look for environmental signs of totemic significance which potentially key the place into the ancestral grid (as Narritjin did in the Snowy Mountains).

The present-day landscape is represented in the myths and simultaneously represents the myth. The metacommentaries of the songs, originally those of the ancestors, represent Yolngu reflections on the environment today. But the environment as a whole also represents the various transformations of the bodies and actions of the ancestral beings. The essence of an ancestral being can be present in any feature of the environment, including colours, tastes, and smells; it is not necessarily represented by the species itself or by anything connected with it in the natural world. In cases where the ancestral being is operating outside its place in the natural world, the ancestral species can find its expression in some other species that today characterizes or is at least present in the particular environment. For example, the river-mouth at Gurka'wuy was created by the fall of an ancestral stringy-bark tree which had been cut down inland by a female ancestral being. The tree rushed headlong down to the sea, creating the channel of the Gurka'wuy river. On the way bits of the tree split off and were scattered about the landscape, and where they fell were transformed into trees. But the particular species of tree that represents them today in any one place is determined by the logic of the ecology. On the beach at Gurka'wuy one of the splinters is represented by a magnificent mangrove tree standing alone on a rocky bar (Fig. 8.4). I was introduced to this tree with the following words: 'See this stringy-bark tree. I know that to you Europeans this looks like a mangrove tree, but really this is a stringy-bark tree.' Again, for example, the shark *maarna* created the river at Wurlwurlwuy in his death throes, and his broken teeth were transformed into the trees that grow on the banks to either

FIG. 8.4. Durndiwuy Warnambi pointing to the mangrove tree on the beach at Gurka'-wuy, Trial Bay, that is a manifestation of the ancestral stringy-bark tree that gouged out the path of the Gurka'wuy river. The river enters the bay beyond the mangrove tree in the distance.

side. The major ancestral beings are in general represented by features of the environment that are like them only by analogy, yet the world which they inhabited is the same world that exists today. It is the present world distanced by its ancestral connection and hence it becomes a source of reflection.

People learn about the ancestral past simply by moving through the landscape. The knowledge they acquire reflects an active relationship between the ancestral past and the land itself. Not only does the landscape change but ancestral presence intervenes to influence human action. Change can be accommodated by its reflection in the transforming nature of the ancestral past. New and different species of tree grow as transforms of the same underlying force. The potential for encoding meaning in place is enormous, and in Yolngu conceptions of landscape, myth and history combine, sometimes to reinforce an image of place, sometimes to present contradictory images. Indeed different people can hold contradictory images about the inherent nature of a particular area of land, and such images play an active role in Yolngu decision-making processes. Present events are used either to confirm or disconfirm alternative images of place. Djarrakpi was chosen as the site for a Manggalili clan settlement. A major camping-place in the past, it is close to a sacred lake which provides a source of conception spirits. However, it is also close to the site of a major burial ground that may have been associated with a major battle some time in the distant past. Certainly the mythology of the place is partly concerned with an ancestral battle and many of the themes of Yirritja moiety mortuary rituals are expressed in the sacred law of the place (see H. Morphy 1977). When the clan re-established the settlement at Djarrakpi, one of the senior clan members refused to go there on the grounds that it was too dangerous a place. Within the next year two members of the clan died. Neither death occurred anywhere near Djarrakpi, but both deaths were associated with the place because it was connected with the conception spirits of the dead. The settlement was abandoned as if the deaths had occurred there. The number of people who viewed Djarrakpi as a dangerous place increased, and it took a long while for people to return there. Even then, only one segment of the clan returned; the other segment argued that the settlement should be built elsewhere. Thus, although no recent deaths had occurred at Djarrakpi, the mythological connotations of the site and the tensions over re-establishing a settlement there kept alive a particular image of the place, and that became a focal point of present-day emotions which were in continuity with the ancestral past.

Conversely, contemporary events can transform the image of a place and give mythological events new connotations. Any site where some catastrophe has occurred, such as a fatal epidemic or a massacre, will become a place to be avoided. But at the same time it is a source of enormous potential power. Eventually such places can again come under human control. The settlement of

Baaniyala, like Djarrakpi, was built near an old massacre site and burial ground. It has become one of the most successful of present settlements and the negative sentiments that were voiced early in its existence have become muted, whereas at Djarrakpi they have been reconfirmed.

Being Born into the Totemic Landscape: The Individual, Kinship, and Ritual

I have so far presented the landscape as it is culturally conceived, as the transformation of the ancestral past having connections with the present through its articulation with group organization, through its interaction with ecology and the natural features of the environment, and through the connotations and memories of the history of events and people associated with place. I would now like to shift focus a little to the social process whereby the individual is born into a landscape and acquires understanding of it through his or her kinship relations with individuals and groups. Finally I will look at the way in which landscape is part of the ritual process, how ritual in turn provides a context for the ordering of the social landscape, and how in mortuary rituals landscape is used both to represent an individual's life and as a means of reabsorbing the social person into the ancestral past. In this way I show how the cultural conceptualizations of the landscape are mediated through *and* are to a degree constitutive of social processes, which in turn are an integral part of their reproduction as concepts.

Yolngu have two words for being born. One literally translated has the prosaic meaning 'come out head first', the other, *dhawal-wuyangirr*, is a compound made out of *dhawal* 'named place' and *guyangirr* 'think of'. Literally, then, the word means 'to think of a named place'. The concept directly associates the birth of the individual with ancestral creativity, and begins the process of positioning the subject within the landscape. Ancestral beings created the world through transforming themselves into named places, and each human life represents a continuation of that process. The ancestral beings are often said to have consciously turned themselves into place just as humans are implicitly born into place. Birth (or, before that, spirit conception) is the beginning of the process of associating a person with a place or set of places, of giving him or her an identity in the landscape just as the ancestral beings gained their identity through being transformed into place. As people grow older they are socialized into a world in which everything of significance in their lives can be associated with named places or referred to in ancestral terms. They are born into a social world, but it is presented as an ancestral world. They chart their own unique course through the ancestral grid, though in Yolngu consciousness this journey is continually transformed into a predestined passage—they are 'following the way of the ancestors' (see Stanner 1984: 169).

Individual identity is so closely associated with the landscape that the one can act on the other. Ill-treatment of the land—the breaking of taboos or disrespect of sacred sites—can result in illness or death for those who were born into that land. Conversely, the death of someone associated with an area of land can cause it to become a dangerous or barren place.

I was once out hunting with a group of Yolngu along the cliff-tops of Yalangbara (Port Bradshaw). We were at a place where the territories of two clans adjoin. One is of the Yirritja moiety and the other of the Dhuwa moiety. One of the hunters, the leader of the Dhuwa-moiety clan, saw a crocodile swimming slowly along in the waters below (Fig. 8.5). He raised his rifle to his shoulder and was taking aim, when suddenly and very dramatically a woman stood in front of the barrel. There was a heated discussion and then the man laid down his rifle. The crocodile had just moved from Dhuwa moiety sea into Yirritja moiety sea. The crocodile is a major ancestor of the Yirritja clan associated with the creation of the land. In normal circumstances it would have been perfectly all right to shoot the crocodile. On this occasion, however, the leader of the Yirritja clan was ill. The woman who stood in front of the gun was his daughter, and she argued that if the crocodile was killed it might weaken her father's spirit. It was the link between the crocodile and the land that was crucial. A short while later, the crocodile turned around and began swimming

FIG. 8.5. Roy Marika on the cliffs at Port Bradshaw has sighted a crocodile in the water (barely visible as a line in the water above the smallest boy's head). His sister-in-law on the right later intervened to prevent the crocodile being shot.

in the opposite direction. Soon the hunter took up his rifle again, took aim, and followed the crocodile along. This time no one intervened as the rules of the encounter had been established. But the crocodile must also have been aware of the rules since it again turned before entering Dhuwa moiety land and the hunter let it be.

Death brings out clearly the close relationship between the individual and the land. Areas of land associated with a person because he or she visited them frequently when alive, or because they are associated with his or her ancestral identity, being the conception place or place from which he or she was named, become closed, sometimes for many months. Animals from certain places cannot be eaten, songs cannot be sung, paintings cannot be produced. The land, like the person, becomes dead. When the memories of the death have faded a little and anger over the death has cooled, the land is opened up again by the performance of ceremonies to 'free' individuals, places, and objects, and to renew them spiritually. The land must first be burnt before it can be safely re-entered. In such ways the identity of the land is firmly associated with the person who has died and the links between people and land are reinforced.

The Landscape as a Sociocentric Grid

Since moiety and clan are mapped on to landscape, an individual, as he[3] acquires knowledge of his kinship to others, can express it in terms of landscape. This, in turn, influences his perception of landscape. Kinship affects where he can go and what he can do at particular places, it can make a landscape, in Biernoff's (1978) terms, safe or dangerous. It is important to distinguish between two related ways in which kinship is mapped on to landscape: there is a sociocentric mapping which appears to flow from the ancestral grid and an egocentric mapping for which the sociocentric map provides a background and a resource and by means of which the sociocentric map is ultimately transformed.

Yolngu clans of the same moiety stand in a particular kinship relation: they are either mother's mother (*maari*), daughter's child (*gutharra*), or sister (*yapa*) to other clans. Clans of the opposite moiety can be referred to as mother (*ngaarndi*), or woman's child (*waku*). Cross-moiety attributions are potential and context-dependent. A clan of the opposite moiety can be both *waku* and *ngaarndi* in relation to another clan depending on context. In the case of the intra-moiety system the relationships are, theoretically, fixed (Fig. 8.6). The sociocentric kin terms applied between clans are directly related to the Yolngu system of bestowal and marriage alliance. The mother's mother and mother's mother's brother are significant relatives in the bestowal system. A man marries his mother's mother's brother's daughter's daughter. A woman plays an important role in the bestowal of her daughter and a man plays an important

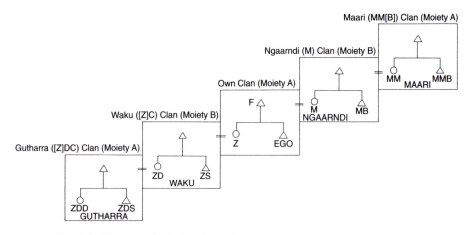

F<small>IG</small>. 8.6. The genealogical basis of the sociocentric clan relationship terms.

role in the bestowal of his sister's daughter. A woman must not marry into her own mother's clan: or if her mother comes from a very large clan she must at least marry into a different lineage of the clan. Hence women are thought to 'pass along' a matriline that connects clans in a chain from mother's mother's (*maari*) clan to sister's daughter's child's clan (*gutharra*). Clans of the same moiety connected by marriage tend to have an invariant relationship in all contexts at any one time: one is always either *maari* or *gutharra* in relation to the other. The sociocentric terms reflect the balance of the individual relationships between members of the respective clans, and marriages that run in the contrary direction will be either rare or absent. However, adjustments in the pattern of marriages between clans occur as political and demographic circumstances dictate, and although the sociocentric system must be a factor in structuring the changes that occur, it too must be subject to modifications so that it reflects the actual balance of relationships between the members of the clans. Sister clans (*yapa*) occupy structurally similar positions within the marriage system: they are likely to call the same set of clans *maari* or *gutharra*.

As an individual ego, a person is connected to a set of clans by marriage or descent, to his mother's clan (*ngaarndi*), to his sister's child's clan (*waku*), to his mother's mother's clan (*maari*), and to his sister's daughter's child's clan (*gutharra*). These individual relations are complemented and amplified by the socially centred relationships, which operate at a group level but also provide a basis for establishing new relationships at an individual level. An individual's own network of connections differentiates him from other members of his clan.

Kinship relations can be mapped directly on to land both at an individual level and at a sociocentric level. An individual will refer to areas of land according to his own kinship relations, as for example 'my mother's country'. People have certain rights in and responsibilities towards their mother's country and the ancestral law associated with it, and this colours their attitude to it. They may have to fire the country after a clansperson has died or give permission for songs to be sung or sacred objects to be made. Kinship gives permission to be in certain places. Because personal names come from the land, particular places gain the connotations of kinship. They remind one of people living and dead with whom one has a close relationship, and they may contain the spirits as well as the memories of the dead.

Yolngu often talk as if kinship relations flowed from the land, and they present a highly systematized account of the correspondence between territorial alignment and marriage patterns (see Williams 1986*b*: 77). Territories are said to be organized in *maari/gutharra*, *ngaarndi/waku* sequences, replicating the pattern of marriage alliances. The orderliness of this pattern can be overstated, but given a regional focus to marriage arrangements and the separation out of clans into non-reciprocal categories it is not surprising that order is always potentially emergent within the system and that Yolngu are able to exploit correspondences between topographical, ancestral, and social orders when they occur. When people camp together they create ideal representations of such order by camping in intermarrying clusters, with the sleeping places of families reflecting the geographical relationship of their clan lands (see Biernoff 1979: 161). Such orderings will clearly vary in detail according to who is present, but the application of the principle reinforces the idea of a prestructured universe.

The Ordering of Landscape in Ritual

Yolngu ritual may be seen from one perspective as the creation of sequences of representations of land. All sacred law is associated with events that are manifest in the form and characteristics of particular areas of land. The land contains the power of the ancestral transformations, and so does the set of representations associated with the land. Yolngu rituals involve the release of that power or its use for particular purposes, such as the strengthening of the individual or the transport of a soul. The power originated in or became accessible to humans through the ancestral transformation into the land and is released or created by representations of that land in the context of ceremonies, sometimes held distant from the land. In Yolngu ritual, the moving of the mountain to Mohammed is achieved figuratively, if not literally. Ceremonial grounds and the constructions that occur on them are stages on which distant landscapes are re-created (Fig. 8.7). The ceremonial grounds are often self-referential: they represent the grounds that the ancestral beings created in particular places, for use in ceremonial re-enactments of their lives. The grounds orientate the ritual action so that it corresponds to the spatial ordering of ancestral events—events that resulted in the creation of place (see Berndt 1974, pls. 44–6).

FIG. 8.7. A sand sculpture made at Yirrkala in 1975 as part of a house purification ceremony. The design belongs to the Yarrwidi Gumatj clan and represents a place at Caledon Bay whose features were formed by the collapse, in the ancestral past, of a house built by 'Dreaming' Macassans (Morphy 1984: 1). The sculpture represents the house posts (the parallel lines in the foreground) surmounted by two rooms (the rectangles above). The sculpture was built outside a house owned by a dead person as part of a purification and commemorative ritual. The dead person's possessions were placed within the sand sculpture for purification or subsequent destruction. On death the person's spirit had been guided in the direction of Caledon Bay.

The sequencing of space in Yolngu rituals is of two kinds: the type depends on the focus or type of the ritual. In what Keen (1988: 284) refers to as regional ceremonies such as the Ngaarra, and in commemorative ceremonies such as the Djungguwan, the focus is on the events that occur on a single ancestral track along much of its length. Although the ceremonies are regional in that they involve geographically widespread groups who are connected by the same ancestral track, they are in some respects essentially inward looking since they are concerned with the spiritual identity of particular places and the relationship between group and place. Each clan associated with, for example, the Djan'kawu sisters (Berndt 1952; Keen 1990) or the dog ancestor (Thomson 1939) enacts the phase of the journey which is located in its own clan lands. Although members of clans of both moieties will take part in the ritual, the main focus of the ritual is on the sacred law of a set of clans of one of the moieties only. The spatial framework shifts as the journey progresses, but in an almost imperceptible way—the representations from two places on the same track often differ only in subtle ways, and to the outsider the performance may seem repetitive (Keen 1978). The ceremonies are highly political since they are a statement of the authority of clan leaders and the rights in sacred objects and law. Such ceremonies represent formal statements of the ancestrally ordained order and of the way human groups fit into that order. They also provide the context for adjustments and for the creation of an appearance of systematic order since there are many other occasions when the different components of the journey are likely to be performed separately.

Mortuary rituals, by contrast, bring together people of many different clans who are linked through their relationship to an individual life (for a detailed analysis see H. Morphy 1984). The objective of the ritual is, in part, to create a unique route across Arnhem Land from the place of death to the final destination of the soul. The burial ceremony provides the spatial and temporal framework within which this journey is enacted. Each stage of the journey involves a different area of land and a different set of ancestral beings—it is a journey that cuts across ancestral tracks. The representations of land from one stage of the journey to the next are almost non-overlapping.

Mortuary rituals provide many examples of the way in which people use the geographical relationships between places to express an individual's kinship relation to other groups and to his ancestral inheritance. Mortuary rituals are concerned in part with the journey of the souls of the dead from the place of death to their conception sites. The journey is undertaken with the assistance of the ancestral beings associated with the land over which the soul is directed. It is accomplished by acting out ritual events belonging to clans related to the dead person. The images evoked throughout the ritual create analogies between kinship and ancestral relations. For example if a dance represents an ancestral being in animal form giving birth to her young, then the mother may be acted by a member of the owning clan and the child by a member of a *waku* clan. At various stages people sing songs of all the clans present to show their relationship to the deceased. The songs will occur in sequences that reflect the *maari/gutharra* relations among clans, ending with the songs of the dead person's clan. Frequently river systems provide a symbolic linking theme, people are said to be 'singing the waters of the clan'. By selecting tributaries appropriately and occasionally bringing in songs from places which are related on a different basis, all the clans present can be included in a sequence of ritual action which organizes the landscape so that an individual's life seems to flow directly out of it, even though the objective, ironically, is to return the individual to the land.[4]

Conclusion: Experiencing the Landscape, Transforming the Ancestral Past

People learn about the land by travelling through it and being introduced to it by members of their individual kindreds—who constitute their 'permission' to be in particular places. Their view of the land becomes enriched with the experiences and associations of their lives. Yet this individual passage is made through a pre-existing grid of named places—coming into being is through 'thinking of a named place'. The ancestral past is learned about during these individual journeys and through participating in ceremonial performances. In some of those performances the presentation of the ancestral past echoes those individual journeys. In mortuary ceremonies a unique path is created, corresponding to the unique characteristics of a person's life, genealogy, and the circumstances of his or her death. In other performances the landscape is presented almost as an abstract ordering of transformations on an ancestral track. The contradiction of the ancestral past is equivalent to the contradiction of the human present: life-experience comes through individual action which is ever changing but which becomes, as it changes, part of an apparently continuing structure. Yet it is through individual lives that the ancestral past is both renewed and transformed. The ancestral past is continuously re-created by the sedimenting of past and present experiences and political outcomes on pre-existing loci. The grid of spaces or named places is at any one point in time occupied by actual or emergent groups connected by individual genealogies, and for any person it is experienced through relations to known individuals. Those connections become part of the value of the place to an individual. Those people are the tangible expressions of the conception spirits of the place, they are the bestowers of wives or competitors for women, they make a place safe or dangerous and give primary connotations to the ancestral dimension of the landscape; they determine whether the shark is 'mother' or 'enemy'.

In reality places are continually being reformed into new sets. New divisions of the landscape are made as clans die out and new ones emerge. The presentation in ceremonies of these new orders of relationship between ancestral past and social group is public confirmation of their existence: it is, simultaneously, a denial that things were ever otherwise. Thus the articulation of social groups with the landscape is always changing, but the mythic screen that covers landscape makes the relationship appear unchanging. The landscape as ancestral transformation is distal from the ancestors, though they created it, and distal from the humans, though they re-create it. It encodes, selectively, their frozen experiences, the images of friends, past deaths, places of birth and ceremony, and these frozen experiences remain as memories while people move on. The acting out of individual lives ultimately produces the cumulative changes which force the ancestral screen to adjust in order to mirror present circumstances. The frozen events of the recent past merge with the frozen events of the ancestral past, to create that timeless sense of continuity that characterizes Aboriginal ideology if not actuality.

There is a continual interaction between the ancestral past and the present which at times threatens to collapse the distinction between the two dimensions in individual consciousness. At other times they are separated out according to the reference point of action: the trajectory may be towards the present from the ancestral past (as for example in marriage) or towards the ancestral past from the present (as for example in ritual). In marriage people will use an image from the ancestral past to represent the present relationship between groups so as to explain where marriage partners come from: for example, 'we follow the line of the shark' refers to the bestowal of women from a clan linked to the ancestral shark. It is almost as if the women were bestowed by the shark. In ritual contexts, on the other hand, the objective of returning something to the ancestral past is often quite explicit. As Stanner (1966) so perceptively pointed out there is an inherent element of sacrifice in Aboriginal religious practice (see also Maddock 1985). On rare occasions there is an element of actual sacrifice. Once after a successful fishing expedition Narritjin buried all the fish that could not be eaten in the sand, in order to return them to the spirit woman Nyapililngu, who was associated with the beach.

The ancestral past, though changed and reproduced through present human action, is absorbed as a precedent for future action, for marrying a particular person, for avoiding a particular place, for disposing of food remains in a particular way. Each generation asserts that it is following ancestrally preordained paths. The ancestral past or Dreaming is simultaneously outside and inside the person: people absorb their identity from the ancestral past and transmit that identity to new generations through performing in ritual and projecting spiritual identity back into the landscape. The landscape, and the associated sacred objects and paintings become the focus for this dual process.

The role of landscape in mediating between present experience and the ancestral past has been a central theme of many recent analyses of central Australian society. As Munn (1970: 144) wrote: 'Since transformations were created in the [Dreaming] but remain visible forever . . . they condense within them the two forms of temporality, and are thus freed from specific historical location. . . . [B]oth human beings and ancestors can be freed from their "historicity" or "mortality".' Landscape is part of peoples' identity but is simultaneously part of the identity of the ancestral beings. Human identity thus is shared with something that has an existence independent of the person and which has the same origin: the ancestral past. In Myers' (1986: 55) words: 'country retains an identity enduring through time as something beyond human choice. Human and Dreaming action each contribute to the definition of landscape . . .' In order to stress the autonomy of the Dreaming Myers almost gives it agency, something that Morton recognizes and endorses. Quoting from Myers, he argues (1989: 288) that 'there is a fundamental sense in which the

Dreaming is not created by "persons", that it is genuinely "not understood by participants as a product of human activity"; and that it really "is articulated as the presence of a self-sufficient reality on which the realm of human life depends" (Myers 1986: 266)'.

In presenting the argument as he does, Morton is trying to come to terms with the psychological and conceptual position of an Aboriginal person with respect to the Dreaming. He also implies a theoretical position which represents ideas and emotions as generators of human action. My only concern with this account is that it tends to privilege religious ideas and grant them autonomy and separateness from more general cultural processes. I would prefer to argue that although the Dreaming is created by persons it is created as part of a cultural process that is not reducible to human agency. The analyst cannot adopt the Aboriginal view of the autonomy of the Dreaming if he or she wishes to determine how the privileged position of the Dreaming is produced.

Anthropologists who analyse symbolic systems, particularly anthropologists of the British tradition in which there is no recent history of a theory of culture, tend to give symbols too central a role in the cultural process of social reproduction—indeed symbol tends to stand in place of culture. The inherent danger of this approach is that it can lead to a variety of forms of reductionism associated with the implicit question 'What does the symbol do?'[5] This particular form of reductionism has 'society' in its Durkheimian mode, 'adaptation' in its cultural materialist mode, 'relations of inequality' in its Marxist mode, or 'individual psychology' in its Freudian mode as the motor force behind particular socio-cultural trajectories. Symbols, however, are constitutive as part of cultural process. The advantage of the more general screen provided by culture (as a system of ideas or body of knowledge connected to praxis, emotion, and the creation of value) as opposed to a privileged subset of cosmological or religious ideas, or a privileged mechanism such as symbolic process, is that it allows for multiple determinacy, for co-evolution, and for a complex and at times potentially chaotic relationship between structure and action, social reproduction and transformation. While I agree with Morton (1989: 292) that part of the determining structure of Aboriginal society is that 'everything and everyone must bear an ancestral identity' it is important to stress that the durability of the connection resides not only in its psychological aspect but also in its relevance to the organization of the relationships between people and place, or in the arrangement of marriages and the organization of trade. Although it is possible both for an Aborigine and for the analyst to abstract the cosmos as a determinant from the processes with which it is connected, in everyday discourse it is more usually presented in connected form: 'we marry [trade, perform ceremonies, live at Y, or have the right to live at X] because of our ancestral identity'. I hope I have shown in this chapter that in the Yolngu case it is not so much the landscape as such or the ancestral past as such that are the determinants of action. Rather, the landscape and the ancestral past are components of wider cultural processes, and action is not determined in any simple or programmatic way by them alone.

Notes

1. I have argued elsewhere (H. Morphy 1984: ix) that Richard Shechner's (1981) concept of restored behaviour is relevant to the analysis of Aboriginal ritual and consistent with Aboriginal concepts of ancestral events as behaviour that can be reperformed at other times and in other places.

2. The non-inflecting particle *bala* has two distinct syntactico-semantic functions. It may be used either as an adverb meaning 'movement away from the speaker/over there' or as a conjunctive particle meaning 'then/next'. There are good independent reasons for postulating that the latter is a development from the former. In Yolngu languages nominals are inflected for a wide range of cases, and the distal determiner *ngunha*, 'there', carries the full set of possible case markers. The ablative form, *ngula-ngur*, 'from there', may be used in the temporal sense 'after that'. 'Time at' (e.g. *walu-y*, lit. 'day-on', 'on that day'), is marked by an archaic form of the locative suffix, and the interrogative *nhaa-tha*, 'when', is simultaneously based on the root for 'what' plus another allomorph of the same archaic locative suffix. Even in these rare instances where the modern languages have a unique suffix for the temporal function, it is derived historically from a locative suffix. For a detailed study of a Yolngu language, Djapu, see F. Morphy (1983).

3. For this section, the perspective of a male ego is adopted, except where explicitly stated otherwise, purely for simplicity of expression. Yolngu kinship terminology assumes the equivalence of siblings, irrespective of their sex. Thus a woman and her brother refer to her children by the same term, *waku*, the term *maari* designates both mother's mother and mother's mother's brother, and a woman and her brother both refer to her daughter's children as *gutharra*.

4. Munn (1973*b*: 199) writes of this process in similar terms among the Walbiri: 'When children . . . are born they have these *guruwari* inside their bodies. When they die, the *guruwari* return to the soil. In this sense, the Dreaming is continually coming out of the ground and being re-embodied as a living entity, as well as continually returning to the ground in death.' One way of reading a Yolngu mortuary ritual is as the representation of a person as landscape.

5. For example the implicit functionalism of Harrison's (1990: 9) generalization that 'the sources of the stability of ritual symbolism must be sought elsewhere, in its uses rather than in its intrinsic characteristics'. My answer on a priori grounds to such dualisms is that both must be involved. Though I accept that balance between cultural ideal and social relations (e.g. the interests of dominant groups) as determinants of a socio-cultural trajectory (which seems to underlie Harrison's opposition), may differ in particular cases, both must be components of any explanation.

References

BERNDT, R. M. (1952). *Djanggawul*. London: Routledge & Kegan Paul.
——(1974). *Australian Aboriginal Religion*. Leiden: Brill.

BIERNOFF, D. (1978). 'Safe and Dangerous Places', in L. R. Hiatt (ed.), *Australian Aboriginal Concepts*, 93–105. Canberra: Australian Institute of Aboriginal Studies.

——(1979). 'Traditional and Contemporary Structures and Settlement in Eastern Arnhem Land with Particular Reference to the Nunggubuyu', in M. Heppell (ed.), *A Black Reality*, 153–79. Canberra: Australian Institute of Aboriginal Studies.

BOURDIEU, P. (1977). *Outline of a Theory of Practice*. Cambridge: Cambridge University Press.

CLUNIES-ROSS, M. (1978). 'The Structure of Arnhem Land Song Poetry', *Oceania*, 49/2: 128–56.

GIDDENS, A. (1979). *Central Problems in Social Theory: Action, Structure and Contradiction in Social Analysis*. Berkeley, Calif.: University of California Press.

HARRISON, S. (1990). *Stealing People's Names: History and Politics in a Sepik River Cosmology*. Cambridge: Cambridge University Press.

HIATT, L. R. (ed.) (1984). *Aboriginal Landowners: Contemporary Issues in the Determination of Traditional Aboriginal Land Ownership*, Oceania Monograph 27. Sydney: Oceania Publications.

KEEN, I. (1978). 'One Ceremony, One Song: An Economy of Religious Knowledge among the Yolngu of North-East Arnhem Land', unpublished Ph.D. thesis, Australian National University, Canberra.

——(1988). 'Yolngu Religious Property', in T. Ingold, D. Riches, and J. Woodburn (eds.), *Hunters and Gatherers: Property, Power and Ideology*, 272–91. Oxford: Berg.

——(1989). 'Ecology and Species Attributes in Yolngu Religious Symbolism', in R. Willis (ed.), *Signifying Animals: Human Meaning in the Natural World*, 85–102. London: Unwin Hyman.

——(1990). 'Images of Reproduction in the Yolngu Madayin Ceremony', in W. Shapiro (ed.), 'On the Generation and Maintenance of the Person', *Australian Journal of Anthropology* (Special Issue 1) 1/2, 3: 192–207.

MADDOCK, K. (1985). 'Sacrifice and Other Models in Australian Aboriginal Ritual', in D. Barwick, J. Beckett, and M. Reay (eds.), *Metaphors of Interpretation*, 133–57. Canberra: Australian National University Press.

MORPHY, F. (1977). 'Language and Moiety: Sociolectal Variation in a Yu:lngu Language of North-East Arnhem Land', *Canberra Anthropology*, 1: 51–60.

——(1983). 'Djapu: A Yolngu Dialect', in R. M. W. Dixon and B. Blake (eds.), *Handbook of Australian Languages*, iii. 1–188. Canberra: Australian National University Press.

MORPHY, H. (1977). 'Yingapungapu: Ground Sculpture as Bark Painting', in P. Ucko (ed.), *Form in Indigenous Art: Schematization in the Art of Aboriginal Australia and Prehistoric Europe*, 205–9. Canberra: Australian Institute of Aboriginal Studies.

——(1984). *Journey to the Crocodile's Nest*. Canberra: Australian Institute of Aboriginal Studies.

——(1988). 'Maintaining Cosmic Unity: Ideology and the Reproduction of Yolngu Clans', in T. Ingold, D. Riches, and J. Woodburn (eds.), *Hunters and Gatherers: Property, Power and Ideology*, 249–71. Oxford: Berg.

——(1990). 'Myth, Totemism and the Creation of Clans', *Oceania*, 60/4: 312–29.

——(1991). *Ancestral Connections: Art and an Aboriginal System of Knowledge*. Chicago: University of Chicago Press.

MORTON, J. (1987). 'Singing Subjects and Sacred Objects: More on Munn's "Transformations of Subjects into Objects" in Central Australian Myth', *Oceania*, 58/2:

100–18.

——(1989). 'Singing Subjects and Sacred Objects; a Psychological Interpretation of Subject into Object in Central Australian Myth', *Oceania*, 59/4: 280–98.

MUNN, N. (1970). 'The Transformation of Subjects into Objects in Walbiri and Pitjantjatjara Myth', in R. M. Berndt (ed.), *Australian Aboriginal Anthropology*, 141–56. Nedlands: University of Western Australia Press.

——(1973a). *Walbiri Iconography*. Ithaca, NY: Cornell University Press.

——(1973b). 'The Spatial Presentation of Cosmic Order in Walbiri Iconography', in J. A. W. Forge (ed.), *Primitive Art and Society*. London: Oxford University Press.

MYERS, F. R. (1986). *Pintupi Country, Pintupi Self: Sentiment, Place, and Politics among Western Desert Aborigines*. Washington, DC: Smithsonian Institute Press.

RUDDER, J. (1977). *An Introduction to Yolngu Science*. Galiwinku: Galiwinku Adult Education Centre.

SCHECHNER, R. (1981). 'The Restoration of Behaviour', *Studies in Visual Communication*, 7/3: 2–45.

STANNER, W. E. H. (1966). *On Aboriginal Religion*, Oceania Monograph 11. Sydney: University of Sydney.

——(1984). 'Religion, Totemism and Symbolism', in M. Charlesworth, H. Morphy, K. Maddock, and D. Bell (eds.), *Religion in Aboriginal Australia: An Anthology*, 137–74. St Lucia: University of Queensland Press.

STREHLOW, T. G. H. (1970). 'Geography and the Totemic Landscape in Central Australia: A Functional Study', in R. M. Berndt (ed.), *Australian Aboriginal Anthropology*, 92–129. Nedlands: University of Western Australia Press.

THOMSON, D. (1939). 'Proof of Indonesian Influence upon the Aborigines of North Australia: The Remarkable Dog Ngarra of the Mildjingi Clan', *London Illustrated News*, 12 August, 271–9.

WILLIAMS, N. (1986a). 'A Boundary is to Cross: Observations on Yolngu Boundaries and Permission', in N. M. Williams and E. Hunn (eds.), *Resource Managers: North American and Australian Hunter-Gatherers*, 131–54. Canberra: Australian Institute of Aboriginal Studies.

——(1986b). *The Yolngu and Their Land: A System of Land Tenure and the Fight for its Recognition*. Canberra: Australian Institute of Aboriginal Studies.

9

Relating to the Country in the Western Desert

===

ROBERT LAYTON

At the time I conducted eleven months' fieldwork in the region of Uluru (Ayers Rock, Australian Western Desert) between 1977 and 1979, half a century had passed since colonization by pastoralists had irrevocably changed the indigenous way of life. Uluru itself had been subject to tourism for twenty years. East of Uluru lay cattle stations while to the west and south, the Petermann and Musgrave Ranges were former Aboriginal reserves which once again belonged to their traditional Aboriginal owners since passage of the Northern Territory Land Rights Act in 1976. One of the purposes of my research was to obtain evidence for a land claim on Uluru and Katatjuta (the Olgas). Much of this claim was unable to proceed because the Federal Government transferred ownership to the Australian National Parks and Wildlife Service before the claim came to court. Surrounding areas were none the less granted to the claimants and title to the Park area was returned to its traditional owners in 1985. The senior men and women with whom I worked were already young adults when they first came into lasting contact with White people. During their adult lives, however, they have seen their way of life transformed in many ways. Although men still hunt regularly, imported flour has largely replaced the wild vegetable foods, traditionally gathered by women, which once provided 80 per cent of the diet. Children are born in hospital rather than in the bush, a change which has created major difficulties for maintaining personal affiliation to the land. Life on settlements has curtailed some ceremonies, while the introduction of motor vehicles has greatly expanded the opportunities for maintaining ceremonial links *between* communities.

From having possessed an autonomous cultural tradition, the indigenous community has become encapsulated in a dominant, often hostile culture. Recollections of childhood, the assertion of ownership rights over places, the continued performance of ritual, and transmission of knowledge are conducted as strategies to sustain identity as a distinctive people. Now all Aboriginal people speak English and the statements presented in this chapter were provided in English or, where indicated, in Pitjantjatjara.

The purpose of this chapter is to explore the links between an everyday knowledge of the land as a source of subsistence and ritual knowledge of the landscape and people as the embodiment of the ancestral heroes of the Creation

Fɪɢ. 9.1. Uluru (Ayers Rock).

Period. How people's continuing mastery of their cultural tradition facilitated successful claims to contemporary ownership is discussed elsewhere (Layton 1983*b*; 1985; and 1986), but it should be remembered that the material presented here was collected in the course of preparing a land claim.

Indigenous and Legal Discourses on the Land

The *Aboriginal Land Rights (NT) Act* was drawn up in response to the failure of the Gove land-rights case. The Gove case had been brought by members of the Yirrkala Aboriginal community against an Aluminium Company mining their traditional land. The case failed because the judge ruled that indigenous links with the land did not embody ownership as it is recognized in British Australian law. While he looked sympathetically on the evidence for what he called a spiritual obligation to care for the land, he found what the witnesses had said about the land being theirs insufficient to demonstrate a proprietory right—a right which he judged to depend on three properties: the right to use and enjoy, the right to exclude others, and the right to alienate (Blackburn 1971: 132; see discussions in Williams 1986 and Layton 1985). The most remarkable feature of the Land Rights Act was its attempt to redress this failure by writing a representation of indigenous land rights into the legal system. In the words of this representation, Aboriginal landownership was vested in local descent groups who held primary spiritual responsibility for sites on the land and whose members were entitled, in Aboriginal tradition, to forage over that land. Subsequent applications of the Act showed, however, that it failed effectively to represent the flexibility of links between people and the land (see Keen 1984 and Layton 1985). In the discourse of the courts exclusiveness played a large part: descent groups were recruited by a unilineal principle, they held rights to mutually exclusive areas of land. In indigenous discourse more than one means of recruitment was recognized, rights overlapped, and the edges of zones of land were often indeterminate.

Thus, driving across the landscape and heading away from Uluru, one might ask, 'Ngura Ulurunya palatja?' (Is this Uluru country?), to be told at first, 'Yes'; but it is impossible to pin down a point at which the answer becomes 'No'. Equally, asking which people look after the country (*wati minymaka nguraku walytja*), elicits a set which appears heterogeneous when judged by the criteria of a Radcliffe-Brownian patrilineage. The same people may prove to be looking after more than one country and many people have the right to forage over particular areas.

The difficulties of representing Aboriginal rights which arose during hearings for the Uluru land claim are discussed in Layton (1983*b*). Both anthropology and the legal system use concepts not exactly matched in local thought and each uses methods for validating those concepts which are foreign to local behaviour (ibid. 226). What criteria had Aboriginal witnesses relied on when they attributed primary spiritual responsibility to one set of people or another and why did statements sometimes appear contradictory? Why was my model of 'ambilineal descent', in which people choose whether to belong to the country of their mother or their father, not always able to predict how people would account for their own affiliation?

The shortcomings of the Act's wording and procedures also point to a more fundamental issue in ethnography, that of whether the translation of culture is possible, or whether cultures are closed to one another. It is this more basic question which the present chapter considers in the light of Foucault's notion of discourse (Foucault 1972).

Discourse on Subsistence

When the landscape appears as an 'object' of subsistence activities in indigenous discourse, there is much in common with Western ecological understanding, even if indigenous discussions are more fine-grained than ours.

When visiting, or talking about places, people will frequently describe the food resources found there: at which waterholes wild figs grow, where possums could be caught before they were wiped out by the fur trade, where hides have been constructed to spear emu as they come to drink in rocky defiles. Some places are named after a characteristic local resource: Kitinya: spinifex gum place; Iriyanya: saltbush place; Ainkuranya: edible mushroom or puffball place (Ainkura was described by Toby Nangina as 'like a pumpkin, long and yellow').

Particular animal species are known to frequent, and plant species to grow in, particular habitats. On *puti* (mulga flats or 'scrub country'), *malu* (red kangaroo) and *kalaya* (emu) are found. At rocky places, *kanyala* (euro), *wayuta* (possum) and *ngintaka* (perentie lizard) can be caught. Among sandhills, perentie may be found hunting for rabbit or small wallaby; also the *kuniya* (python), *kurkati* (sand goanna), and *mala* (hare wallabies).

People speak of how, during the pre-colonial way of life, they retired to a base camp adjacent to permanent water in times of drought, but after rain they moved about, meeting up with those living at neighbouring base camps and travelling between adjacent *ngura* ('countries' or estates). The movement of *ngangkali* (rain clouds) across the desert signals where fresh green plants will spring up; after rain is the time of *ukiri pulka*, the 'big green grass'. Not only was it said that the uneven and sporadic occurrence of plant foods compelled movement, it was considered a good thing to visit relatives living in other countries or camps (*ngura*).

Tjukurpa *as Discourse*

The Western Desert landscape is not spoken of purely in terms of subsistence. It is fundamentally determined by the actions of beings during the *tjukurpa*, the 'time of the law'. Many places are named after the *tjukurpa* being on whose route they lie: Malutja Uril (Red Kangaroo Plain); Kalaya Murpu (Emu Ridge). This discourse appears far more alien to our own way of speaking about the environment. In one important legend, for instance, the Red Kangaroo travelled with the Euro, even though the two animals are found in different habitats. They were accompanied, moreover, by their *kamaru* (uncle, mother's brother), the Owl, a night-time creature. Rocks and waterholes are spoken of as relatives, or as embodying ancestral beings.

How can a bridge be effected between the two discourses, indigenous and Western? For Foucault (1972) discourses such as natural science, psychiatry, or economics each have certain 'objects' around which discourse takes place: the species, madness, the market. The rules of a discourse determine which statements are sensible and which are deemed irrelevant, marginal, or unscientific. The rules specify what is possible. 'How wide is a dreaming track?' is, for instance, a nonsensical question within discourse on the Dreaming, though it was one posed at an earlier land claim hearing. Discourses also determine who is allowed to speak or who speaks with authority and where he can speak (Foucault 1972: 53): both important considerations in indigenous discourse about the landscape of the Western Desert. Most can be said about a place when at that site, and by someone linked to it in a recognized way. If another spoke, he would be usurping an authority to which he is not entitled.

Foucault believes that, in general, 'objects' cannot be translated from the terms of one discourse to the terms of another. The 'objects' of nineteenth-century psychiatry cannot be projected back on to earlier discourses; before madness was linked to criminality, for example, it was a different 'object'. Foucault writes that, while it would be possible to do so, he will not attempt to discover the *meaning* given at a certain time to the word 'neurosis', because that would not be relevant to understanding how, at a certain time, criminality became an object of medical expertise *within* psychiatric discourse (ibid. 48).

He none the less makes two important concessions. First, he distinguishes between the internal relations of a discourse, and relationships that exist outside it. Factors outside discourse can be seen as its formative elements (ibid. 69). These include the role of discourse in the decisions of government and in political struggles, and the appropriation of discourse (who takes the right to speak); these are regulated ways of practising its possibilities. The relationship between the bourgeois family unit and nineteenth-century French law, for instance, can be studied 'in its own right', independently of how legal discourse talked about relations between family life and normal behaviour (ibid. 45). Such external relations define a space articulated with possible discourses, just as discourse about the 'time of law' is articulated within the space of Aboriginal politics, which confers the right to display knowledge. Secondly, Foucault does present mania, delirium, and melancholia as objects which exist outside a particular discourse when he poses the question of how we can identify the appearance of a new discourse such as psychiatry. His answer is that, 'what had been said on the subject of mania . . . (etc.) by the doctors of the classical period in no way constituted an autonomous discipline' (p. 179). This is a remarkable admission because, even if mania and the others can be shown to reappear in different discourses, they are obviously, as constructs, artefacts of culture, and contrast, for instance, with spirit possession, which is an 'object' within a different discourse.

Places are 'objects' of indigenous discourse on the *tjukurpa* ('time of the law'). At Witapula, for instance, the Kungarangkalpa, or Seven Sisters, built a *yuu* (windbreak) where they camped for the night. This became the steep slope on the south-west side of the soak. It was pointed out to me by the men who took me to the site that the wind must have been blowing from the south-west on the night the young women camped there. At Taputji the Mala women prepared food before going to dance at Tjukutjapi. Holes in the roof of the rock shelter at Taputji show where they treated *mayi itunypa*, the berries of *Solanum coactiliferum* which contain a bitter juice that must be squeezed out or destroyed by cooking. The digging stick of one young woman lies, as a long boulder, outside the entrance to the rock shelter. Sometimes the passage of a *tjukurpa* hero is marked by a bright colour, or wavy lines, in the rock. At

FIG. 9.2. Witapula: looking from the low ridge which was the Seven Sisters' windbreak, on to the soak marking the overnight camp (trampling by cattle has eroded the surrounding vegetation). In the distance stands Atila (Mt Conner), created by the Ice Men and associated with winter frosts.

Urkuntja a wavy mark is the foot of Walawuru the Wedge-tailed Eagle, who camped there with his two wives, the old crow and the beautiful young cockatoo.

A crucial difference between hard (Derrida-inspired) and softer postmodernists hinges on whether they accept the possibility of referential meaning. Reference is 'the way in which we use language to draw attention to what we are talking about' (Rommetveit 1987: 86). Referential meaning is that meaning, from out of the range of possible meanings, that a word or phrase might have, which is determined by the context in which the word or phrase is produced. While Sarup shows how Derrida apparently disregards referential meaning (Sarup 1989: 58–62), both Eco (1990) and Foucault (1972) allow the possibility of this escape from the closed world of the text, allowing us to draw correspondences between 'objects' of different discourses.

Although Derrida does not accept that speech is more immediate or effective than writing, once the possibility of referential meaning is accepted, it becomes clear that speaking to someone face to face should allow us to discover whether we have got our message across more effectively than if we write our message to them from a distance. While Derrida is right to argue that use of the spoken word is, in our culture, likely to be affected by earlier written texts and therefore not (in one sense) privileged, this is clearly not true of oral or non-literate cultures studied by anthropologists. Derrida's theory is itself ethnocentric. Ricoeur (1979) gives a preferable model for ethnographic fieldwork. According to him, social interactions as they are carried out are *performances* in which the participants have some access to each other's fleeting, subjective references (see the examples of mapping and collecting genealogies given above). If the listener responds inappropriately, the speaker can try again, or realize that his question is inept within the local discourse. In Pitjantjatjara, for instance, *punganyi* may signify either to hit or to kill by striking. Suppose a man sees his favourite dog stealing meat hanging in a tree and shouts to the anthropologist (in Aboriginal English) 'kill that dog' . . . the anthropologist will quickly discover whether he has interpreted the instruction correctly. For Ricoeur, it is only when interactions are externalized that they become texts. It is at that stage that we attempt to construe the text in terms of our inferred understanding of the 'possible world' of meaning inhabited by the performers. Here however we risk, as writer, taking refuge in the technical terms of our familiar discourse or, as reader, in analogies from our own experience: especially if we have never been to the Trobriands, the Western Desert, or the Sudan.

Derrida considers meaning only in the dictionary sense: words are defined only with reference to other words; but dictionary meanings are inherently circular. During fieldwork, on the other hand, we interact with people in an environment that has meaning for them and which is perceptible to us, even if only perceptible in the terms of a particular discourse. Yet, when we hear:

> 'That man is my father' (but genealogy shows him to be an uncle, or not biologically related at all)
> 'That rock is my father' (but we do not speak of rocks as relatives),

the disjunction between our discourse and that of those we are working with is forced upon us. When we participate in performances of culture, language is being used to do practical things.

Derrida cites Pierce as an authority on the indeterminacy of textual interpretation but this, as Eco comments (1990: 35), is ironic. It suggests that Derrida regards his own reading of Pierce as somehow privileged above other possible misreadings. Moreover, Eco argues, Pierce does not support Derrida's view that there is nothing outside the text. On the contrary, Pierce contends that meaning purposefully refers to something outside language. What this referent is can only be known via the way in which we represent it, but the thought or opinion that defines reality must belong to an intersubjective *community of knowers* and their universe of discourse (ibid. 28, 39). The passages cited above suggest that Foucault also recognizes the possibility of referential meaning, but (just as importantly) argues that reference to objects can only be made by means of cultural representations of those things (i.e. by means of what Foucault terms 'objects').

Eco parallels Foucault in arguing that while something can be truly asserted within a given universe of discourse, this does not exhaust the other, potentially infinite determinations of 'that object' (Eco 1990: 37). Thus in Aboriginal discourse it can truly be said, 'That is the Kingfisher Woman'; while in Western discourse it can be said, 'That is an exfoliated boulder of dune-bedded sandstone.' None the less, as we stand there talking, we know we are talking about the same *apu* (rock). The normal ethnographic task, for the anthropologist, is to learn the rules of Aboriginal discourse that make the exotic representation of the rock truthful.

The greater problem, I argue, lies with the text we write based on our fieldwork. How can we discourage unintended readings? How can we render local discourse into 'objects' of comparative ethnography, such as 'local descent group' or 'territory'? If Evans-Pritchard had described what the Azande do as 'small-group psychotherapy' rather than 'witchcraft' we would feel very differently about it. Do we read Lienhardt's account of the 'congregation' that performs a Dinka 'sacrifice' the way a Dinka would read it (Carrithers 1990: 268)? Only by attempting to recreate in our account the original referential context can we overcome these difficulties. This is the intention of the remainder of the chapter.

Going into the Ground

Although Strehlow, in his accounts of Aranda religion, refers to ancestral heroes emerging from the ground as well as sinking back at the end of their journeys (e.g. Strehlow 1964), emergence played little part in the narratives I was given. The most important sites are those where *tjukurpa* figures went into the ground: *piti tjarpangu*, 'hole go into'. It is at these places that their fecundity is concentrated. Three examples follow: Arutju Piti, near Mitchell's Knob in the Musgrave Ranges, is the place where Paddy Uluru was born. It is where a large group of *mingkiri* (mice) went into the ground. In Paddy Uluru's presence his friend Pompy Wanampi cleaned away dead vegetation from the dry soak, commenting 'I'll make him *mingkiri*, plenty.' He then sang the ceremonial songs for the site and threw handfuls of dry soil from the hole into the air. Ngintaka Piti, near Apara, also in the Musgraves, is the place where a *ngintaka* (perentie lizard) went into the ground. He was chased by a big mob of brush-tail possum men from Wayuta Piti. Reaching the hill called Pala, Ngintaka paused and looked round to make sure he was not closely followed, then went into the ground. Dark lumps incorporated into the bare rock of the hillside are his footprints and white veins the track of his tail. Tommy Minyungu demonstrated how people rubbed a stone on the hillside to increase *ngintaka*. Piles of stones on a rock platform at the base of the hillside were kept heaped up and hit with sticks to make many, fat perentie. Once underground, Ngintaka became a *wanampi* (water snake or rainbow serpent) and now releases water into the soak, Ngintaka Piti.

The Kuniya pythons went into the ground at Kuniya Piti, at the eastern end of Uluru. Undulating lines on the flank of Uluru show where they passed as they came across from Mutijulu, while their bodies are long, cylindrical

FIG. 9.3. Kapi Yularanya Pulka, a rock hole 20 km. north of Uluru and one of the temporary water sources traditionally visited during foraging expeditions from Uluru. Two ancestral tracks cross here; one is that of the 'Devil Dingo' on his way to Uluru. Uluru can be seen in the distance.

boulders. One Kuniya woman buried the eggs she had carried to Uluru here. Paddy Uluru and Nipa Winmati took two *nyitiyara* (boys aged about 12 years) to Kuniya Piti, where the men cleared away grass around the boulders. Paddy Uluru described how his father's youngest brother had left Areyonga to die here and become a 'proper Kuniya'. The boys were told to sit astride one of the boulders while Paddy Uluru brushed it with a bunch of grass. Both men then rubbed the stone with their hands. One explained, *Kuka ngalkuntjara alatji*, 'meat' 'eat + having' 'like this' (see also Layton 1986: 16).

A negative instance of such increase sites is that of Kurpany, the 'Devil Dingo' at Inintitjara, on the north side of Uluru. Kurpany was created by the Wintalka (Tingari) men of Kikingkura to punish the Mala when they refused to attend the Wintalka men's ceremony (see ibid. 5–7). Kurpany emerged from the ground at Pulpayala, in Kikungkura country, a hole lined with rock containing distinctive green crystals, and attacked the Mala as they slept in their camp at Uluru at midday. Tired from having killed and eaten two young Mala men, Kurpany himself slept for a while at Inintitjara. Only his head, the tip of a large boulder, projects above ground. The long grass growing on it must not be disturbed, otherwise one would make a proper (live) *mamu* (evil spirit).[1] When Kurpany woke, he followed the trail of the Mala over Uluru, attracted by the scent of a new-born baby. The Mala fled southward.

Two men, on different occasions, asserted that Uluru was more closely associated with Kuniya than with the Mala, because the Kuniya went inside the rock, while the Mala merely ran on.

The Source of Personal Identity

Relationships between living people and ancestral beings are said to be established in several ways. Each individual is first identified with one of the *tjukurpa* beings at birth, according to where the *pulyi* (stub of their umbilical cord) fell off. Their personality, *kurunpa* (spirit, will, self), is expected to follow that of the hero they embody, and people may be spoken of as if they were the being in question. Paddy Uluru's father was Lungkata Tjukurpa (Blue-tongue lizard Dreaming). Spencer and Gillen seem to have met this man when they visited Uluru in 1894 (Layton 1986: 31). According to Strehlow, who visited the area in the 1940s, the Mala were led to Uluru by a man named Lungkata Tjukurba (Strehlow 1969: 14). In the narrative as told today at Uluru Lungkata killed an emu who was being hunted by the Bell Bird brothers. They had tracked it from Antalanya, near Paddy Uluru's birthplace, where it had been disturbed by a woman dropping her headpad. As the emu ran ahead of the hunters toward Uluru, Lungkata killed it and hid the meat. On one occasion Paddy Uluru and Pompy Douglas told me the story in the following terms (see Layton 1986: 9):

FIG. 9.4. Men belonging to the Kikingkura country, near Docker River. They are the living embodiments of the Tingari, who quarrelled during the 'time of law', and sent the 'Devil Dingo' to punish the Mala Wallaby people of Uluru for not attending their ceremony. The men are standing on a sand dune which is part of the Tingari legend.

P.U. Lungkata was my father.

P.D. He stole Kalaya meat from Antalanya. He was the owner of Uluru. He killed an emu belonging to that other bloke, and he planted [buried] him [it] at Kalaya Tjunta . . . His father is Lungkata Tjukur.

P.U. My boss.

Pompy Douglas and Toby Nangina, born on the same night at two places associated with the two boys who built Uluru from mud, are the two boys of the legend. Since in the legend the boys quarrelled, Pompy and Nangina were told they would quarrel, but became good friends, a fact from which they took pleasure. Some of the most dramatic identifications between people and their *tjukurpa* were given by men from the Petermann Ranges. The Tingari men made preparations for the ceremony to which the Mala were invited, but during a discussion fighting broke out. A line of stones shows where the men sat down to talk. Senior men pointed out individual stones identified with their fathers: *Mama ngayuku palatja*, 'father mine just there', said one.

A large stone shaped like a double cylinder marks the place where one of the men and his nephew were killed by the *tjukur* of another of those present.

Further on, the most senior of the men showing me the area sat astride a seven-foot long boulder. This is his *tjukurpa*, where he died. A small flat rock half under the stone has the black-outlined silhouette of a footprint, his footprint. Another man, in the narrative, saw that he was dead and ran off. He is another stone, about eight feet away.

Discourse and Practical Habit

Beyond the notion that context itself restricts plausible interpretations, Eco cites a further reason for questioning whether Pierce provides a good authority for Derrida's claim that 'there is nothing outside the text' (Derrida 1976: 158). Pierce argued that if interpretation of a representation does not produce a successful practical habit, semiosis has failed (Eco 1990: 29). In the Western Desert, the scarcity of water and the unpredictability of foods are considerations to which Dreams must adapt through practical habit, or be broken. While a person is affiliated to his or her birthplace, the significance of this link to the land depends on whether or not it proves to fall in the locus of his or her life movement. It is a kind of initial hypothesis or opening gambit. A baby's mother may carry a child to a place before the *pulyi* falls off (as happened in the cases of several Petermann men, and Toby Nangina), to ensure they embody the being associated with that site (cf. Tonkinson 1978: 51). Some people, however, are born while their parents are away from their country foraging, or attending a ceremony. If this happens the 'birthplace' may be regarded as that person's country only in an *unytju* (trivial) sense. Nipa Winmati said, 'I would have been born in the cave at Kantju [on the north side of Uluru] only no water there; my mother went round to Mutitjulu.' Hence Nipa's Dreaming is Kuniya, one of the *tjukurpa* at Uluru.

Peter Bulla was born at Katulkira, near Pantu (Lake Amadeus). 'There's good water there. . . . I should have been born somewhere around Ayers Rock, Mt Olga, but . . . they all been walk about in good season time, green time.' His mother later brought him back to Katatjuta (Mt Olga). The *tjukurpa* at Katulkira is the same as that for places just west of Katatjuta, his mother's country (a group of lizards including the Thorny Devil, Ngiyari, and Central Bearded Dragon, Ngapala). This provides a way of speaking of Peter's association with Katatjuta. Peter's older brother Ngapala Jack was born where Ngapala left her eggs at Utiti, just west of Katatjuta, and they therefore identify with a single legend.

Paddy Uluru, on the other hand, was born while his parents were attending a ceremony at Yunanpa (Mitchell's Knob), and gained a Dreaming that has no connection with Uluru. Although his *tjukurpa* was Minkiri (mouse), he emphasized that the emu killed by Lungkata also came from Yunanpa country. Pompy

Douglas defended Paddy Uluru's claim to hold Uluru: 'Never mind this Uluru Paddy him been born that way . . . his family been go that way; still belonging to him Ayers Rock. His brothers all been born there [at] Ininti [on the north face of Uluru]. Been gone [died] his brothers . . . he's taken their place now.'

An interesting process arose in the identification of men with the left-handed Mala who speared Tjintir-Tjintir the Willy-Wagtail woman at Ininti (Layton 1986: 14). Paddy Uluru told me this man was his 'brother' (first cousin), Lungkata's nephew Muraku. He had been left-handed and had died at Wilpiya, near Angus Downs. While Peter Bulla once spoke of the man who speared Tjintir-Tjintir as Paddy Uluru's brother, on another occasion Peter indicated Paddy and said *he* was that man. After Paddy Uluru's death Ronny Russell told me that Paddy himself, whom Ronny classed as *tjamu* (grand-father), had been the left-handed Mala man. The deceased cousin Muraku, as far as I could establish, died childless. This process of shifting identification with legendary heroes parallels the construction of social kinship to be dis-cussed below.

Conflicting constructions of the cultural landscape may occur at two levels: the attribution of people to places, and the legendary significance of sites. During my work at Uluru, the birthplace of one man was repeatedly in con-tention. The man in question maintained that he was born at Uluru, that his *tjukurpa* was the new-born baby smelt by the 'Devil Dingo'. He asserted rights of ownership to Uluru on that basis and had done so since the 1930s (see Layton 1983*b*: 228–9). Other men associated with Uluru were adamant that he was born to the south, in the Musgrave Ranges, and contested his claim to belong to Uluru (see ibid. 228–9). This dispute was bound up with claims to present the significance of sites at Uluru. Early during my fieldwork I was taken to visit sites on the south side of the Rock. An elongated boulder standing upright and half buried in the sand was described by the man whose birthplace was in contention as the firestick of Pulari, a heroine who gave birth in a small cave several hundred metres further west, where he himself claimed to have been born. Paddy Uluru was furious, retorting that the stone was the body of Lungkata, where he fell after being burnt in his boughshade by the Bell Bird brothers. Other senior men present discretely commented, as we walked away, that Paddy Uluru was looking after the place for his father and his version was correct. It agrees, in fact, with documentation by Harney and Mountford, who relied on other informants (Layton 1986: 9–10, 120). Less overt disagreement centred on several sites on the north face of Uluru which three brothers claimed to belong to the Kuniya python legend, contrary to the usual interpretation that these were *mala* (hare wallaby) sites. This disagreement was not confronted in public during my fieldwork, but in such dispute the testimony of someone who is *ninti* (familiar with, has experience of) carries more weight than someone who is *kulira* (had heard or taken notice of the tradition).

Looking After a 'Country' (Ngura)

How, then, do people speak of their rights to a country? Each permanent water associated with a base camp, and the surrounding temporary waters, forms a *ngura* (camp or country). Places within the orbit of a particular base camp are *ngura kutju*: one country (Layton 1983a: 15–20). Ramifications of the key terms *ngura* and *walytja* (kinsman) are extensively analysed by Myers (1986a: 54–9, 101–11, 151). A person, I was told, 'holds' a country (*ngura witini*) by living in it, by making their base *nguranka nyinanyi* ('camp + at' 'sitting') and by looking after its sacred traditions. People who go to Alice Springs abandon their *tjukurpa*; people who live in the bush now hold those traditions (cf. ibid. 68, 129, 145–6).

One of the distinguishing features of Western Desert kinship is that a child inherits rights in both his mother's and father's *ngura* (Layton 1983a: 24–30; Myers 1986a: 128–30; Tonkinson 1978: 51–2). A man's sons and his sister's sons learn the same *tjukurpa*. But someone can not look after a *ngura* if he has not learnt the ceremonial songs. His responsibility is to protect the *inma* (songs, ceremonies) and sacred objects in that country. If he fails to do so, he 'gives the country away'.

Anyone who regularly forages in a country (even if it is not his or her own) also needs to be acquainted with the songs. Ideally a man learns all the *tjukurpa* traditions in his region. You cannot go into a country until those who hold it have displayed its sacred objects to you and brought you into contact with them (cf. Myers 1986a: 151; Tonkinson 1978: 53). Nipa Winmati said all the people of Katatjuta, Uluru, and Atila have to know the *tjukurpa* for all three countries, because after rain people camp throughout that area.

When sacred objects are revealed, those about to see them for the first time stay outside the site with guardians until the objects have been set out on a bed of branches. They are then summoned forward. Verses describing the events depicted on the objects are sung, with additional spoken explanation. Those who have seen them for the first time are then invited to help return them to storage.

To 'hold' a country you must therefore both know its law and make it the base for your life movements; 'You can't just say "that's my country", you must stay in it.' It is possible to hold both your mother's and your father's countries, or you can 'pick one out'. A person cannot hold a country as a child, only when they become big (*pulkaringu*). Those who hold an estate have pre-eminent rights to it at three levels. First, they control access to the country in general, by yielding access to its religious traditions (cf. Myers 1986a: 91). 'Even a brother-in-law', I was told, 'can't go into a country (for the first time) without an owner to take him in.' Secondly, when people from another country hunt in your *ngura*, they must give something to your people, especially to the old men too aged to hunt for themselves (cf. Layton 1986: 39–40). Thirdly, it is the custodians' responsibility to punish trespass by unauthorized individuals on sacred sites (ibid. 45).

Kinship in the Country

Can we speak of 'local descent groups', as defined in the Land Rights Act, in the Western Desert? The collectivity, or coalition of people belonging to a country such as Uluru or Katatjuta are *utulu*, a group or band of people living together. By accepting responsibility to look after places in that country they have, moreover, become relations to, or have come to care for, that country, or *ngura walytjaringanyi*, 'country' 'kinsman/carer + become'.

The mapping of people on to the landscape thus has a further basis in practical habit. That the term *walytja* can make reference to both people and places as 'objects' is central to the character of Western Desert discourse. Their equivalence is consummated after death, when a person becomes, or returns to the ancestral figure embodied within a place in their country. Social kinship is predicated on attachment to country. Although, statistically, most people hold the same country as one of their parents, this is not necessarily the case. In principle a person inherits rights from their grandparents, conferring potential rights to four countries. The terms *kami*, or grandmother, and *tjamu*, or grandfather, refer equally to relatives on the mother's and father's side. Transmission thus follows the generational moieties: 'a young person who needs help to speak about his country will sit with his grandparents' (cf. Tonkinson 1988: 157). And failure to look after a country leads to a loss of productivity: 'when a people leave their country the permanent water fails' (said of Kulpitjata, in the northern Musgraves).

Kinship between Countries

Walytja denotes a kinsman, someone you care for. Both adjacent countries and the people who look after them are spoken of as kinsmen. Thus the people of Uluru and Apara were spoken of by Paddy Uluru as, 'one family, *nganampa walytja* [our kin] same grandfather, half and half'. Ngapala Jack described Katatjuta and Uluru as 'like cousins', while Uluru and Atila were said to be 'brothers, those two hills'. The same kin terms, *kuta* (elder brother) and *malanya* (younger brother), were applied to both full siblings and close collateral relatives, both parallel and cross cousins. Members of more distant countries on the track of the same *tjukurpa* heroes are also regarded as siblings.

Kinship with the country is expressed in the rule that a person should marry someone from a distant country (cf. Myers 1986*a*: 71, 175). 'If someone tried to get married in their own family, they would be killed.' Regular alliances between particular estates are not the norm, although a number of marriages between those affiliated to Uluru and Kikingkura have occurred in recent generations.

A survey of marriages among senior living people and their deceased parents gave the results at Table 9.1. Despite the small size of the sample, a marked preference emerges for marriage to someone from a distant estate. The one exception to the rule prohibiting marriage within the same estate was obtained while compiling genealogies. I was unable to interview the people in question although the son of this couple was still alive.

The Western Desert marriage rule is markedly different from those among communities which rely on section or subsection systems, where marriage to a particular category of relative in the opposite patrimoiety is prescribed. Section and subsection systems are anchored to local groups in such a way as to create a chequer-board pattern where members of adjacent estates belong to opposite moieties and, in a subsection system, alternating semi-moieties (see Morphy, Ch. 8, for an example from northern Australia). A person's social kinship is predicated on the identity of the land to which he is attached.

How do Pitjantjatjara, lacking such systems, interact with one another in the idiom of 'kinship'? Belonging to a particular country predicates relationships of siblingship or affinity with those belonging to other estates, depending on whether they are near or distant. Although the operation of this process is illustrated in Fig. 9.5 it is a difficult one to elucidate through genealogies because people constantly tend to speak of more distant collateral genealogical relationships of cousinship as the closer ones of siblingship. The collateral relationship, *sibling's child*, is similarly merged into the lineal relationship *own child*. Billy Kaiyipipi was explicit about this tendency when he described how when he was a child, he and his family used to visit Muntaruwa, where he had a lot of cousins whom he addressed as 'brother'. Paddy Uluru called Ngapala Jack and Tjalkalyiri Tiger brothers because his father Lungkata and their mother Antumara, although cousins (Lungkata was Antumara's mother's brother's son), 'were like brother and sister . . . always travelling together' (cf. Myers 1986a: 192–5). The small sample at Table 9.2 illustrates this tendency.

Four cases were noted in which people claimed a brother-in-law (*marutju*) relationship although neither had married the other's sister. In one case the two men were from adjacent estates, but in three the men's estates were separated

TABLE 9.1. *Marriage and residential propinquity*

Husband and wife from				
Same estate	Adjacent estates	1 estate between	2+ estates between	TOTAL
1	2	8	22	33

(a) 4– and 8– section systems

'sib'	affine	'sib'
aff.	**EGO**	aff.
'sib'	aff.	'sib'
aff.	'sib'	aff.

☐ own moiety

▨ opposite moiety

'sib' = classified as lineal relative (i.e. sibling)

aff. = classified as affinal relative

note - as a result of cross-cousin marriage, affine
       is synonymous with matrilateral relative in 4-
       and 8- section systems.

(b) Western desert

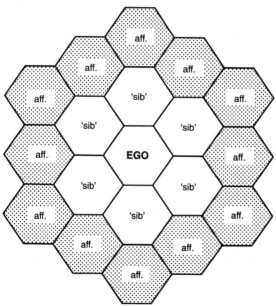

FIG. 9.5. Social kinship between local groups: (*a*) four- and eight-section systems;
(*b*) Western Desert.

TABLE 9.2. *People other than actual siblings claiming a sibling relationship*

Affiliation	No specifiable genealogical connection	Collateral genealogical connection (i.e. cousins)
Same estate	2	2
Adjacent estates	7	5
1 estate between	2	1
2+ estates between	–	–
2+ estates between but on same *tjukurpa* path	3	–

by two or more intervening countries. There is thus a general tendency for people who interact closely as members of adjacent estates to speak of each other as siblings. Such people would regularly have foraged in each other's countries, probably often as members of the same band. Those from distant estates are treated as potential affines with whom actual marriage links may be contracted. Such marriages will offer the children options to develop local allegiances in two widely separated areas. The role of looking after estates on the same *tjukurpa* track is selectively relied upon to extend classificatory siblingship beyond adjacent estates (cf. Myers 1986*a*: 154–5, 184 ff.). The concept of places as kinsmen is thus congruent with the relationships forged between those who forage in them. In the myth of the Kangaroo, Euro, and Owl, mentioned earlier, the two young men are being taken through a distant country by the man who will later find them a wife.

Conclusions

Can we therefore now transpose the terms of indigenous discourse into the 'objects' of a more familiar way of speaking? One way of attempting this is to consider what people say about access to places and foods in the light of socio-ecological theory, arguing that both the indigenous and Western discourses speak, through corresponding 'objects', of constraints external to both, so making indigenous and Western discourses congruent.

It can be argued, along these lines, that hunter-gatherers throughout the Western Desert and northern Australia exploit two types of resource with very different distributions. In both, water is distributed in a dense and predictable fashion at widely scattered soaks, rock holes, and occasional wells. Sacred sites, as noted above, always occur near water. Although access to the water itself is not physically defended, access to sacred sites is a right vested in those holding the estate. Plant and animal foods, on the other hand, are dispersed and

unpredictable in their distribution. Reciprocal rights of access between neighbouring estates guarantee mutual rights to exploit temporary abundances following rain. The structure of social kinship can be argued to express the mutual
advantages of allowing reciprocal access to temporally abundant resources, of
accepting indebtedness when goods are shared, but guarding rights to scarce
permanent water and religious knowledge (Myers 1986*a*: 97–9, 1986*b*: 189–90;
Layton 1989: 447–51). Myers suggests that it is during drought, when social
relations are most subject to stress, that being able to retreat to a base camp with
one's close kin is most important (Myers 1986*b*: 183). Counterbalancing this,
the network of ancestral tracks, personal identification with particular ancestral
heroes, and kinship between neighbouring estates creates the sense of a wider
living community whose members' destinies are intertwined. The *tjukurpa*
thus underpins two complementary modes for speaking of access to subsistence
resources: one inclusive, one exclusive.

The Western Desert is distinguished from northern Australia, however, by
the very irregular pattern of rainfall and the absence of seasonality (see Layton
1986: 24–8, 34–5). One range of hills may endure several years' drought while
the next enjoys good conditions. It was a traditional strategy for the entire
population of a range experiencing drought to leave the area and move to
another range of hills. During the first thirty years of the present century
movements occurred at different times between the Mann and Petermann
Ranges and the Musgrave and MacDonnell Ranges. Such movement may
exploit existing links of marriage. It also provides the context for new marriages
to take place: Pitjantjatjara from the Petermanns married Aranda in the
MacDonnells or Yankunytjatjara in the Musgraves. This strategy appears to
underlie the strong preference for avoiding marriages between the same or
adjacent estates, and instead to establish more distant alliances, which is distinctive of the Western Desert, as against those areas with section and subsection systems. The nexus of localized clans linked by ancestral tracks and flexible
band membership may thus be interpreted as the source of cultural adaptations
common to central and northern Australia, while the distinctive marriage rule
of the Western Desert offers a solution to the particular problems of surviving
in a semi-arid landscape. Such an explanation attempts, in Foucault's terms, to
define an ecological space within which Western Desert discourse on the
landscape takes place. It cannot claim that the conceptual forms of that discourse are *determined* by the ecology.

An alternative way of bridging Western and indigenous discourse is not to
explain but to search for familiar interpretive analogues, such as Evans-
Pritchard's 'witchcraft' or Lienhardt's 'sacrificial congregation', which seek
parallel concepts in our own discourse. One such interpretation would be to
construe Western Desert paintings as maps of the landscape. Depictions of the
landscape in Australian Aboriginal art are notable for the bird's-eye view they
adopt. This is a quite different convention to the view from a single point

located within the landscape characteristic of European art. Whereas farming communities construe the landscape from a fixed point of order, their own village surrounded on the horizon by the unknown, chaotic, or unseen (see Introduction and Chapters 3 and 10), nomads seem to adopt a decentred perspective in which numerous points are attributed equal value (see Chapters 6 and 8). A particularly strong contrast exists between the Pitjantjatjara and Umeda, described by Gell in Chapter 10. Pitjantjatjara life is highly visible. People traditionally light fires to signal their presence on foraging expeditions so as not to be suspected of theft or vengeance. In camp, people sit outside their boughshades as much as possible to proclaim their sociality. Munn argued that a key concept in Pitjantjatjara and Walbiri cosmology is the transformation of creative acts into visible objects (Munn 1971). The Umeda, by contrast, live in a world of invisible objects, where sounds become the primary manifestation of behaviour. European commentators on central Australian paintings commonly write that sacred sites and the ancestral tracks linking them are laid out as on a map. A key can be provided, explaining that concentric circles denote sites while tracks of various forms denote kangaroo, snake, possum, etc. Michaels has, however, derided this cartographic interpretation as an exercise in cryptography, which 'reduces the mystery of the ambiguous so that the European observer is able to construct a readable text' (Michaels 1987: 156).

Is it possible to go beyond the cartographic interpretations? A number of speakers at the original Anthropology of Landscape Conference remarked that in understanding how the landscape is conceived within a cultural tradition it should not be thought that the landscape is merely a mnemonic, or metaphor, for processes that are really going on at some independent level: the land itself as socially constituted plays a fundamental role in the ordering of cultural relations (see Introduction and Chapters 2 and 8). This observation is applicable to the Western Desert. The concept of the creation period, and its ongoing presence as a state of being in indigenous Australian cultures, transforms fluid social processes into the realization of a continuing structure of predictable social relationships (see Chapter 8, and Myers 1986*a*: 47). A more productive parallel than the idea of painting as map might be to compare the landscape to an abacus on which people are beads whose 'value' (cultural identity) is determined by their position on the board, a board whose structure is in turn determined by the places and journeys of the *tjukurpa*. Sacred sites are fixed reference points to which individuals and coalitions are anchored (compare Tonkinson 1978: 105), and permit what Myers terms the precarious achievement of society in an environment where dispersal is the norm and the problem is how to draw sufficient people together to facilitate social interaction (Myers 1986*a*: 48, 154). Sacred sites are places where the creative and mundane planes of existence intersect. The strange forms and colours in the rock can therefore also be conceived, via another Western discourse, as perturbations in the space–time continuum where creative energy is transformed into matter.

Each of these interpretations changes the way we evaluate indigenous discourse, just as we respond differently to the Azande according to whether we regard them as practising 'witchcraft' or 'psychotherapy'. The choice of analogous 'object' from our professional discourse is a political act which determines whether writing be oppression or liberation. It is only by participating in indigenous discourse that we can attempt an appropriate interpretation.

Note

1. *Irati* (killing magic) is infused in the rock at a *liru* (poisonous snake) site on the south side of Uluru (cf. Mountford 1977: 50, 54, 60).

References

BLACKBURN, J. (1971). 'Milirrpum v. Nabalco Pty. Ltd. and the Commonwealth of Australia', *Australian Law Report (NT Supreme Court)*, 4–154.

CARRITHERS, M. (1990). 'Is Anthropology Art or Science?', *Current Anthropology*, 31: 263–82.

DERRIDA, J. (1976). *Of Grammatology*. London: Johns Hopkins University Press.

ECO, U. (1990). *The Limits of Interpretation*. Bloomington, Ind.: Indiana University Press.

FOUCAULT, M. (1972). *The Archaeology of Knowledge*. London: Tavistock.

KEEN, I. (1984). 'A Question of Interpretation: The Definition of "Traditional Aboriginal Owners" in the Aboriginal Land Rights (NT) Act', in L. R. Hiatt (ed.), *Aboriginal Landowners*. Sydney: Oceania.

LAYTON, R. (1983a). 'Ambilineal Descent and Traditional Pitjantjatjara Rights to Land', in N. Peterson and M. Langton (eds.), *Aborigines, Land and Land Rights*, 15–32. Canberra: Australian Institute of Aboriginal Studies.

——(1983b). 'Pitjantjatjara Processes and the Structure of the Land Rights Act', in Peterson and Langton, ibid. 226–37.

——(1985). 'Anthropology and Aboriginal Land Rights in Northern Australia', in R. Grillo and A. Rew (eds.), *Social Anthropology and Development Policy*, 148–67. London: Tavistock.

——(1986). *Uluru, an Aboriginal History of Ayers Rock*. Canberra: Australian Institute of Aboriginal Studies.

——(1989). 'Are Sociobiology and Social Anthropology Compatible? The Significance of Sociocultural Resources in Human Evolution', in V. Standen and R. Foley (eds.), *Comparative Socioecology: The Behavioural Ecology of Humans and Other Mammals*, 433–55. Oxford: Blackwell.

MICHAELS, E. (1987). 'Western Desert Sandpainting and Post-modernism', in *Yuendumu Doors: Kuruwari*. Warlukurlangu Artists. Canberra: Aboriginal Studies Press.

MOUNTFORD, C. P. (1977). *Ayers Rock, its People, Their Beliefs and Their Art*, 2nd edn. Adelaide: Rigby.

MUNN, N. D. (1971). 'The Transformation of Subjects into Objects in Walbiri and Pitjantjatjara Myth', in R. Berndt (ed.), *Australian Aboriginal Anthropology*, 141–63. Nedlands: University of Western Australian Press.

MYERS, F. R. (1986*a*). *Pintupi Country, Pintupi Self*. Canberra: Australian Institute of Aboriginal Studies.

—— (1986*b*). 'Always Ask: Resource Use and Land Ownership among Pintupi Aborigines', in N. Williams and E. Hunn (eds.), *Resource Managers: North American and Australian Hunter-Gatherers*, 173–95. Canberra: Australian Institute of Aboriginal Studies.

RICOEUR, P. (1979). 'The Model of the Text: Meaningful Action Considered as a Text', in P. Rabinow and W. M. Sullivan (eds.), *Interpretive Social Science: A Reader*, 73–101. Berkeley, Calif.: University of California Press.

ROMMETVEIT, R. (1987). 'Meaning, Context and Control: Convergent Trends and Controversial Issues in Current Social-Scientific Research on Human Cognition and Communication', *Inquiry*, 30: 77–99.

SARUP, M. (1989). *Post-Structuralism and Postmodernism*. London: Harvester-Wheatsheaf.

STREHLOW, T. G. H. (1964). 'Personal Monototemism in a Polytotemic Community', in E. Haberland (ed.), *Festschrift für Ad. E. Jensen*, 723–53. Munich: Renner.

——(1969). 'Mythology of the Centralian Aborigine', part I, *Inland Review* (June/August), 11–17. Alice Springs.

TONKINSON, R. (1978). *The Mardudjara Aborigines: Living the Dream in Australia's Desert*. New York: Holt, Rinehart and Winston.

——(1988). ' "Ideology and Domination" in Aboriginal Australia: A Western Desert Test Case', in T. Ingold, D. Riches, and J. Woodburn (eds.), *Hunters and Gatherers: Property, Power, and Ideology*, 150–64. Oxford: Berg.

WILLIAMS, N. (1986). *The Yolngu and Their Land*. Canberra: Aboriginal Studies Press.

10

The Language of the Forest: Landscape and Phonological Iconism in Umeda

═══

Alfred Gell

It might seem odd to raise the question of linguistic iconicity—the diagram-like or mimetic attributes of language—in the context of a work on landscape and culture. But I hope to show that my choice of subject-matter is not as arbitrary as it might appear, and that there may be, indeed, an intimate relationship between the cultural factors shaping the phonology of certain natural languages, and the particularities of the landscape setting within which the speakers of these languages live. My thesis is that people who live in dense, unbroken jungle, such as the New Guinean peoples I shall discuss, speak languages that are unusually rich in phonological iconisms, and that this association between forest habitats and iconic languages can be theoretically accounted for. Phonological iconisms are instances in which there are interpretable relationships between speech sounds or articulatory 'gestures', and the semantic meanings conveyed by words in speech.

The simplest form of phonological iconism is onomatopoeia, which motivates such common English forms as 'hiss', 'buzz', 'crunch', etc., a device which is also present in the New Guinean languages I am dealing with; but in these languages intelligible sound/meaning relationships are carried much further, into semantic domains in which there is no obvious relationship between 'natural' sounds and speech sounds, and the force of the iconisms involved is only apparent in the light of a much more complex cultural analysis. Our culture, for instance, supplies no answer to the question, 'What is the sound a mountain makes?' English mountains make no sounds, and consequently, there is no basis for linking the concept 'mountain' to the specific speech-sounds which have to be enunciated in order to say the word 'mountain'. English 'mountain' is an 'arbitrary sign' conforming to the general principle of the arbitrary nature of all spoken signs proposed by de Saussure (1966) and since then overwhelmingly accepted by linguists, with only sporadic murmurs of dissent (Sapir 1929, Jakobson and Waugh 1979). I believe that in Umeda, things are otherwise, and that the Umeda word for 'mountain' (*sis*) should be understood precisely as 'the sound that a mountain makes', or more precisely, 'the shape in articulatory/acoustic space' made by a mountain.

The ethnographic material I shall explore in this paper is the articulatory symbolism of Umeda 'landscape' concepts (such as 'mountain') in the context of Umeda culture, which is keyed to sound-symbolism at a very basic level, as I have attempted to show more than once already (1975; 1979). But I also have in mind to do rather more than describe an interesting (questionable) linguistic phenomenon; my primary objective is to explain just why it is that it is the Umeda (and other people who live in an Umeda-like landscape) who resort to expression in the phonological-iconic mode, and why other people, who inhabit different landscapes, do not do so.

It would be a hopeless proposition to attempt to demonstrate a clear 'statistical' correlation between the New Guinea forest habitat and phonological iconism, even if one suspects, as I do personally, that such a correlation exists. I shall attempt no such demonstration, whose hopelessness resides in the fact that most ethnographers simply do not consider the possibility of a profound relationship between landscape, cognition, and language, and do not construct indigenous 'culture' in the light of this unexamined possibility. Nor do linguists commonly describe languages with this in mind, even in those instances in which they are simultaneously interested in the cultural context of the language they are studying. It was mere accident which led me to devote as much attention as I did to iconism in Umeda while I was in the field; and I never explicitly focused attention on 'sounds' in Umeda culture, apart from speech sounds (Gell 1975: 120). Because of this methodological deafness, I could not advance my study of Umeda sound-symbolism beyond the point I reached in 1979, which was only to show to my own satisfaction that the pervasive presence of articulatory/phonological iconism in Umeda constituted a unique 'poetic language' so that to speak Umeda was to speak poetry, as envisaged by Rousseau (Gell 1979: 61). I had no positive explanation whatsoever to offer for this marvellous state of affairs, though I thought I could explain why Umeda had not ceased to be poetic, as most languages have.

Subsequent developments in Melanesian anthropology have altered the situation. Two ethnographies have now been published which specifically seek to reveal the auditory domain, including natural sounds, language, and song, as cultural systems in their own right, and not just as adjuncts to culture at large, but as foundations, thematic at every level of cultural experience. I refer to Steve Feld's (1982: 3) path-breaking study dealing with 'sound as a cultural system' among the Kaluli of the Great Papuan Plateau and the more recent and theoretically elaborated work of James Weiner (1991) on Foi language and ethno-poetics. Both of these 'ethnographies of sound' (dealing with different language-groups, hundreds of miles from Umeda, and separated by the central highlands of New Guinea) come independently to similar conclusions about phonological iconism to those advanced by me. I draw some encouragement from this convergence of opinion, which, it seems to me, supports the inference that phonological iconism in New Guinea languages is probably widespread, but that it requires a particular ethnographic approach, that is, sensitivity to the acoustic domain as a fundamental constituent of culture, to reveal it. But this also means, unfortunately, that for a 'statistical' demonstration of the pervasiveness of phonological iconism in New Guinea languages, one would have to envisage a large cohort of Felds and Weiners committed to providing particularistic studies of the iconic systems of each of New Guinea's multitudinous cultures, since languages can be equally 'iconic'—in the sense here discussed—without bearing the least mutual resemblance one to another (see below). Similarity of landscapes does not imply 'surface' similarity of languages, because the landscape/language relationship is crucially mediated by cultural factors which may vary extensively. Extracting the inbuilt 'poetics' of languages (at every level, including the phonological, morphosyntactic, etc.) is in every case a new enterprise. But what may be emerging is that the enterprise is, at least with respect to a delimited category of languages, theoretically feasible and analytically fruitful.

The aim now is to delimit the kind of parameters which circumscribe the languages which are likely to show pronounced phonological iconicity. I exclude from consideration the other kind of iconicity which all languages probably do manifest, namely syntactic iconicity. Syntactic iconicity covers the kinds of relationships which exist between syntax (the rules governing the arrangement of main and subsidiary clauses within the sentence, and other grammatical features) and semantics or sentence meaning. A paradigm case of syntactic iconism is Caesar's famous sentence 'Veni, vidi, vici,' where the order of verbs mirrors the order of Caesar's actions, and the terseness of the entire construction figures the ease and rapidity of his successful military operations (Jakobson 1965). Syntactic iconicity in New Guinea languages has been examined recently by Haiman (1985), and this work has been incorporated into ethno-poetics by Weiner (1991: 87). This kind of iconicity does not breach the principle of the arbitrariness of the spoken sign, which applies not to sentences but to words and morphemes. Phonological iconism is much more problematic, since it depends on tracing connections between the sound-substance of individual words and morphemes and their meanings. As a culturally elaborated expressive mode it is probably quite rare, if only because the regular processes of sound-shift which all languages undergo would ensure, other things being equal, that phonologically iconic forms evolved into non-iconic ones after a lapse of time. Only where things are not equal, that is, where there are specific cultural vectors tending to preserve, generalize, and intensify expressivity against the countervailing forces of morphological change, should one expect to encounter elaborate phonological iconism as opposed to sporadic onomatopoeia.

Now I do not think it is a matter of chance that the New Guinea languages which have seemed susceptible to analysis as systems of phonological symbolism (so far, Umeda, Kaluli, and Foi) are situated in 'marginal' areas, away from the more populous and socially dynamic central highlands and maritime/riverain belts. Kaluli and Foi are in the sparsely inhabited and thickly forested slopes to the south of the central highlands (where lowland forest cover gives way to more open grassland) and Umeda occupies a similar niche in the hill country to the north of the Sepik bend, where, once again, population is very thin and livelihood depends on exploiting the forest and only minimal horticulture. What I have to say depends crucially on this common factor of forest habitat, as opposed to grassland/riverain/coastal habitats. I propose that the primary forest environment imposes a reorganization of sensibility, such that the world is perceived in a manner which gives pride of place to the auditory sense (and another sense we hardly use, olfaction: Gell 1977), and that this transformed sensibility has manifold consequences in the domain of cognition, tending to promote phonological iconicity in language.

Nor is this all. The value systems of New Guinea 'forest' cultures seem to emphasize sentiment, or (a better word, perhaps) 'sympathy', more than the cultures of the open plains and the coastal and river flats. Here, in the vibrant, tactile, scented gloom is the landscape of nostalgia and abandonment, so well described by the ethnographers of Kaluli and nearby societies (Feld 1982; Schieffelin 1976; Wagner 1972; Weiner 1988, 1991). I suspect that there is an intrinsic connection between the cultural bias towards the expression of heightened sympathy towards community members (see below on Foi/Kaluli poetics) and the predominance of hearing over seeing, which, I argue, also distinguishes these cultures. Hearing is (relatively) intimate, concrete, and tactile, whereas vision promotes abstraction; iconic language is, likewise, 'concrete' (in the sense of Goldstein and Scheerer 1971; cf. Merleau-Ponty 1962) whereas arbitrary language, in which sign and meaning belong to entirely separate codes, is abstract. Forest habitat, language iconism, and the 'culture of sympathy' I will touch on later, all seem to be linked together in a way I hope to clarify as I proceed. The Umeda share some features of this cultural pattern, though I placed little emphasis on 'sympathy' in my account of Umeda culture (1975) partly because of my visualist bias, and partly because emotionality was of little theoretical interest to me in the early 1970s. At this stage it suffices to say that my argument is not just about language and the forest habitat, but also raises the question of the relationship between language and 'sociality', as it has come to be known.

Briefly, I define my problem as follows: there are, in New Guinea—and perhaps also beyond New Guinea, wherever suitable natural and cultural environments coexist—certain languages which show marked phonological iconism (of a type to be specifically described below). I propose that these languages correspond to certain forest habitats and lifestyles which privilege audition and olfaction and which de-emphasize vision, especially long-range vision. These are 'auditory' cultures which also show certain ideological continuities (i.e. sympathy). I have, first of all, to sketch in the phenomenology underlying these claims. Having done so, I will attempt to explain these facts cognitively, by arguing that where signs and their signifieds are coded in the same sensory modality, there is an inbuilt tendency towards iconic expressions.

Umeda: An Auditory Culture

Let me introduce my subject-matter by means of a brief autobiographical reflection. During my fieldwork in Umeda (West Sepik district, now Sandaun Province, Papua New Guinea) in 1969–70, I suffered from many forms of frustration. One of the most annoying and insurmountable problems I encountered was my inability ever to obtain a decent view of the country in which Umeda is situated. In the end, I spent fourteen months in visual surroundings limited to tens of metres, and at most, half a kilometre or so. (There was one exception to this which I will go into later.) I found these restricted horizons profoundly unsatisfactory. Like all middle-class Britishers, I share our national obsession with views and panoramas, despite having to peer at them through ever-thickening spectacles. No hill is too rocky, jungly, sun-baked or wind-swept to deter me if I fancy that I can indulge my craving for distant prospects by ascending it. But Umeda was purgatory in this respect. The surrounding country is by no means flat and there are a number of hills in the vicinity over which I passed frequently on hunting trips or on my way to the patrol post. But on none of these hills was the forest cleared in such a way as to afford a 'view' despite my best efforts to find a suitable spot. To this day, I do not know what Umeda village looks like from a distance.

At the time, I endured my unconsummated craving for a view of Umeda as just one more of the many trials which constitute an ethnographer's lot. I was not aware that this problem had any deeper significance, though in the light of subsequent developments, it certainly had. My inability to encompass Umeda as a visualizable totality offered a direct challenge, at an experiential level, to my theoretical ambition which was to 'encompass' Umeda as an intellectually constructed whole. Please remember that this was long ago, before 'visualism' had been made a culpable offence in enlightened circles. I was perfectly confident that the objective of anthropological research was to make visible, in the form of a predominantly geometric/spatial model, the totality of Umeda social relations. Because I happen to be a pronouncedly visual thinker, I was quite successful at this, but now my self-critical middle age is upon me and I can see that there are certain disadvantages inherent in the notion that anthropological understanding is coterminous with the provision of a visual/spatial *Gestalt*. Making use of geometrical diagrams and analytical figures, and a descriptive language continually emphasizing visual forms, this is, none the less, what I set out to do, and what, to some extent, I did. I was already in possession of the elements of the visual model of Umeda social relations while I was in the field, and my unavailing efforts to encompass Umeda in a 'view from afar' (Lévi-Strauss 1985) were motivated, not just by cultural predilection, but also by a more ambitious desire to project my intellectual construction of Umeda on to the physical terrain.

The point is that, in hindsight, this preoccupation with the visual and the visualizable may have been misplaced. The very fact that Umeda was invisible and that vision itself was of rather restricted use for a lot of the time ought to have alerted me to the possibility that the balance between vision and other sensory modalities was differently struck where the Umeda were concerned. As it was, there were a number of odd things I could not help noticing.

I was very intrigued, for instance, by a story I was told by a young man who had been a member of the first group of Umeda to visit the coast, where they had been imprisoned for a period, returning to Umeda shortly before I arrived there myself. On arrival at Vanimo (on the coast, where the prison was located) the Umeda were lined up on the sloping beach, facing out to sea. Between the Umeda and the shoreline stood a policeman. The Umeda had never seen the sea before, or any large body of water, and they had never seen a distant, flat, horizon. So rather than perceive the sea receding in the horizontal plane, they perceived it as a huge vertical wall of water, sticking up into the sky and clearly higher, from their point of vantage, than the head of the policeman facing them on the foreshore. They were afraid that he was about to be engulfed by an immense wave, and would be rapidly followed by themselves. They could not understand why the expected wave did not come.

I think that, for Umeda, whatever was visible was, *ipso facto*, relatively close. This may explain their extraordinary courage, not to say foolhardiness, in attempting to walk from Wewak (a coastal town about 150 km. away) to Umeda, after a mass break-out from the labour compound there. This famous escapade (in New Guinea it is an adventure to pass 10 kilometres through enemy territory, let alone 150) was undertaken, so participants told me, because they had been able to see the whole country through the windows of the aeroplane which flew them from Imonda (near Umeda) to Wewak. They had seen the line of the Torricelli mountains and the valley of the Sepik on the other side. These they followed during the return journey, taking many weeks, during which they were mostly captured and one of them was shot as a presumed witch. They had no idea of the actual difficulty of the journey, which they undertook only because they were deluded into thinking that the distance was very much shorter than it was in reality. I believe that this arose from their habitual tendency to assume that the distance between any two intervisible points would be short and easily traversed.

Another line of evidence that the Umeda operated a different perceptual framework from the Western norm, was the way in which they were always much more aware of their acoustic and olfactory surroundings than I was. Mostly this goes without saying. Hunting (and also raiding and escaping from raids) in dense forest places a premium on hearing as the main sensory modality for detecting objects and events at some distance, where they are invariably out of sight. Out hunting, I could never find game for myself, because I tended to look for it; the Umeda listened, and of course knew exactly what to listen for. In the bush, they travelled with eyes downcast, looking for thorns and obstacles on the path (and other signs, such as tracks) while they 'surveyed' their surroundings with their ever-receptive ears. Because hearing had such acute functional saliency for them, they observed a discipline about noise which was very marked; either they were very quiet, or they were very noisy, but they did not tolerate intrusive unsocial background noise, which we take for granted. This feature is well brought out in the Umeda origin-myth which accounts for the existence of white men, who are defined, characteristically, as producers of noise-pollution. The myth begins, as usually for myths of this genre in New Guinea, by relating that there were two brothers, the older one black-skinned and stupid, the younger one white-skinned and intelligent. The elder lived like an Umeda, hunting in the forest, while the younger stayed behind in the village and made things. My informant specified that the things that the younger brother made were kettles, spoons, knives, tin plates, and saucepans. He made them by bashing metal with a hammer. The elder brother came back from hunting weary and wishing to sleep, but the younger brother persisted with his metal-bashing operations. The elder brother found the clatter unbearable so he rose up in his wrath and drove his brother from the village. The younger brother took his metal objects and descended into a hole which led to the interior of the earth. That is where white men live to this day, underground, bashing metal, and making a terrible noise.

Of course, vision as well as hearing is necessary in hunting and raiding, especially at the climax of events. But the point I am making here is not that the Umeda did not see things, or relied on hearing to the exclusion of all else, but that the relationship between the visual and auditory components of their ambience was differently evaluated than it is with us. For an Umeda an audible but invisible object was entirely 'present' in a way difficult for us to grasp, in that for us such an object is 'hidden', however perceptible. The concept of 'hiding' in Umeda culture was, in fact, quite different from our own. The Umeda term for 'hidden(ly)', *maksmaks*, implies, not invisibility, but the concealment of auditory clues, as in the silent approach of an assassin. An individual who approached audibly, even if concealed the while in thick bush, would not be 'hidden' at all in their terms. The Umeda expression applies to clandestine (silent) movement, and also to concealment of the truth in speech, that is, lying, prevarication, depriving the interlocutor of the auditory information needed to perceive the true state of affairs.

For us, invisible objects are deeply problematic, but not for the Umeda, who defined objective existence in terms of audibility, not visibility. This came out in conflicts over 'evidence' which I often had with my informants. Once an Umeda man I knew well came into my house looking as if he had just had the fright of his life and bursting to tell me about the harrowing experience he had just had. He had been on a forest path leading to the village and he had been chased up and down by a *yawt*, a horrifying kind of ogre in whom all Umeda firmly believe. The dusk had fallen and the forest was plunged in more than the usual darkness, but, yes, the ogre had been there all right, waiting. He had heard it panting *hu-hu-hu*, and he had raced up the path to escape it, but the ogre had doubled round, hiddenly (*maksmaks*) and before he knew it, the thing was right in front of him, going *hu-hu-hu* again and he had had to cut through the forest to avoid it. Finally, rejoining the path, he had made it home as quick as his legs would carry him. 'Yes, yes,' I said, cutting him off, 'but did you actually see the ogre?' My informant looked at me in perplexity. 'It was dark, I was running away, it was there on the path, going *hu-hu-hu*' . . . I came away from this conversation, and from similar ones, as puzzled as ever about how such sensible people as the Umeda could remain so credulous on the subject of ogres and other terrifying apparitions. When, I wondered, was an Umeda going to admit to actually seeing one of these monsters? But that, of course, was a misapprehension bred of a visually based notion of the real. For Umeda, hearing is believing, and the Umeda really do hear ogres, or what they take to be ogres.

It is relevant here to note that strong emotion makes Umeda 'deaf' rather than 'blind'. Where we would say somebody was 'blind' with rage, or 'could not stand the sight of' some other person, the Umeda say they cease to hear, or wilfully won't hear one another, because they are 'deaf' (*agami*, 'closed ears').

Umeda treat sight, not as a basic evidential sense, but as a climactic sense with connotations of intimacy and danger. As is common in New Guinea, ordinary conversations do not require sustained eye-contact, while intimate or confrontational conversations do. Direct sustained eye contact between a man and a woman implies sexual solicitation or complicity. The aim, in dancing, or simply ogling any passing female, is to capture the woman's glance, because everything depends on seeing and being seen. Besides being the organ of seduction, the eye (especially of a senior kinsman) which gives an angry glance, terrifies and demoralizes the victim of a sorcery attack. This is the Umeda version of the belief in the 'evil eye', but the point is that it works only at close (genealogical) range, between agnatic kin, while lethal sorcery (and actual violence) is carried out invisibly, by means of night-attacks from affinal and enemy villages.

The visual world is close-range, intimate, but it is very far from being the whole world, very far from being anything like what we could recognize as a 'landscape' since it is only a sequence of partial glimpses, which do not cohere around any central point of vantage. In the 'village' one sees the hamlet one happens to be in, not the 'village' as a whole. Looking out, one sees the tops of the nearby trees, but not the gardens, paths, streams, hunting tracts, sago-stands, and so on which really constitute 'the bush'; these are hidden below, though one can hear bush activities in progress; chopping, pounding sago, and the standard location-giving 'whoops' uttered by parties of Umeda on the move. In 'the bush' one never sees the village, or indeed, any but the most adjacent surroundings, most of which are irrelevant. There is nothing to bind all this together, no privileged 'domain-viewing' point, like the view from the keep of a castle. Bound together it is, though, but in a quite different way. Lacking a visual landscape, what the Umeda have instead, I would say, is a 'landscape of articulation', a landscape which is accessible, primordially, in the acoustic modality. This landscape is constructed out of the interface between two kinds of experience; distally it comprises a codification of ambient sound, that is, a soundscape, proximally it comprises the basic unifying armature of the body as a sounding cavity, sensitive to sound and, through the autokinetically sensed experience of verbal and mimetic vocalization, productive of sound.

The Articulatory Landscape

Merleau-Ponty (1962: 184) says, 'The spoken word is a gesture, its meaning, a world.' One can indeed imagine the Umeda world/landscape as a series of mappings between articulatory gestures, syllabic shapes moulded within the oral tract (microcosm) and the macrocosm consisting of the body, social relationships mediated through the body, and other natural forms, particularly trees, and the encompassing physical ambience. The oral tract (fulfilling both vocal and gustatory functions, emitting and receiving) is a little landscape in itself (cf. Mimica 1981) but not a stationary one. Moving and shaping, transforming itself from within, its various positions correspond to particular physical and social vectors: constriction and restraint, above and below, centrality and distance.

The Umeda language is richly provided with onomatopoeic words (e.g. *huf*, the name of the wooden trumpets Umeda play, which make a noise exactly like that). Even more so, there is a large class of vocal 'sound-effects' which are used in narratives to punctuate and illustrate the action. These can be used without any additional explanation. For instance, in one myth, the hero has been abandoned at the top of a tall, unclimbable tree. At this point the story goes into pure sound effects, *w-w-w-ba* . . . One just has to know that this is the noise of the hero's tears dripping softly down from on high, striking leaves as they fall, alerting the friendly snake who will rescue him. But these onomatopoeic words and sound-effects are not what constitutes the basic system, which is not confined to contexts in which sounds are directly represented, albeit in terms which are only transparent to members of the culture.

The fundamental schema of Umeda phonological symbolism can be derived from the following basic mappings. Front (alveolar) consonants are associated with centrality (*edi* = man, *edie* = middle, *edtodna* = male/central moiety) while velar (back) consonants are associated with peripherality (*agwa* = woman, *aga* = ear, *agea* = arm/branch, *agwatodna* = female/peripheral moiety). This basic opposition is aligned with another, which opposes nasalized front bilabials and alveolars which denote 'soft' nutritive/gustatory objects and experiences (*mo* = fruit, *mol* = daughter/vulva) to hard back consonants associated with hard objects (*ke* = bone) and velar affricates associated with disgust (*ehe*). Umeda lexemes are commonly built up from morphemic elements each of which may be found in diverse combinations. Thus, for instance, an entity which combines, say, centrality/masculinity with disgustingness, must combine an element featuring one of the alveolar consonants, with an element featuring one of the velar affricates. Such an entity is easily identified; it is the species of blindworm (actually a legless lizard) which lives inside the hollow interiors of old palm trees, living on the ants which are to be found there. The name of this creature, of which the Umeda are extremely fearful, is *eliehe*, a long, pink, self-propelled phallus which sometimes emerges when palms are cut down (cf. Gell 1975: 240). The name *eliehe* decomposes into *eli* + *ehe*; *eli* being a variant of *edi* (replacing the alveolar stop with the corresponding glide) plus *ehe*, which we have already met. *Eliehe* is more than a neutral phonic sign, it is a 'gesture' delineating its object in articulatory space, which is simultaneously mapped on to social and emotional space. As Merleau-Ponty (1962: 179–87) writes:

the meaning of words must finally be induced from the words themselves, or more exactly their conceptual meaning must be formed by a kind of deduction from a gestural meaning which is immanent in speech . . . The gesture brings certain perceptible bits of the world to my notice, inviting my concurrence in them . . . the gesture does not make me think of anger, it is anger itself . . . [the 'conceptual and delimiting' meanings of words are arbitrary, but this] . . . would no longer be the case if we took in the emotional content of a word, what we have called above its 'gestural' sense which is all-important in poetry for example. It would then be found that words, vowels and phonemes are so many ways of 'singing' the world, and their function is to represent the world, not, as naïve onomatopoeic theory had it, by reason of an objective resemblance, but because they extract, and literally express, their emotional essence.

These remarks of Merleau-Ponty may seriously overstate the role of phonological iconism in most languages, but I hold them to be almost literally true of Umeda (serendipitously, *The Phenomenology of Perception* was among the small collection of books I carried into the field). Let me examine another example of 'gestural' meaning, this time specifically to do with 'landscape' in the sense we would understand. I said, at the outset, that there was no culturally obvious way in which 'mountain' in English could be phonologically motivated. English mountains are silent and immobile, and it is hard to imagine that there could be any one vocal 'gesture' which would communicate the essence of mountainhood better than any other. In Umeda, things are otherwise, though it requires a cultural interpretation to bring this out. The Umeda word for mountain is *sis*. Umeda 'mountains' are really ridges, with sharp tops, and they define the boundaries of territories, particularly to the north and west, where the major enemies of Umeda reside. The sibilant 's' is uniformly associated with (*a*) male power and (*b*) with sharp, narrow things like pointed sticks (*sah*). Male power comes from the coconut *sa*, and the ancestors *sa-tod* (village/male/central). Sharp things like bamboo knives are *sai*, *sa* plus the constricted, 'narrow' vowel 'i'. *Sis*, a symmetrical arrangement of sibilants and the narrow 'i', is very appropriate for an Umeda 'mountain', that is, a narrow ridge, associated with masculine pursuits, danger, etc. As a ridge, it is opposed to *kebe*, a flat-topped knoll of the kind Umeda hamlets are built on, which combines the hardness-implying 'k' sound with *ebe* (bilabial) meaning 'fat' (prosperous).

One can carry the analysis of *sis* as 'a mountain made audible' one stage further. I mentioned that there is one exception to the generalization that no landscape features distant by more than half a kilometre or so are visible from Umeda. The exception is the *awsis*, a tall ridge to the north of Umeda, marking the boundary between Umeda territory and the territory of the 'Waina-Sowanda' groups who share the same culture and language (the Umeda's 'minor' enemies and affines) and the Wasengla valley people to the north and west, 'major' enemies, who before the imposition of the colonial peace often threatened to overwhelm the Umeda. In traditional times, no Umeda had ventured beyond this ridge into the Wasengla valley. The name *awsis* decomposes into *aw* + *sis*. *Aw* plays an independent role in the language; as the maximally 'open' vowel 'a' followed by the rounded, constricted, or restraining semivowel 'w', *aw* is a component of words indicating encircling limits; thus one has *awda* = a fence, and *popaw* = a river dam: *po* = water + *aw*. (Cf. also *yawt*, the encircling ogre of the forest.) The *awsis* is thus the vertical restraining fence or wall around the Umeda world, perhaps the real progenitor of the vertical wall of water the prisoners saw when they looked out to sea on Vanimo beach.

Umdakebe, the village knoll, and *awsis* mark, respectively, the core and the periphery of the Umeda articulatory landscape; but what stands between foreground and background? The Umeda landscape, formed as it is out of transient sounds and articulations, has to be understood dynamically, rather than as a fixed array of visual/spatial objects. Landscape features are grasped as movements rather than as forms. Take, for instance, a common feature of Umeda country, the kind of pools known as *pwiob* which form where springs emerge through rock. Such a pool consists of a narrow passage from which water emerges (under slight pressure) and the surrounding, swelling, pool itself. As an articulatory gesture, *pwiob* has two parts, *pwi* + *ob*. *Pwi* belongs to the class of words all of which imply upward growth; *wi* = cucurbit (symbol of growth, taboo to children for that reason, cf. Gell 1979), *wis* = moon (growth), *pwi* = growth shoot, pitpit (tall spindly edible cane), *pwie* = tall. This corresponds to the 'forced upward growth' of the water emerging from the rock. *Ob*, on the other hand, belongs to the class of articulatory gestures of 'swelling', usually with 'a' or 'e', thus *ab* = ripe (also *abwi*), *kabwi* = big, fat, *ebe* = fat, *pab* = penile erection, *popab* = highwater, flood. All of these words featuring vowel + b involve an articulatory 'swelling' in that to utter them one must allow the cheeks to distend with air while voicing the bilabial (this resonation is acoustically what is distinctive about this type of consonant). Finally the rounded vowel 'o' seems to mimic round shapes, the round shape of the pool in this instance (cf. *mol* = fruit, *mo* = gullet, vulva, word, etc.). Thus, taken as a whole, the word *pwiob* provides a dynamic moving image of a spring-fed pool as a process rather than a thing; an articulated demonstration of the water spurting up through the rock, and the swelling, rounded pool forming around it.

There is a more encompassing sense of 'movement' in the Umeda acoustic/articulatory landscape which opposes above and below, complementing the axis of centrality/peripherality which has already been described (for further details see Gell 1975: 133–7 and 1979: 46). The above/below axis is linked to the phonological contrast between the low/back vowels 'u' and 'o' and the high/front vowels 'a' and 'i'. If we start at the top, we have the empyrean (*pai*). The stars are *painauf*. Stars are also the penises of the ancestors, the penis itself being *paiha*. Closing off the uppermost realm we have the clouds *awfie* (another of the group of -*aw*- words). *Awfie* means 'on top'.

The element for 'up' is *ap*, Umeda being one of those languages in which the word for 'come' implies upward motion (come up, *idapiav*) and the word for 'go' implies downward motion (*iduiav*). When upward motion is rapid and explosive, *ap* is inverted and becomes *pa*, as in *hotamovie pa!* ('he scrambled up the *hotamov* tree'). In general, superiority expressed by the open/front vowel 'a', as in *sa-tod* = ancestor, mentioned previously. Senior male agnates are *at*, which is also usable as an 'up' deictic. I was occasionally addressed as *at* by Umeda, not because they wanted to claim kinship with me, but because I was taller than them; sometimes kinship term and deictic expression would fuse entirely, as when they were attempting to point me in the right direction to shoot some bird concealed above in the foliage (*at-at-at* . . . 'up there, uncle, up, up . . . '). *Pat* is the roof beam of a house, *asi* senior affines and grandparents, *na* mother's brother, and so on.

Downward movement is indicated by -u- as in *iduiav* (go down). The bush, which is 'low' in relation to the village, is *sugut*. The lowest part of the bush are swamps: *pud*. 'Inferior' social roles are marked by the same 'u' vowel symbolism; *mugtod* = bachelor, from *mug* = leg, foot; *ipudi* = son; *tuda* = child; *ude* = little sister, dog. But the canonical downward movement is that of water, falling from the skies and flowing down the many streams; all these are *po*. The general down/bush direction is indicated as *pokwie* or *sugwie*. When the *po* falls in quantity, the floods rise, *popab*, from *pab* = erection (cf. above on 'swelling' words). These falling/rising watery motions have the standard sexual/

cosmological significance. The earth is female and womb-like; transfixed by earthworms (*subul*) of which the Umeda are extremely afraid, its properties as a womb (*uda*: also 'netbag') are particularly concentrated in the deposits of white kaolin clay hidden underground, which are a prime magical material. The term for this magical kaolin is *urugubwe*, a most magical sound, delivered *sotto voce*.

These notes on the articulatory landscape of Umeda must suffice for the present; I might prolong them, since the entire vocabulary of the Umeda language constitutes a 'landscape' in the sense I am driving at. I have already published much additional material and there seems no point in duplicating it. However, to afford a further glimpse of the system, and for the enjoyment of puzzle addicts, I reproduce an illustration which I devised for the article I published in 1979, which maps a number of the most important Umeda terms on to the composite man/tree/society, forming the 'triple analogy' at the heart of the system (Fig. 10.1). I trust that what I have said here, in conjunction with what I have said in earlier publications, will have been enough to lend plausibility to my basic contention that the Umeda language is pervasively iconic at the level of phonology and articulation. Now, having established my ethnographic point, I want to put forward an explanation for this relatively unusual, or at least unfamiliar, state of affairs.

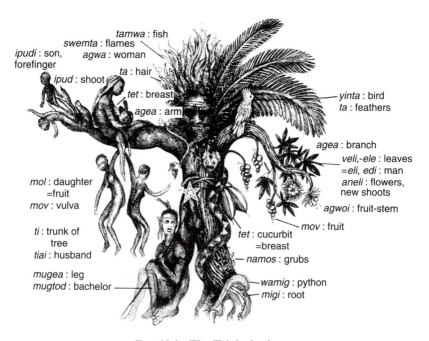

FIG. 10.1. The Triple Analogy.

Sensory Modality and Language Iconism

In the New Guinea forest habitat, I have argued, hearing is relatively dominant (over vision) as the sensory modality for coding the environment as a whole. What I aim to do now is to propose a general principle which would explain why 'acoustic' cultures might be particularly liable to invent, elaborate, and preserve linguistic phonological iconisms, by contrast to speakers of the languages of non-acoustic, or 'visual' cultures. The principle involved is this: where there is uniformity between the dominant sensory modality for registering 'the world', and the sensory modality used in linguistic communication, iconism will tend to prevail; but where this uniformity of sensory modality does not exist, phonological iconism will tend to be less well marked or entirely absent.

The normal sensory modality for language is hearing; language is acoustically coded. But whereas in 'visual' cultures—which, for the purposes of argument can be taken to include all cultures in which vision is the main distal sense—there has to be a cross-over between the sense modality of the (visual) world evoked by language, and the (acoustic) code of language, in primarily acoustic cultures there is no such cross-over; the dominantly acoustic 'world' is directly evoked in the same sensory modality, in the acoustic code of language. In other words, Umeda, and languages like Umeda, are phonologically iconic, because they evoke a reality which is itself 'heard' and imagined in the auditory code, whereas languages like English are non-iconic because they evoke a reality which is 'seen' and imagined in the visual code.

Why should uniformity of sensory modality between the sign and signified give rise to iconism? Is this in fact true? Let us consider English, for a start. English has two main kinds of phonologically iconic words, onomatopoeias (squeak, hum, rumble, etc.) and a more problematic category of 'expressive' like the set of words ending in 'sh' which denote sudden destructive action: bash, crash, crush, smash, etc. (Fudge: 1970). Maybe these latter are not motivated at all, but only appear to us to be so, by what I have called elsewhere 'a posteriori iconism', i.e. by being associated with their meanings (Gell 1979: 57, 59). Let us say, therefore, that the only indisputable instances of phonological motivation in English are actually onomatopoeias, i.e. words which denote sounds, and to some extent actually resemble those sounds (so that one could anticipate that non-English speakers, presented with the words 'squeak' and 'hum' and a selection of actual squeaks and hums, could sort them out correctly according to the English taxonomy of sounds). This is good evidence for my proposition, because it shows that, in a language like English, where, exceptionally, the meaning of a word is actually a sound, then 'the arbitrariness of the sign' is suspended, and the language preserves a thriving subset of phonological iconisms, through all the historical vicissitudes which otherwise beset sound/meaning relationships. But the huge majority of words in English do not denote

sounds and are not onomatopoeic, and thus the whole question of onomatopoeia is relegated to the sidelines. It is too obvious and trivial to merit much
consideration.

But perhaps the 'obvious' can teach us a lesson. If words for sounds continue
to be iconic even where there is no pervasive tendency to phonological iconism
elsewhere in the language, then at the very least it suggests that in this domain
(i.e. the linguistic coding of acoustic experience) there is a principle of 'least
effort' at work in the deployment of expressive resources; if an onomatopoeic
expression is intrinsically feasible (because of the uniformity of the sound-
substance of language and the acoustic reality being evoked) then an onomatopoeic form is likely to emerge and be preserved. We only need to expand the
scope of what, for any culture, counts as 'acoustic reality' to find the explanation for pervasive phonological iconism, i.e. generalized onomatopoeia.

Unfortunately, in the history of attempts to criticize the Saussurean postulate of the 'arbitrariness of the sign' the obvious has been lost sight of. Following the work of Sapir (1929), some linguists and psychologists have sought to
explain phonological iconism by means of 'synaesthesia', that is, certain natural
propensities we may have to associate qualities in one sensory modality with
corresponding qualities in another (Peterfalvi 1970: 47). Thus comparative
studies have been carried out to link 'bigness' with open vowels and littleness
with narrow vowels, as in the French pairing *grand* versus *petit*. Or we have
Köhler's famous experiment in which respondents were invited to decide
which of the two forms shown below (Fig. 10.2) was TAKETE and which was
MALUMA (Peterfalvi 1970: 33). These studies are predicated on the notion that
'spatial' (visual) qualities are intrinsically associated with acoustic (articulatory)
qualities by 'synaesthesia'. This, I think, is a mistake, not because these exper-
iments have failed to demonstrate certain uniformities in human intuitions, but
because they have assumed that phonological iconism, above the level of 'mere'
onomatopoeia, necessarily involves associative links between vision and hearing, or some other pairing of different sense modalities. I would interpret the
Köhler experiment differently. I believe that respondents see the 'takete-ob-
ject' not as a silent, spiky, thing, but as an object which makes the sound 'takete'
(e.g. if one attempted to bowl it along the floor), and ditto the soft, rubbery,
maluma-object. So 'takete' and 'maluma' are really onomatopoeic, and respondents tended to identify them correctly, not on the basis of acoustic/visual
associations, but because of sedimented (and cross-culturally uniform) knowledge of the kinds of sounds objects make. This analysis also applies to the
kinaesthetic sensations generated in the oral tract while articulating, in that
auditory awareness is a specialized 'tactile' sense anyway, and 'inside the head'
tactile and acoustic sensations are indissociable, not two separate sensory
modalities.

One can approach the problem of uniformity and non-uniformity between
the sensory modalities of sign and signified from the opposite direction. As is

FIG. 10.2. Köhler's figures.

well known, there has been much debate among specialists in the education of the deaf about lip-reading, finger-spelling, and other communicative modes which allow the deaf to access spoken language indirectly (via a visual channel) versus sign-language, which was developed in institutions for the deaf, by the deaf, primarily for the purpose of communicating with one another (the history of the subject is summarized in Sacks 1989). (These deaf-community sign-languages have to be distinguished from sign-languages used by hearing people to communicate unspeakingly, or with deaf individuals in their midst.) The best known of the sign-languages developed within deaf communities, which exclude hearers and have frequently been repressed by well-meaning but insensitive authorities, is American Sign Language (ASL). The world of the deaf is a visual one. ASL, despite what its detractors once said, is a fully functional communication system, capable of transmitting all the semantic representations of spoken language, except, of course, the ones appertaining to acoustic experiences. It is just as 'good', just as 'advanced', as spoken language. But even the briefest study of the standard work on ASL (Klima and Bellugi 1979) suffices to show that (visual) iconisms are not just frequent, but pervasive throughout the entire language.

Klima and Bellugi note that there are some arbitrary signs in ASL, and that the frequency of arbitrary forms seems to be increasing as time goes by, but they are in no doubt that iconicity has been, and remains, a constitutive principle in acquiring, using, and developing ASL, and that this arises from the 'cognitive naturalness' of imitative signing (ibid. 21–6). In terms of the theory being advanced here, the pervasive iconism of ASL is the predictable consequence of the uniformity between the sensory modality used in signing (vision) and the sensory modality which dominates in the deaf world (also vision). That is to say, the principle of least effort (or 'naturalness') in expression, leads to the production of visual iconisms which are easier to interpret, remember, and innovate than arbitrary signs. They also permit greater flexibility of paralinguistic expression (e.g. emphasis, stylization, comic effects, etc.) as is well brought out in Klima and Bellugi's chapter devoted to ASL signed poetry (ibid. ch. 14).

Such, then, is the suggested cognitive explanation for the pervasiveness of phonological iconisms in Umeda. Because, in the forest habitat, there is relative dominance of the acoustic modality as the distal sense in terms of which experience is organized and concepts are formed, it follows that (relatively speaking) there is uniformity in sensory modality between signs and signifieds, and consequently phonological iconisms are favoured on the basis of 'natural-ness' in the employment of expressive means.

It would be interesting to enquire further as to whether the pervasive iconicity of ASL as the cognitively most natural mode of communication among the deaf is associated with a specific set of value orientations, as I shall claim below that phonological iconism is associated with a value orientation stressing 'sympathy'. The resilience of ASL over nearly a century of outright suppression (after 1880: Sacks 1989: 27) suggests that it fulfilled an emotional as much as a practical or instrumental need among the deaf in institutions. And the very marked suitability of ASL for the expression of moods and feelings might suggest that this is a language which mediates egalitarian social solidarity particularly well, whatever else it may be able to do with respect to the com-munication of abstract information. So there may be a deep connection here, but it would require a more extended analysis to do full justice to the problem. Let me return therefore to phonological iconism and landscape in New Guinea, this time in a slightly wider comparative perspective.

Concluding Comments: Language and Ethno-Poetics

The significance of Feld's Kaluli 'ethnography of sound' in the context of the present discussion lies less in what he says about phonological iconism as such, which I shall come to in due course, than in his original and highly successful attempt to focus on sound as a formative element in culture. Feld is able to do this because of the conjunction of two factors; first of all the Kaluli environ-ment, and secondly certain thematic elements in Kaluli culture, which are equally well brought out by Schieffelin (1976). The Kaluli occupy the slopes of Mount Bosavi, on the Great Papuan Plateau (which is very far from being flat). This is an enormous expanse of very densely forested and thinly settled terri-tory, ecologically not unlike the Border Mountains region where Umeda is situated, and, like the Umeda, the Kaluli exploit sago extensively (and, like the Umeda, sing sad songs while they do so: Feld: n.d.). The Kaluli forest is full of voices; these voices are birds, particularly the Muni bird whose song, descend-ing D–C–A–G, is the prototype of Kaluli 'sung-texted-weeping' (Feld 1982: 32–3). Birdsong, Feld shows, is a basic key to Kaluli culture, since it is as birds/mourners that Kaluli seek ritual apotheosis in the Gisaro song ceremon-ies described in Schieffelin's work (1976), and in fact, after death, they become birds, travelling from place to place and singing, as in life. Birds are simultan-eously part of the world of the living and the world of the dead, but not as tangible things, only as disembodied songs. 'To you they are birds, to [us] they are voices in the forest,' as one Kaluli put it to Feld (1982: 45). Bird classification, he goes on to show, is based not on what birds look like, but on the kinds of songs they have (ibid. ch. 2). All this strongly underlines the claim I am making that certain forest cultures are disposed to order reality in the acoustic code, or, to be more precise, it was as a result of reading Feld that this possibility occurred to me.

Birdsong is not the only kind of sound which is thematic in Kaluli culture. The other very important source of acoustic coding of the environment is noise produced by watercourses and particularly waterfalls. The descending movement of Kaluli song is the sung equivalent of a waterfall, and particular streams and falls are perpetually evoked in the texts of Kaluli songs, which are typically 'journeys' through the remembered forest, in search of lost companions (ibid. 107 ff.). Place, sound, and social memory are fused together in Kaluli poetics. It would certainly be correct to suppose that the acoustic landscape of Kaluli constitutes their 'world' in the fullest sense; and that their rituals, in which visual display, though present, is subordinated to a cataract of sheer sound, evoke a heard rather than a visible transcendence.

Of the presence of a degree of acoustic dominance in Kaluli there can perhaps be no doubt; what remains to be asked is whether the Kaluli language shows the same pervasive iconism as I have claimed is the case in Umeda. I cannot say whether this is so in relation to the language as a whole, but Feld is quite specific in noting the presence of phonological symbolism in song texts. The device is known as 'sound words', and employs specific vowels to communicate environmental features and qualities (ibid. 144–50). These symbolically employed vowel sounds (in combination with appropriate consonants) evoke birds, water, and forest. For instance *gi-ge* 'is the sound of trees turning with the change of season . . . the forest hums and buzzes as some leaves fall dramatically with crisp sounds and others drop softly and continuously' (ibid. 146). Poetic 'sound words' based on *-u-* evoke waterfalls, thunder, falling trees, *-o-* words the flight of birds, and so on.

These forms also play a part in ordinary speech, though they are treated differently from a grammatical point of view in their poetic and ordinary language uses. What is not perhaps clear from the discussion is whether they are a delimited class, or whether many more words in the language employ the same kind of vowel symbolism than the ones particularly used in song texts. It could be that 'sound words' are just that, words for sounds, and more comparable to the 'sound-effects' one finds in Umeda myths (cf. above) rather than to the bulk of the Umeda examples considered hitherto. On the other hand, they are clearly much more systematic and integrated into the language than is commonly the case.

Any such doubts are removed in connection with the Foi, who occupy (less mountainous) territory on the eastern edge of the plateau, near Lake Kutubu. Weiner (1991) is quite explicit in identifying phonological iconicity as a general feature of Foi language, much exploited in poetry. Weiner cites my 1979 paper and quotes certain of my comments, though I am sure he would have arrived at exactly the same conclusions had he lacked this particular stimulus. Weiner devotes whole sections of his book to exploring different types of iconisms in Foi, for example space/time deictics (ibid. 72 ff.), movement and rest, emotional qualities of tenseness and intimacy appertaining to kinship relations (81 ff.). However, he makes a very important point that has surfaced already, namely, that languages which are iconic are not necessarily iconic on the same basis; there is far from being any 'universal' system of iconisms. Thus he notes that Umeda has a 'k' sound in the first-person pronoun (*ka* = I) whereas in Foi, *ka* (for entirely different reasons) is 'woman'. The basis for the Umeda first person pronoun is the cultural postulate that 'bone' (*ke*) is the core of the person: the self is a hard, resistant, core of bone surrounded by flesh (*nih*). Hence the maximally hard consonant, 'k'. Whereas in Foi 'k' words all imply restraint, constraint, factors which inhere in affinal relationships, hence, *ka*.

Weiner concludes that one source of phonological iconism is the tendency of languages to develop sets of allied words on the basis of shared sound-associations (what I called 'a posteriori iconism', Gell 1979: 59; Weiner 1991: 84). That is to say, once a term is ensconced in the language, sound and meaning, even if arbitrarily conjoined initially, will henceforth be associated, so that new terms may accrete around the original one, exploiting the same established resonances. The reality of this phenomenon is not in doubt (Weiner cites English examples from Bolinger 1965) but I prefer to think that it is not the principle which is responsible for iconism in 'acoustic cultures'—or at least, not entirely. Even so, Weiner does not seem to discount 'a priori' iconism of the kind I was keen to demonstrate in Umeda. This question is obviously open to further debate.

But perhaps the most important theoretical development in Weiner's work, which I would like to take up in these closing remarks, is the analysis he provides of the relation between language and sensibility. Weiner takes a strongly Heideggerian stance in interpreting Foi sensibility (revealed particularly in their poetics) as an existential quest, to which he attaches absolute significance. Drawing on Heidegger's metaphor of language as the 'house of being' (1971: 132) he argues that poetic evocation of the world in language 'desevers the distances between us and things in their true being' (Weiner 1991: 200). Just as houses are not separate from their occupants but part of their personality, so languages are not a neutral tool, useful for describing a world 'out there' but are constitutive of the world itself. To have a house, a language, is to have a world. Foi poetic texts are journeys through this linguistic 'house', which are enacted inside a (long-) house which is itself metaphorically linked to the totality of the Foi territory and landscape (ibid. 64–70, 185–95). Running through all this is a critique of Cartesianism and 'Western' rationalism. Weiner contrasts the home-grown pathos of Foi poetry, which arises directly from the experience of loss and abandonment, with the alienated character of Western art, which is produced by virtuosi for an audience screened from the processes of art-making itself. Foi poetry abolishes the distance between subject and object, our art establishes and reinforces this distance (ibid. 202). He also cites Heidegger's claim that 'for speakers of modern European language, the existential link between poetry (art), life, and thinking has been lost' (ibid. 201). Among the Foi, this 'link' is still intact.

Weiner's commentary on Foi poetics raises a number of very interesting issues. The whole thrust of his book is to show a linkage between Foi poetics and a set of social attitudes, which may best be labelled 'sympathetic'. Foi culture, in its moments of self-revelation (when the songs of loss and abandonment are sung) culminates in the elicitation and display of sympathy for the dead, and sympathy for the survivors who remain behind to mourn their departure. The same can be said of the Kaluli, who express their sentiments in very similar poetic and institutional forms. 'Sociality', in Foi and Kaluli terms, is crucially bound up with the demonstration of sympathy, and given that (sung) poetry is the supreme instrument for the social communication of sympathy, there is reason enough to describe these as 'poetic' societies, invoking Heidegger, as Weiner does.

The interesting point for us, however, is that the culture of sympathy conducts itself in a tightly restricted code, a highly invariant musical idiom (well described by Feld) and an equally simplified poetic format. Claiming to discover in this restricted domain something amounting to the 'essence' of poetry, of art in general, seems to run the risk of romantic idealism. Weiner himself is forced to recognize that poetry, in this vein of artless truth, is only half of what Foi culture is about. Only women compose poetry (though men sing it) while male verbal art consists of spells whose efficacy reposes precisely in the fact that they subvert lived experience and impose a barrier between the apparent and the real (ibid. 16–17). Magic is not real poetry, says Weiner, but this is a question of critical dogma, and hardly consistent with the more commonly held view that verbal magic works through powerful metaphors, and is hence decidedly poetic, whether or not it is intended to be emotionally expressive. The same can be said of the poetics of political rhetoric, and other male verbal arts, in which dissimulation and concealment often play a marked role.

Weiner's conception of poetry as the spontaneous revelation of being, and nothing else, is too one-sided. The poetics of loss and abandonment which he and Feld describe so well is only one facet of Foi/Kaluli culture, for all that it is a facet they and their ethnographers choose to emphasize particularly. As such, it cannot be made into a touchstone for determining what ought to count as 'authentic' art, for them or for us. Rather than appeal to the universality of Heideggerian romantic notions of 'human nature' (ibid: 13) it seems better to construct theories which locate poetic practices, not in relation to 'being' but in relation to context, more narrowly understood. Because it is here, in the relation between landscape, personhood, and language, that the factors which are responsible for the genesis of particular poetic forms are instituted.

The approach to ethno-poetics implied in this paper rests on this more local foundation. I agree with Merleau-Ponty (and oppose Heidegger) in emphasizing the crucial role of the body, perception, and the composite formed out of the body in its perceptual environment, in the grounding of language. Language is not the 'house of being', in any absolute sense; if anything, the body is that, and language is one function of the body. But there is no 'absolute' body, either; the body is a locality, an ambience, and a certain perceptual regime imposed by that ambience and inculcated over a lifetime. I trace the roots of Foi poetics not to language itself, therefore, but to this perceptual surround. The prevalence of iconisms is a diagnostic feature, not just of a style of life destined to culminate in a certain type of poetic expression, but also of a certain type of sociality which culminates in the expression of sympathy. The linguistic devices and predominating themes of this poetry share a common origin, that is, the contingencies, the characteristic instability (demographic, residential, political) of the marginal forest habitat.

Although I did not focus attention on it, the theme of 'sympathy' is equally prominent in Umeda culture, and the sung poetry of the Umeda is also comparable in style and tone. Like the Foi/Kaluli, the Umeda engaged in passionate, formalized, keening over the dead, the women sang dirges, and one whole night of the *ida* ceremony was entirely devoted to singing songs which, as far as I can reconstruct from wholly inadequate notes, very strongly resemble the kind of nostalgic, bird-infested songs described by Weiner and Feld (Gell 1975: 199–201). So, on the one hand, iconicity is peculiarly associated with marginal-forest habitat and with the expression of the 'concrete' attitude of 'sympathy'; while on the other, the marginal forest habitat elicits 'sympathy' as a social necessity, since the vicissitudes of forest existence impose an inescapable instability on the collective institutions on which life depends.

This is a narrow, and, if you like, environmental-determinist theory of ethno-poetics. I insist on it only in so far as I believe cultural theories ought to be anchored in the specifics of physical localities, technologies, lifestyles, rather than seeking to appeal to absolutes and essences. It seems to me quite misguided to point to the languages of the Foi, Kaluli, or Umeda as exemplary poetic languages, superior to our own (on Heideggerian grounds) since their poetic characteristics are strictly local, having no counterparts in the kinds of perceptual, social, and linguistic experiences which are conducive to poetic expression hereabouts. The peculiar interest of these exotic poetic traditions and poetic languages lies in their rootedness in a certain landscape and a certain perceptual style, which we can appreciate (from afar) but in which we are debarred from full participation by virtue of the extraordinary gulf between our experience and theirs. But, even so, I admit that there is much we can learn from them when it comes to enlarging our conception of what is humanly possible. Even vicarious participation in alterity is subversive of the conceptual restrictions which motivate our own sense of the real, and by derivation, our conceptions of the poetic.

References

BOLINGER, D. (1965). *Forms of English*. Tokyo: Hokouo Publishing Co.

FELD, S. (1982). *Sound and Sentiment: Birds, Weeping, Poetics and Song in Kaluli Expression*. Philadelphia: University of Pennsylvania Press.

——(n.d.). 'Wept Thoughts: The Voicing of Kaluli Memories'. Unpublished manuscript.

FUDGE, E. (1970). 'Phonological Structure and "Expressiveness"', *Journal of Linguistics*, 6: 161–88.

GELL, A. (1975). *The Metamorphosis of the Cassowaries*. LSE Monographs in Social Anthropology, 51. London: Athlone Press.

——(1977). 'Magic, Perfume, Dream', in I. Lewis (ed.), *Symbols and Sentiments*. London: Academic Press.

—— (1979). 'The Umeda Language Poem', *Canberra Anthropology*, 2/1: 44–62.

GOLDSTEIN, K., and SCHEERER, M. (1971). 'Abstract and Concrete Behaviour', in Kurt Goldstein, *Collected Papers*, ed. A. Gurwitsch. The Hague: Martinus Nijhoff.

HAIMAN, J. (1985). *Natural Syntax: Iconicity and Erosion*. Cambridge: Cambridge University Press.

HEIDEGGER, M. (1971). *Poetry, Language, Thought*. New York: Harper & Row.

JAKOBSON, R. (1965). 'In Search of the Essence of Language', *Diogenes*, 51: 21–37.

—— and WAUGH, L. (1979). *The Sound Shape of Language*. Brighton: Harvester Press.

KLIMA, E., and BELLUGI, U. (1979). *The Signs of Language*. Cambridge, Mass.: Harvard University Press.

KÖHLER, W. (1930). *Gestalt Psychology*. London: G. Bell.

LÉVI-STRAUSS, C. (1985). *The View From Afar*. London: Penguin Books.

MERLEAU-PONTY, M. (1962). *The Phenomenology of Perception*. London: Routledge & Kegan Paul.

MIMICA, J. (1981). 'Omalyce: An Ethnography of the Ikwaye View of the Cosmos'. Unpublished Ph.D. thesis. Australian National University.

PETERFALVI, J.-M. (1970). *Recherches Expérimentales sur le Symbolisme Phonétique*. Paris: Centre Nationale de la Recherche Scientifique.

SACKS, O. (1989). *Seeing Voices: A Journey into the World of the Deaf*. Berkeley, Calif.: University of California Press.

SAPIR, E. (1929). *Language*. New York: Harcourt, Brace & World.

SAUSSURE, F. DE (1966). *Course in General Linguistics*. New York: McGraw Hill.

SCHIEFFELIN, E. (1976). *The Sorrow of the Lonely and the Burning of the Dancers*. New York: St Martin's Press.

WAGNER, R. (1972). *Habu: The Innovation of Meaning in Daribi Religion*. Chicago: University of Chicago Press.

WEINER, J. (1988). *The Heart of the Pearl Shell: The Mythological Dimension of Foi Sociality*. Berkeley, Calif.: University of California Press.

—— (1991). *The Empty Place: Poetry, Space and Being among the Foi of Papua New Guinea*. Bloomington, Ind.: Indiana University Press.

INDEX

Note: References in italics denote Figures in the text.